Managerial Decision Analysis Series

Risk Management

David E. Bell • Arthur Schleifer, Jr.
Harvard Business School, Boston, MA

Course
TECHNOLOGY

Course Technology, Inc. One Main Street, Cambridge, MA 02142
An International Thomson Publishing Company

I(T)P

Albany • Bonn • Boston • Cincinnati • London • Madrid • Melbourne • Mexico City
New York • Paris • San Francisco • Singapore • Tokyo • Toronto • Washington

Risk Management is published by Course Technology, Inc.

Managing Editor	Mac Mendelsohn
Production Editor	Christine Spillett
Text Designer	Susannah K. Lean
Cover Designer	John Gamache

© Copyright 1995 Course Technology, Inc.
A Division of International Thomson Publishing, Inc.

For more information contact:
Course Technology, Inc.
One Main Street
Cambridge, MA 02142

International Thomson Publishing Europe
Berkshire House 168-173
High Holborn
London WCIV 7AA
England

International Thomson Publishing GmbH
Königswinterer Strasse 418
53227 Bonn
Germany

Thomas Nelson Australia
102 Dodds Street
South Melbourne, 3205
Victoria, Australia

International Thomson Publishing Asia
211 Henderson Road
#05-10 Henderson Building
Singapore

Nelson Canada
1120 Birchmount Road
Scarborough, Ontario
Canada M1K 5G4

International Thomson Publishing Japan
Hirakawacho Kyowa Building, 3F
2-2-1 Hirakawacho
Chiyoda-ku, Tokyo 102
Japan

International Thomson Editores
Campos Eliseos 385, Piso 7
Col. Polanco
11560 Mexico D.F. Mexico

Case material of the Harvard Graduate School of Business Administration is made possible by the cooperation of business firms and other organizations which may wish to remain anonymous by having names, quantities, and other identifying details disguised while maintaining basic relationships. Cases are prepared as the basis for class discussion rather than to illustrate either effective or ineffective handling of an administrative situation.

Library of Congress Catalog Card no.: 94-74892

Trade Marks

Course Technology and the open book logo are registered trademarks of Course Technology, Inc. I(T)P The ITP logo is a trademark under license. Microsoft Excel and Windows are trademarks of Microsoft Corporation.

Some product names used in this book have been used for identification purposes only and may be trademarks or registered trademarks of their respective manufacturers and sellers.

Disclaimer

Course Technology, Inc. reserves the right to revise this publication and make changes in content from time to time without notice.

1-56527-276-5
Printed in the United States of America
10 9 8 7 6 5 4 3 2 1

To our parents George and Constance Bell and Arthur and Miriam Schleifer

FROM THE PUBLISHER

At Course Technology, Inc., we believe that technology will transform the way that people teach and learn. We are very excited about bringing you, professors and students, the most practical and affordable technology-related products available.

The Course Technology Development Process

Our development process is unparalleled in the higher education publishing industry. Every product we create goes through an exacting process of design, development, review, and testing. Reviewers give us direction and insight that shape our manuscripts and bring them up to the latest standards. Every manuscript is quality tested.

The Course Technology Team

This book will suit your needs because it was delivered quickly, efficiently, and affordably. In every aspect of our business, we rely on a commitment to quality and the use of technology. Every employee contributes to this process. The names of all of our employees are listed below:

Tim Ashe, David Backer, Stephen M. Bayle, Josh Bernoff, Ann Marie Buconjic, Jody Buttafoco, Kerry Cannell, Jim Chrysikos, Barbara Clemens, Amy Clemons, Susan Collins, John M. Connolly, Kim Crowley, Myrna D'Addario, Lisa D'Alessandro, Jodi Davis, Howard S. Diamond, Kathryn Dinovo, Joseph B. Dougherty, Karen Dwyer, MaryJane Dwyer, Kristin Dyer, Chris Elkhill, Don Fabricant, Viktor Frengut, Jeff Goding, Laurie Gomes, Eileen Gorham, Catherine Griffin, Tim Hale, Jamie Harper, Roslyn Hooley, John Hope, Marjorie Hunt, Nicole Jones-Pinard, Matt Kenslea, Susannah Lean, Kim Mai, Margaret Makowski, Tammy Marciar, Elizabeth Martinez, Debbie Masi, Don Maynard, Dan Mayo, Kathleen McCann, Sarah McLean, Jay McNamara, Karla Mitchell, Mac Mendelsohn, Kim Munsell, Amy Oliver, Michael Ormsby, Debbie Parlee, Kristin Patrick, Charlie Patsios, Darren Perl, Kevin Phaneuf, George J. Pilla, Cathy Prindle, Nancy Ray, Laura Sacks, Carla Sharpe, Deborah Shute, Jennifer Slivinski, Christine Spillett, Michelle Tucker, David Upton, Mark Valentine, Karen Wadsworth, Renee Walkup, Tracy Wells, Donna Whiting, Janet Wilson, Lisa Yameen.

CONTENTS

▼ CHAPTER 2 Hedging

▼ CHAPTER 3   Risk versus Return

▼ CHAPTER 4 Personal Risk

▼ CHAPTER 5 Multi-Period Risks

▼ CHAPTER 6   Multi-Person Risks

OVERVIEW

This book is one of a series entitled Managerial Decision Analysis. This series of four books represents the output of three long-term course-development projects with which we have been associated at Harvard Business School. Both of us spent several years, at various times, heading the semester-long Managerial Economics course, required of all 800 first-year MBA students. We have separated this material into two parts, according to whether it concerns a decision made under conditions of complete knowledge (Decision Making Under Certainty) or a decision made under some degree of uncertainty (Decision Making Under Uncertainty). The first of these two books covers topics such as relevant costs, net present value, and linear programming. The second covers material on decision trees, simulation, inventory control and cases involving negotiation and auction bidding.

Both of us have also taught elective courses to second-year MBA students. Schleifer developed a course on Business Forecasting that is the foundation of our third book, Data Analysis, Regression, and Forecasting. Bell developed a course that integrates approaches to decision making under risk, whether business, personal, or societal. This material is presented in our fourth book, Risk Management.

Together, these four books provide unprecedented case coverage of issues, concepts, and techniques for analyzing managerial problems. Each book is self-contained and can serve as a stand-alone text in a one-semester course (which is how the material was used in our classrooms) or as a supplemental volume for those seeking a set of demanding real-world applications for students in a more traditional text and lecture course.

Learning concepts and techniques through the case method may be a new experience for some. It takes time to adjust to the notion that problems do not always have neat, clear solutions, and, more profoundly, that learning is often greater when they don't. We believe that this set of material covers not only what a future manager should know as an intelligent user of quantitative methods but also as an intelligent consumer of analyses others have done.

As the reader will see, some of the cases and notes were prepared by our colleagues; we are grateful for the opportunity to use them. What will not be apparent is the debt we owe to those of our colleagues that have gone before us in heading the Managerial Economics course: Robert Schlaifer, John Pratt, John Bishop, Paul Vatter, Stephen Bradley, and Richard Meyer. We also thank the Division of Research at the Harvard Business School for their financial support of all the course development reflected in these volumes. Finally, we wish to express our appreciation to Rowena Foss and Laurie Fitzgerald of the Harvard Business School, and to Mac Mendelsohn of Course Technology, for their substantial efforts both keeping this project on track and contributing to its quality. Rowena Foss has been our secretary, at times individually, but for the most part jointly, since 1978. To her we owe a special debt of gratitude.

PREFACE

Managerial Decision Analysis
Risk Management

In many discussions of business problems, whether in the classroom or in the boardroom, risk is mentioned as being an important issue, but since no-one has a concrete way to think about it, it is left as an intangible. This book brings together a broad collection of intriguing real-life problems in which risk plays a central role. The problems are drawn from a wide range of contexts: business, personal and societal. By making risk the central focus of discussion in case after case, we find that a coherent framework for risk management emerges. The net result is not that all business problems should be regarded as exercises in risk management but rather that by developing this skill, managers will have a new, additional way, to invent and to evaluate alternatives.

It is an over-simplification to think of risk as a one-dimensional concept, captured by a measure of variability in some statistic such as profit. Risk is created by unpredictability in the value of an outcome as measured by the decision maker's objectives. Unless these objectives—and the tradeoffs between them—are thoroughly understood, actions taken to manage risk could easily make a situation worse. Moreover, by the non-repetitive nature of risk-taking (a decision taken repeatedly can't be all *that* risky), it is extremely difficult to learn risk management by experience.

We may regard the value of a firm as being a function of its level of return and of its level of risk. This book adopts the perspective of a manager with a primary interest in the minimization of risk, rather than in the maximization of return. It is not the intent of the book to produce specialists of this type, but it is expected that managers who are trained to look at problems from this additional vantage point, will identify new and creative ways to permit a company to expand its capacity for risk-taking by improving the management of those risks, and opportunities, that it currently faces.

The book covers the following broad topics:

1. What risk is and why businesses and individuals tend to be averse to it.
2. The alternatives that are available for managing risk and how to use them.
3. The extent to which unaided intuition is adequate for managing risks.
4. Whether and when quantitative methods are useful for managers facing risky decisions.

In addition to case problems, there are many notes, exercises and readings. The notes cover topics such as diversification (including portfolio construction and the capital asset pricing model), life insurance, hedging, the futures and options markets, and capital budgeting.

Together the materials promote discussion and learning that encompass three different strands of academic research into risk:

1. Decision analysts have developed techniques, including decision trees, subjective probability distributions and preference curves, to aid a manager in choosing between risky alternatives.

2. Financial theory has provided techniques for establishing fair market equilibrium prices for risky assets and tools such as the capital asset pricing model, risk-adjusted discounting, and option-pricing formulas.

3. Psychologists have studied how people actually behave when confronted with risk and have identified systematic cognitive biases that lead to the drawing of false conclusions in problems involving uncertainty. Just as the eye can be fooled by the refraction of light as it passes from water to air, so the mind can be fooled by dilemmas involving uncertainty. And just as the mind can be trained to correct for the refraction bias, so too can it be trained to avoid the cognitive pitfalls that impede effective decision making.

Outline of the Book

The book has six chapters, covering various aspects of the risk management problem:

Chapter 1   Diversification (Mean-Variance Analysis, the Capital Asset Pricing Model)

There is a natural tendency to assume that the best way to manage a risk is by reducing or eliminating it. The book begins by showing that this is not always true. Risks may be attractive if they are negatively correlated with existing holdings. Also, because some risky investments can be traded, people with a relative high tolerance for risk may find it worthwhile to take on risk, due to the attractive returns implicit in the market-clearing prices.

Chapter 2   Hedging Exposure (Multiple Objectives, Futures Contracts)

The measurement of exposure is fundamental to the management of risk. A person or company is *exposed* to an uncertainty if he/she/it is affected, in a significant way, by the outcome of that uncertainty. Future values of foreign exchange rates are uncertainties to us all, because none of us know in advance what they will be, but only those of us whose financial welfare is affected by their levels are exposed to them. Many of the cases in this segment illustrate the difficulties of measuring exposure. In each there is no secret about the uncertainty involved, nor about the significance of that uncertainty to the company in question. Rather the difficulty is in determining which outcomes are good and which bad; does a company want the exchange rate to go up or down? The basic hedging device of this segment is the futures contract.

Chapter 3 Risk versus Return
(Insurance, Preference Curves)

In this third chapter of the book the fundamental dilemma of risk management is tackled: to what extent should return be sacrificed for a reduction in risk? The cases and exercises in this chapter show just how risk averse managers are in the face of significant downside risk. Each of the three cases in this segment are related to the insurance industry. Together with an exercise, they illustrate the purpose, usefulness, and limitations of preference analysis.

Chapter 4 Aversion to Risk
(Psychological Concerns, Tradeoffs)

Up to this point in the book the fundamental problem of exposure has been examined, along with two quite different methodologies for determining whether a given enterprise offers sufficient return to be worth the risk involved. The fourth chapter explores the reasons behind personal aversion to risk in more detail. The purpose is to uncover various intangible components of risk aversion and thereby offer an explanation of why actual behavior does not always match economically "rational" behavior. This aim is achieved by leading off with two medical situations[1] in which patients (the reader) must choose between alternative treatments, each of which has many extreme possible outcomes, including death. It is readily apparent that obvious quantifications, such as probability of survival, do not capture the essence of the problems and that we are not effective in thinking these problems through "rationally." The reader will see that psychological concerns affect judgment when the stakes are high, and no less so when the extreme consequences are financial rather than medical.

Chapter 5 Multi-Period Risks
(Options, Capital Budgeting)

Up to this point all the problems have been of the one-period type; you face a decision, take an action and observe the result. In many situations there is no such single go/no-go point; decision and corrective actions may be taken at any time. The first half of the fifth chapter looks at the value of contingent strategies in risk management. The material on traded options not only provides readers with another hedging instrument but also primes them to recognize one of the benefits of risk taking, namely the creation of options. The second half of the chapter is concerned with the evaluation of risky cashflows and shows not only when and how risk-adjusted discounting may be used, but also the importance of the timing of information about the size of those cashflows. A primary goal of this segment is to illustrate the interaction, in a single problem, of the tools designed for the analysis of traded and nontraded risks.

---

[1]Only one, "John Brown," is actually contained in this book. The second is described only in the Teacher's Manual.

Chapter 6 Multi-Person Risks
(Incentives, Cost-Benefit Analysis)

The final chapter deals with situations in which the management of risk requires thought about how other parties will be affected by and respond to, your actions. Part of the chapter looks at the problem of creating appropriate incentives to ensure that all parties to the contract, each with a portion of the risks to manage, will act in the common good. We also discuss why it is that people are very averse to some personal dangers such as nuclear power, but oblivious to others such as driving without seatbelts. It is important to understand how people think about such issues, for a manager is often called upon, implicitly if not explicitly, to trade off the company's financial well-being against the health and safety of its employees. One case illustrates that employees will make extraordinary sacrifices to keep their jobs. As with financial risk-taking, a manager cannot always rely on his or her subordinates to make effective decisions in the face of risk.

A few of the cases have substantial amounts of accompanying data. For these the data is available on a data diskette in spreadsheet form. This diskette is available with the Teacher's Manual or by calling 1-800-648-7450. The Teacher's Manual also contains an analysis of each case and suggestions for teaching the material.

READ THIS BEFORE YOU BEGIN

To the Student

A few of the cases have substantial amounts of accompanying data. The data is available on the *Data Diskette* in spreadsheet format. If your instructor does not provide you with the disk, it may be obtained from Course Technology, Inc., by calling 1-800-648-7450 or by sending a FAX to (617) 225-7976.

To the Instructor

Data Diskette: The instructor's copy of this book is bundled with the *Data Diskette* which contains data in a spreadsheet format for some of the cases in this book.

Instructions for installing the files contained on the Data Diskette are found in the README.TXT file on the disk. The README.TXT file may be opened by using the Windows Notepad.

DIVERSIFICATION

There is a natural tendency to assume that the best way to manage a risk is by reducing it or eliminating it. Not all risks are bad. In this chapter we examine the potential for risks to "average out" when viewed as a portfolio. The portfolio view of risk is fundamental to the development in this book. We begin with a motivational case, followed by a note and exercises that will establish and explain the concepts involved.

BREAKFAST FOODS CORPORATION

John Morgan, CEO of Breakfast Foods Corporation (BF, makers of "Wheatflakes" and others), had just come back to his office from lunch when the phone rang to announce Ron Sykes, his marketing VP:

"John, I told our sales force to keep their ears to the ground regarding any possible move by MC (Morning Cereal, Inc., BF's principal competitor) to start a price war. They are just crazy enough to do that even though it would hurt both of us. I told the sales force that if a price war is going to happen, it's an enormous advantage to be the first one to start. So we wanted to know the minute there are signs that MC is ready to move. Well, Fred Sharp called me fifteen minutes ago. He has a contact inside one of the major networks who tells him that MC has just booked large blocks of advertising space starting two weeks from today. Now you and I know that there's no way MC wants big blocks of advertising space unless they're announcing price reductions."

"Ron, how sure are you that Sharp is reliable as a source? We wouldn't want to jump to hasty conclusions."

"Well, normally I wouldn't pay much attention to a report like this except that Fred reminded me, with some acerbity I thought, of three previous occasions when he correctly called a major move by MC. I checked the files and, indeed, he had given us significant information before those three occasions. John, I think we should take this seriously and beat them to the punch."

"O.K., Ron, bring me a proposal before six o'clock."

John turned to a report on his desk from David Baker, a recent graduate of the Stanford Business School whom John had hired as a general assistant. This report concerned John's desire to fire one of BF's three wheat price forecasters. Every three months, for nearly ten years, BF had received from these men best-guess forecasts of wheat prices three months hence as part of BF's desire to reduce its purchase costs. BF relied exclusively on these forecasts since the experts had already assimilated information from such sources as futures prices, econometric models, and so on.

Harvard Business School case 9-182-202. This case was prepared by Professor David E. Bell. The first of the two issues in this case is adapted from an example in *Judgement and Choice*, by R.M. Hogarth, John Wiley & Sons, 1980. Copyright © 1982 by the President and Fellows of Harvard College.

However, their ten-year tenure had led the experts to be overly exacting in their demands for retaining fees, and John felt that firing one of them would not only cut costs directly by about a third, but indirectly it would send the message to the remaining two that no one was indispensable. He had asked David to evaluate which one should get his marching orders.

David's memo read as follows:

> I dug out the forecasts made by our three experts and compared them with the actual prices that resulted three months later (Exhibit 1). I plotted a distribution of errors for each of them (Exhibit 2). Clearly what we want is to fire the expert with the widest spread (variance) of errors. The graph shows that this is Harry.

Exhibit 1

ERROR (ACTUAL PRICE — FORECAST PRICE TO NEAREST CENT/BUSHEL)

Forecast #	Tom Smith	Dick Wilson	Harry Simpson
1	–3	–3	23
2	–13	–4	22
3	5	7	1
4	13	0	–16
5	5	–4	–31
6	4	2	1
7	–4	6	11
8	–13	6	36
9	–8	–7	–5
10	0	5	1
11	0	4	–2
12	5	8	–24
13	1	–4	15
14	–6	–10	15
15	–13	–15	11
16	3	3	3
17	2	3	–10
18	7	0	–6
19	–1	–3	–5
20	–4	–4	17
21	4	–8	–25
22	2	0	–19
23	0	3	–9
24	–5	–12	7
25	1	8	0
26	–10	–9	11
27	–7	0	21
28	–3	3	33
29	2	–4	–22
30	2	4	–12
31	–3	–4	12
32	10	0	–41
33	–10	–12	9
34	8	19	–17
35	–8	6	8
36	2	–7	–6
37	–3	–10	–10
38	2	6	–4
39	–8	–13	–6
40	3	2	–12

A Month Later

John read two memos on his desk. The first was from Ron Sykes:

> We should really give Fred Sharp some kind of bonus or recognition. As you recall he was the one that told us about MC's booking of advertising space two weeks before we would have seen it for ourselves on TV. Because of him we beat them to the punch. What do you think?

The second memo was from David Baker:

> I thought you'd be amused to hear that Harry Simpson has been retained by MC as part of their forecasting team. Not only did we get rid of him, MC actually hired him. Let's hope they're paying him some outrageous salary.

Exhibit 2

DISTRIBUTION OF ERRORS

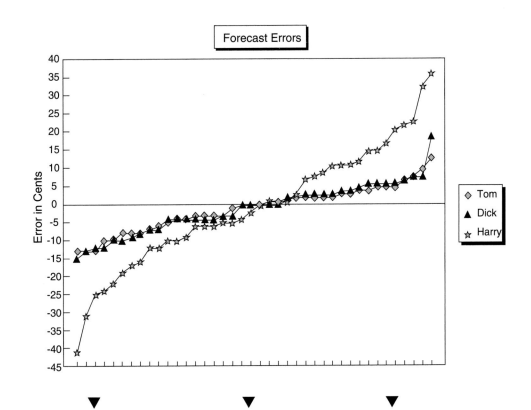

DIVERSIFICATION AND INVESTMENT RISK

In an earlier book in the *Management Decision Analysis* series we described decisions in terms of probability distributions of return. This is quite a reasonable procedure when choosing among a small number of alternatives, but in problems such as selecting a portfolio from among hundreds of stocks, the computational burden of calculating complete probability distributions and evaluating them one by one is too great. In this chapter we present, in detail, a framework for analyzing portfolios of risks. The details are important even for those only wanting to build an intuition for the subject.

The fundamental assumption is as follows:

Mean-variance assumption

In comparing risky alternatives it is sufficient to know the mean and variance of the probability distributions of return.

The variance is simply the square of the standard deviation[1] and is a measure of the risk in an alternative. It is simple to construct examples where knowing *only* the mean and variance can lead you into patently absurd decisions[2], but for most real-life situations where the probability distributions have the normal s-shaped appearance the mean-variance assumption is quite reasonable.

One of the great advantages of summarizing an alternative by two statistics is that it is possible to make a two-dimensional graph of alternatives. Figure 1.1 shows the average return (EMV) on the vertical axis and standard deviation (rather than variance) on the horizontal axis for 10 hypothetical investments.

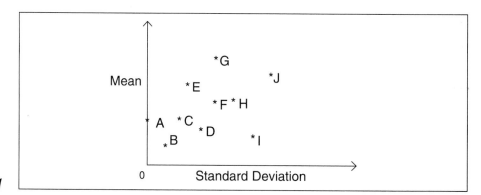

Figure 1.1

If you were permitted to invest in one and only one of these ten alternatives, you would certainly not want to pick alternative *F*, since *E* has a higher return and lower risk. Also, *E* is superior to *H*. Only *A*, *C*, *E*, and *G* are *efficient* (or Pareto optimal) in that they are undominated by other alternatives. Each investor must decide whether the extra average return in *G* compensates for the increased level of risk associated with it.

Harvard Business School note 9-183-047. This note was written by Professor David E. Bell. Copyright © 1983 by the President and Fellows of Harvard College.

---

[1] These and other terms are illustrated with sample calculations in Appendix A to this note.

[2] Further amplification of this point is to be found in Appendix B. Appendix B is optional reading.

The problem changes drastically if you are allowed to subdivide your investment and take *shares* in any or all of the ten alternatives. It is remarkable, but not even alternative *I* can be ruled out from our portfolio on the basis of the graph. It could be that *I* is perfectly negatively correlated with *G*, and that some combination of *I* and *G* is risk-free, with a higher return than, say, *A*.

For example, let's consider two investments I_1 and I_2 which are both determined by the outcome of a single coin toss (Table 1.1).

The means of I_1 and I_2 are $3 and $2 respectively. Their variances are 9 and 1, respectively, for standard deviations of 3 and 1. A risk/return graph looks like Figure 1.2.

Table 1.1

	I_1	I_2
COIN LANDS HEADS	$6	$1
COIN LANDS TAILS	$0	$3

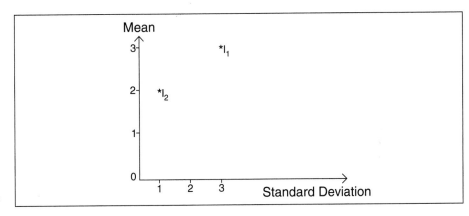

Figure 1.2

Let's construct portfolios $I_3 = \frac{3}{4}I_1 + \frac{1}{4}I_2$, $I_4 = \frac{1}{2}I_1 + \frac{1}{2}I_2$, and $I_5 = \frac{1}{4}I_1 + \frac{3}{4}I_2$ (Table 1.2).

Table 1.2

	I_3	I_4	I_5
Heads	4.75	3.50	2.25
Tails	.75	1.50	2.25
Mean	2.75	2.50	2.25
S.D.	2	1	0

The graph now looks like Figure 1.3 in which I_1 and I_2 are perfectly negatively correlated.

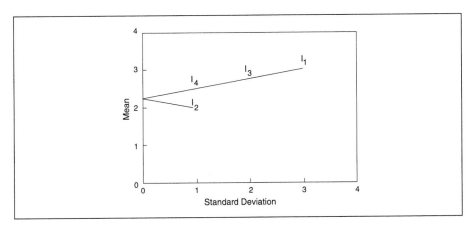

Figure 1.3

The curve connecting the five portfolios illustrates all those points in risk/return space that are achievable by simple combinations of investments I_1 and I_2.

Now consider the same initial diagram as Figure 1.2, but with the returns shown in Table 1.3.

Table 1.3

	I_1	I_2	I_3	I_4	I_5
Heads	$6.00	$3.00	$5.25	$4.50	$3.75
Tails	$0.00	$1.00	$0.25	$0.50	$0.75
Mean	$3.00	$2.00	$2.75	$2.50	$2.25
S.D.	$3.00	$1.00	$2.50	$2.0	$1.50

This table gives the graph in Figure 1.4 in which I and I_2 are perfectly positively correlated.

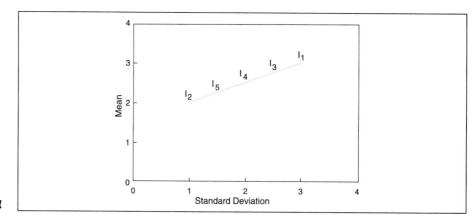

Figure 1.4

The curve of possible portfolios is now a straight line. For the sake of completeness we will draw the graph of the case where I_1 and I_2 are independent (not correlated). This requires the toss of two coins (Table 1.4).

Table 1.4

	I_1	I_2	I_3	I_4	I_5
Heads, Heads	$6.00	$3.00	$5.25	$4.50	$3.75
Heads, Tails	$6.00	$1.00	$4.75	$3.50	$2.25
Tails, Heads	$0.00	$3.00	$0.75	$1.50	$2.25
Tails, Tails	$0.00	$1.00	$0.25	$0.50	$0.75
Mean	$3.00	$2.00	$2.75	$2.50	$2.25
S.D.	$3.00	$1.00	$2.26	$1.58	$1.06

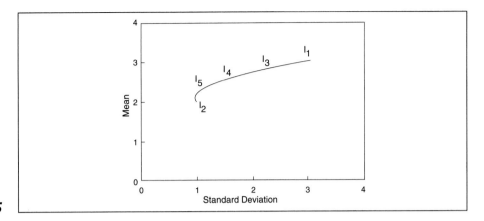

Figure 1.5

Comparing Figures 1.3, 1.4, and 1.5 you see that if you were permitted to select whether the investments would be positively correlated, negatively correlated, or independent, you would probably choose negatively correlated, because its curve of efficient portfolios lies entirely to the left of those in Figures 1.4 and 1.5. That is, with negative correlation, you can have the same mean return but with a lower standard deviation.

It is not necessary to perform explicit calculations of the variance for each potential portfolio. There is a simple formula that gives the mean and variance for combinations of two investments as a function of the means, variances, and correlation of the component investments.

Mean and variance of a portfolio

If Investment 1 has mean r_1 and standard deviation s_1, and Investment 2 has mean r_2 and standard deviation s_2, and if the correlation between the two is c, then a portfolio consisting of a fraction k of Investment 1 and $1-k$ of Investment 2 has

$$\text{Mean} = kr_1 + (1 - k)r_2 \qquad\qquad \text{(Formula 1)}$$

and

$$\text{Variance} = k^2 s_1^2 + (1 - k)^2 s_2^2 + 2k(1 - k)cs_1 s_2 \;. \qquad \text{(Formula 2)}$$

Some special cases are worth noting. If $s_1 = s_2$ and $c = 0$ then the variance is $[k^2 + (1-k)^2]s_1^2$. If $k = \frac{1}{2}$ then this is $\frac{1}{2}s_1^2$. That is, a 50-50 combination of two equal, but independent, investments has half the variance of its components. Another special case is $s_2 = 0$, for then the variance is $k^2 s_1^2$. The standard deviation of the portfolio is simply proportional to the amount invested in the risky alternative.[3]

Figure 1.6 shows the set of all portfolios which combine a risk-free alternative with mean r_F and standard deviation 0, with investment I_1. The dotted line indicates portfolios that may be constructed by borrowing at the risk-free rate and investing that money in more shares of I_1.

---

[3] In general, if you have a fraction k_i in investment I_i which has mean r_i and standard deviation s_i, then the portfolio mean is $\Sigma k_i r_i$ and the portfolio variance is

$$\sum_{i=1}^{n} \sum_{j=1}^{n} k_i k_j c_{ij} s_i s_j \quad \text{where } c_{ij} \text{ is the correlation between investments } i \text{ and } j.$$

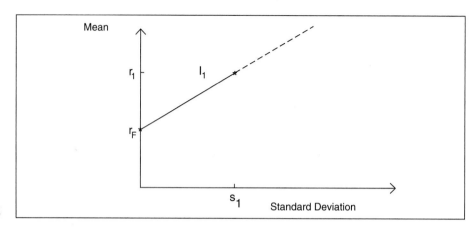

Figure 1.6

Finding the Minimum Variance Portfolio

Exhibit 1 graphs the variance of a portfolio as a function of k for different values of the correlation. A relevant question is: for any particular value of the correlation, what choice of k minimizes the portfolio variance (standard deviation)?

The answer may be derived mathematically[4] and is

$$k = \frac{s_2(s_2 - cs_1)}{s_1^2 + s_2^2 - 2cs_1 s_2} \quad .$$

Perhaps the most important insight to be gained from this formula is the answer to the following question: Given an existing portfolio, how can you tell whether a new potential investment would be useful for diversification purposes (that is, would reduce the variance of the existing portfolio)? We will restrict attention to cases where the new investment cannot be sold short.

If your existing portfolio is Investment 2 (I_2) and if I_1 is the new investment, then you want some of I_1 in your portfolio if the minimum variance portfolio has $k > 0$. It can be shown that the denominator of the formula for k is always positive, so k is positive when $s_2 > cs_1$.

Diversification formula

A new investment is of diversification value (will reduce the risk in a portfolio) if and only if:

Existing Portfolio S.D. > New Investment S.D. × Correlation   (Formula 3)

That is, if:

$$Correlation < \frac{Existing\ Portfolio\ S.D.}{New\ Investment\ S.D.} \quad .$$

In particular a new investment will always be of diversification value if it is independent of or negatively correlated with the existing portfolio.

---

[4] Further amplification of this point appears in Appendix B.

Note that reduction of variance isn't the sole criterion for decision; if the new investment has very low returns, it may not be worth the reduction in risk that it brings. However, in the special case where the mean return of the portfolio and of the new investment are equal, minimizing the variance does become the sole criterion.

Example

You hold a cash/stock portfolio with mean return 8% and standard deviation 15%. A new investment with a mean return of 8% and a standard deviation of 40% is offered to you. The correlation between the new investment and your existing portfolio is 0.3. Are you interested?

The breakeven correlation is:

$$\frac{Old\ Standard\ Deviation}{New\ Standard\ Deviation} = \frac{15}{40} = 0.375 \ .$$

Anything less is good, anything more is bad. Hence the new investment is a good idea.[5]

Appraising New Investments with Different Means

Surprisingly, the problem of deciding whether a new investment with a different mean return is worth including in your portfolio is essentially the same as the above, after using a trick. First though, we will formally assume the existence of a risk-free investment.

Assumption of a risk-free rate

There exists an investment with mean r_F (which is positive), and standard deviation 0 that can be bought or sold.

From now on let's assume that the portfolio that you currently hold is called I_2 with mean return r_2 and standard deviation s_2. The potential new investment is I_1 with mean return r_1 and standard deviation s_1. The correlation between I_2 and I_1 is c. We know that if $r_2 = r_1$ then I_1 is desirable if $cs_1 < s_2$.

If r_1 does not equal r_2, the trick is to borrow (or lend) at the risk-free rate until the leveraged version of I_1 *does* have the same mean as I_2. Then you can apply the formula we already know to see if we want some of the leveraged I_1. It turns out [6] that we do if:

$$\frac{r_1 - r_F}{s_1} > c\frac{r_2 - r_F}{s_2} \qquad \text{(Formula 4)}$$

or, in words, if:

$$\frac{New\ Risk\ Premium}{New\ S.D.} > \frac{Current\ Risk\ Premium}{Current\ S.D.} \times \text{Correlation}$$

---

[5] Using the minimum variance formula we would divert

$$\frac{15(15 - 0.3 \times 40)}{225 + 1600 - 360} = \frac{45}{1465} = .03 = 3\%$$

of our portfolio into the new project.

Example

You currently hold a cash/stock portfolio with mean return 8% and standard deviation 15%. The risk-free rate is 6%. A proposed investment for your portfolio has mean return 7% and standard deviation 40%. The correlation between your existing portfolio and the new investment is 0.15. Are you interested?

For your current portfolio:

$$\frac{Risk\ Premium}{Standard\ Deviation} = \frac{2}{15}\ .$$

The new investment has:

$$\frac{Risk\ Premium}{Standard\ Deviation} = \frac{1}{40}\ .$$

You are interested if $2/15 \times$ correlation $< 1/40$, which will be the case if the correlation is less than 0.1875. Hence, you do want to invest in the new opportunity.

So far the argument has only shown that if the new investment satisfies the inequality then it is attractive. We haven't actually shown that if it *fails* the test then it is *not* wanted. This cannot be simply asserted because the optimal portfolio depends upon the preference of the investor for risk and return. If the new investment satisfies Formula 4, then *every* investor holding I_2 will want some of I_1. However, it might be that even if I_1 doesn't satisfy Formula 4, there might be some investor with particular risk/return preferences who does want some of I_1.

One more assumption eliminates even this possibility.[7]

Assumption that current portfolio is correctly leveraged

No matter what portfolio of risks an investor has, we assume that he or she has taken maximum advantage of the ability to borrow or lend at the risk free-rate.[8]

Formula 4 can be rewritten in an especially suggestive manner as:

$$r_1 > r_F + \frac{cs_1}{s_2}\left(r_2 - r_F\right),$$

and even more suggestively if we denote $\dfrac{cs_1}{s_2}$ by the Greek letter β:

$$r_1 > r_F + \beta(r_2 - r_F) \tag{Formula 5}$$

First main result

If the investor holds portfolio I_2, correctly leveraged with available risk-free funds, and if that investor is only concerned with the mean and variance of returns, then a new investment I_1 will be attractive if and only if Formula 5 holds.

---

[6] Further amplification of this point appears in Appendix B.

[7] Further amplification of this point appears in Appendix B.

[8] Note that this does not say that the investor is currently holding the best portfolio of available investments, only that whatever portfolio is being held is correctly leveraged.

Optimal Portfolios and the Effect of Markets

Figure 1.1 was drawn assuming investments A through I were mutually exclusive. If we allow mixtures of all risky investments (B through I), the set of possible portfolios will look something like the shaded area in Figure 1.7.

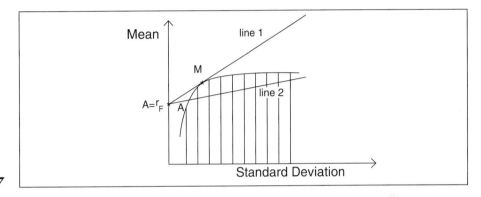

Figure 1.7

Recalling Figure 1.6, if we now allow portfolios to be leveraged with the risk-free asset, then we can have any portfolio on a straight line connecting A to any point in the shaded area. If you think about the portfolios on line 2, it is clear that you can always find one on Line 1 that is better. Line 1 connects A to the tangent point M in the shaded area. Depending on your level of risk aversion (and thus the degree of leverage you adopt), your *optimal* portfolio will be some combination of M and the risk-free asset.

Market agreement on means and variances

We assume that all investors agree on the mean and variance of every potential portfolio.

This assumption means that *every* investor is looking at the *same diagram* (Figure 1.7). Moreover, they all conclude that they should hold portfolio M, leveraged to some degree depending upon their particular risk aversion.

Second main result

All investors hold the same portfolio but with different degrees of leverage in the risk-free asset.

Consider what happens when a new investment I_1 comes on the market with return r_1 and standard deviation s_1. Suppose an investor holds exactly the portfolio M with no leverage. He or she will like I_1 if:

$$r_1 \; > \; r_F \; + \; \beta(r_M \; - \; r_F) \qquad\qquad \text{(Formula 6)}$$

where

$$\beta \; = \; \frac{cs_1}{s_M} \quad .$$

Hence, the investor modifies M to include I_1. Since we know everyone holds the same portfolio, this means that *everyone* modifies their portfolio to include I_1.

It is clear that an investment offering will be sold out immediately if Formula 6 holds, and will never sell at all if $r_1 < r_F + \beta(r_M - r_F)$.

Thus the correct price for investment I_1 will be the one that makes:

$$r_1 = r_F + \beta(r_M - r_F) \qquad .$$

If the price is any lower, demand will raise it; any higher and lack of demand will cause it to fall. This conclusion is called the Capital Asset Pricing Model. If a new investment is uncorrelated with the market, then $c = 0$, so that $\beta = 0$. If $\beta < 1$ ($cs_1 < s_M$), the investment will be priced so that $r_1 < r_M$. If $\beta > 1$, the investment will be priced so that $r_1 > r_M$. If $c < 0$, so that $\beta < 0$, we would have $r_1 < r_F$.

This analysis has reduced what looked like a horrendous computational problem into one that says, "Hold the market, suitably leveraged."

As we increased the number of assumptions, the formulas became less and less generally applicable. If you don't believe that standard deviation is an adequate measure of risk, none of this work applies to you. If you don't believe that all investors think the means and variances of investments are the same, for example if they have different tax situations, then the last section of the note can be discarded. If you believe that the uncertainty of inflation means that even T-bills are not risk-free, then most of these results are wrong. But as with many *models*, if the assumptions are approximately true then so too are the implications.

It is important to understand that the elegance of the Capital Asset Pricing Model derives from the simplifying assumptions that were made to produce it. Earlier in this series we allow general risk preferences and make no presumption that people view the world identically or that they are perfectly diversified. However, generality has its price in computational burden. To select portfolio M still requires a choice of appropriate leverage for the portfolio.

Choosing Between Efficient Portfolios

Suppose you want to decide between two efficient portfolios, with mean and standard deviation r_1, s_1 and r_2, s_2 respectively. We will assume you have a preference curve (see Exhibit 2) for total return from the chosen portfolio. We will not pursue, in this note, the question of where this curve comes from, or whether a preference analysis is appropriate.

A simulation program would simply draw random numbers from a probability distribution with the parameters of Portfolio 1, convert the random return into a preference number, do the same for Portfolio 2, and repeat 100 times. Whichever portfolio yields a higher average preference is the one to be preferred.

If the calculation is to be done by hand, the following table of bracket medians (Table 1.5) will be useful. The medians are given as a function of the mean r and standard deviation s.

Table 1.5

No. of Bracket Medians	Representative Values
1	r
3	$r + .965s, r, r - .965s$
5	$r + 1.28s, r + .525s, r, r - .525s, r - 1.28s$
10	$r + 1.645s, r + 1.035s, r + .675s, r + .385s, r + .125s$ $r - .125s, r - .385s, r - .675s, r - 1.035s, r - 1.645s.$

Example

Which is better? Portfolio I_1 with $r_1 = 10$, $s_1 = 20$, or I_2 with $r_2 = 8$ $s_2 = 10$? The preference curve is shown in Exhibit 2. Using a 5-bracket median approximation we have the values in Figure 1.8.

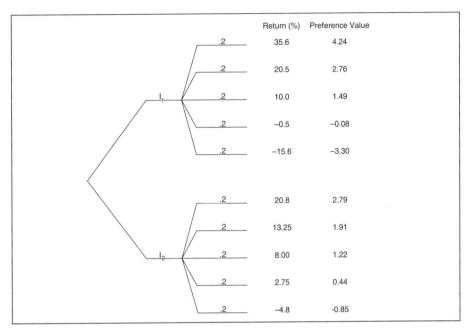

Average Preference for $I_1 = 1.02$ (C.E. = 6.65)
Average Preference for $I_2 = 1.10$ (C.E. = 7.15)
This suggests Investment 2 is better.

Exhibit 1

VARIANCE OF A PORTFOLIO BY SHARE OF EACH OF TWO INVESTMENTS AND BY THEIR CORRELATION

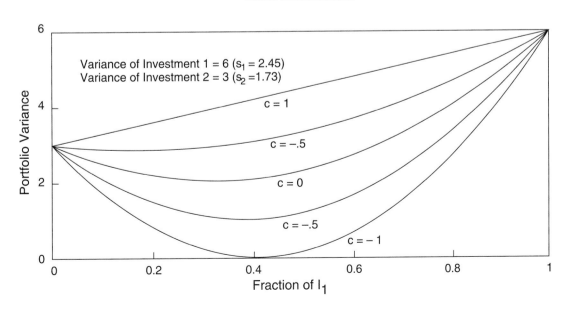

Exhibit 2

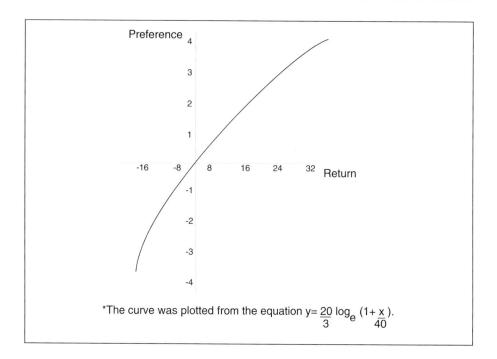

*The curve was plotted from the equation $y = \dfrac{20}{3} \log_e (1 + \dfrac{x}{40})$.

APPENDIX A: RISK ANALYSIS FOR TWO INVESTMENTS

Table 1.6

CONSIDER THE FOLLOWING TWO INVESTMENTS ALONG WITH THEIR 10 POSSIBLE JOINT OUTCOMES.

	1	2	3	4	5	6	7	8	9	10
I_1	10	4	2	9	15	11	7	10	8	14
I_2	5	2	3	4	10	7	5	3	4	7

The mean of I_1 is: $\dfrac{10 + 4 + 2 + 9 + 15 + 11 + 7 + 10 + 8 + 14}{10} = 9$

The mean of I_2 is: $\dfrac{5 + 2 + 3 + 4 + 10 + 7 + 5 + 3 + 4 + 7}{10} = 5$

By removing the means (Table 1.7) we can concentrate on the risks associated with the investments:

Table 1.7

	1	2	3	4	5	6	7	8	9	10
I_1	1	–5	–7	0	6	2	–2	1	–1	5
I_2	0	–3	–2	–1	5	2	0	–2	–1	2
$I_1 \times I_1$	1	25	49	0	36	4	4	1	1	25
$I_2 \times I_2$	0	9	4	1	25	4	0	4	1	4
$I_1 \times I_2$	0	15	14	0	30	4	0	–2	1	10

The variance of I_1 is: $\dfrac{1+25+49+0+36+4+4+1+1+25}{10}=14.6$.

The standard deviation of I_1 is: $\sqrt{14.6}=3.82$.

The variance of I_2 is: $\dfrac{0+9+4+1+25+4+0+4+1+4}{10}=5.2$.

The standard deviation of I_2 is: $\sqrt{5.2}=2.28$.

The covariance of I_1 and I_2 is: $\dfrac{0+15+14+0+30+4+0-2+1+10}{10}=7.2$.

The correlation of I_1 and I_2 is:

$$\frac{Covariance}{Product\ of\ Standard\ Deviations} \quad = \quad \frac{7.2}{3.82\times2.28}=0.83 .$$

The correlation can range in value from –1 to 1.

A value of 0.83 means the investments are highly correlated. A visual inspection of either Table 1.7 or Table 1.8 shows that I_1 and I_2 tend to be high or low in synchronization.

If we construct a portfolio investment, I_3, consisting of one-half of I_1 plus one-half of I_2, we can calculate its mean and standard deviation as shown in Table 1.8.

Table 1.8

	1	2	3	4	5	6	7	8	9	10
I_3	7.5	3	2.5	6.5	12.5	9	6	6.5	6	10.5

The mean of I_3 is: $\dfrac{70}{10}=7.$

The variance of I_3 is:

$$\frac{0.5^2+4^2+4.5^2+0.5^2+2^2+1^2+0.5^2+1^2+3.52^2}{10}=8.55$$

The standard deviation is: $\sqrt{8.55}=2.92$.

As a cross-check of the formulas given in the text we may calculate directly

$$\tfrac{1}{2}r_1 + \tfrac{1}{2}r_2 = \tfrac{1}{2}9 + \tfrac{1}{2}5 = 7 \text{ for the mean}$$

and

$$\sqrt{\tfrac{1}{4}s_1^2 + \tfrac{1}{4}s_2^2 + 2c\tfrac{1}{4}s_1 s_2} = 2.93 \text{ for the standard deviation.}$$

APPENDIX B: AMPLIFICATION OF RISK ANALYSIS

Footnote 2. Suppose we have an alternative with mean 10 and standard deviation equal to 20 which is considered undesirable by a decision maker. The following gamble shown in Figure 1.9 can be calculated as also having mean 10 and standard deviation 20.

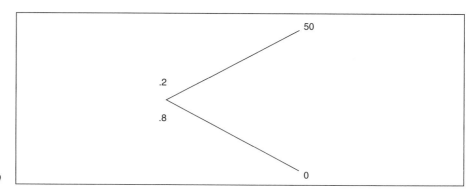

Figure 1.9

It is obviously desirable.

If *r* and *s* are the mean and standard deviation of a gamble, then so long as *r* is positive it is always possible to construct a gamble with these statistics that is desirable. See Figure 1.10 for a general example.

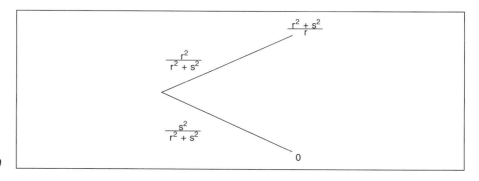

Figure 1.10

These examples suggest that variance is not a very satisfactory statistic for risk in cases where the distribution of returns is far from "normal."

Footnote 4.   Formula 2 gives the variance as:

$$k^2s^2 + (1 - k)^2s_2^2 + 2k(1 - k)cs_1s_2$$

which may be rewritten as

$$s_2^2 + 2k(cs_1s_2 - s_2^2) + k^2(s_2^2 + s_2^2 - 2cs_1s_2) \quad .$$

For those who know calculus, this expression may be differentiated with respect to *k* and equated to zero as follows:

$$2(cs_1s_2 - s_2^2) + 2k(s_1^2 + s_2^2 - 2cs_1s_2) = 0 \quad .$$

The solution is $k = (s_2^2 - cs_1s_2)/(s_1^2 + s_2^2 - 2cs_1s_2)$.

This is the formula given in the text. Substituting this value of *k* into Formula 2 gives us an expression for the minimum variance:

$$\frac{s_1^2 s_2^2 \left(1 - c^2\right)}{s_1^2 + s_2^2 - 2cs_1s_2} \quad .$$

Note that the optimal value of *k* might be less than 0 or greater than 1. If short selling or borrowing are not permitted, the minimum variance *k* cannot range below 0 or above 1. The expression for the minimum variance k will be between 0 and 1 if $cs_1 < s_2$ *and* $cs_2 < s_1$.

Footnote 6. Suppose $r_1 < r_2$. If we leverage I_1 by borrowing $\$b$ at the risk-free rate and investing $1 + b$ in I_1 we get an investment with mean return $-br_F + (1 + b)r_1$ and standard deviation $(1 + b)s_1$. In order that $-br_F + (1 + b)r_1 = r_2$ we must have $b = (r_2 - r_1)/(r_1 - r_F)$. Thus the standard deviation of the leveraged I_1 is:

$$1 + \left[\frac{(r_2 - r_1)}{r_1 - r_F}\right]s_1 = \left[\frac{r_1 - r_F + r_2 - r_1}{r_1 - r_F}\right]s_1 = \left[\frac{r_2 - r_F}{r_1 - r_F}\right]s_1 .$$

The leveraged I_1 is desirable if:

$$c\left[\frac{r_2 - r_F}{r_1 - r_F}\right]s_1 < s_2 .$$

When rearranged, this is Formula 4.

Footnote 7. A portfolio of k_1 parts of I_1, k_2 parts of I_2 and $(1 - k_1 - k_2)$ of the risk-free rate will have mean

$$k_1 r_1 + k_2 r_2 + (1 - k_1 - k_2)r_F \qquad \text{(a)}$$

and variance

$$k^2_1 s^2_1 + k^2_2 s^2_2 + 2k_1 k_2 cs_1 s_2 . \qquad \text{(b)}$$

A portfolio created by borrowing b parts of the risk-free rate to invest $1 + b$ in I_2 gives a portfolio with mean:

$$-br_F + (1 + b)r_2 \qquad \text{(c)}$$

and variance

$$(1 + b)^2 s^2_2 . \qquad \text{(d)}$$

The logic of the proof will be to show that if I_1 fails the test of Formula 4:

$$\frac{r_1 - r_F}{s_1} < c\frac{r_2 - r_F}{s_2}$$

then any portfolio containing positive amounts of I_1 is strictly worse than a portfolio of the same mean created by a simple leverage of I_2. That is, whatever is achieved by investing in I_1 could be achieved even better by simply leveraging the existing portfolio. To do this, I will show that whenever (a) = (c), (b) is greater than (d).

If (a) does equal (c), then

$$k_1 r_1 + k_2 r_2 + (1 - k_1 - k_2)r_F = -br_F + (1 + b)r_2$$

or

$$b(r_2 - r_F) = k_1 r_1 + k_2 r_2 + (1 - k_1 - k_2)r_F - r_2$$

so that

$$1 + b = k_2 + k_1 \frac{r_1 - vr_F}{r_2 - r_F} \quad .$$

If k_1 is positive and

$$\frac{r_1 - r_F}{s_1} < c \frac{r_2 - vr_F}{s_2}$$

then $1 + b < k_2 + k_1 \dfrac{cs_1}{s_2}$ so that (d) is less than

$$(k_2 + k_1 \frac{cs_1}{s_2})^2 s_2^2$$

or

$$(k_2 s_2 + k_1 c s_1)^2.$$

This in turn will be less than (b) if:

$$(k_2 s_2 + k_1 c s_1)^2 \leq k_1^2 s_1^2 + k_2^2 s_2^2 + 2k_1 k_2 \, cs_1 s_2$$

or

$$k_2 s_2^2 + k_1^2 c^2 s_1^2 + 2k_2 k_1 \, cs_2 s_1 \leq k_1^2 s_1^2 + k_2^2 s_2^2 + 2k_1 k_2 cs_1 s_2$$

which will be so if $c^2 \leq 1$, which is of course, true.

To summarize, a portfolio containing I_1 is worse than one of the same mean created by simply leveraging I_2. But we already know that leveraging I_2 is suboptimal. Hence I_1 is undesirable.

CASE

GOLDEN GATE BANK RETIREMENT FUND

In May 1979, the Golden Gate Bank of San Francisco set up an Investment Management Division to manage the assets of large pension funds and endowments. Prior to this time, although the bank had a sizable and profitable personal trust business, it had not managed institutional assets of any size, and the contribution to earnings of the institutional management activities was negative. Moreover, the investment environment of the previous five years had been such that its institutional investors had not had good investment returns. This performance in the investment management business was typical of the bank's past performance in general, and the bank's poor financial position had led to the appointment of a new president in March of 1979. One of his first actions was to hire Janet Beach, formerly an investment analyst at a New York bank, to set up a new group to court aggressively institutional money-management business.

By November of 1981, Janet had good reason to feel some satisfaction with her progress. Not only were returns on assets managed by the bank competitive with those of other money management institutions, but her group had succeeded in building the volume of assets under management for major corporate clients to over a billion dollars.

It had been Janet's idea to use an International Index Fund as a means of distinguishing Golden Gate's services from other investment management companies. A company in Geneva had for some years published an index of worldwide stock values, but no one had thought of operating a fund indexed in this manner. Golden Gate's International Index was now a major component of many of the bank's significant pension funds. The index was calculated by adding the stock market indexes of several major countries (not including the United States) weighted proportionally to the total capital that each market represented. For example, Japan had twice the weighting of the United Kingdom which had 10 times the weight of Singapore. Had the United States been included on the same basis, its weight would have been twice that of Japan's.

One client that had not been approached to adopt the International Index was Golden Gate's own Retirement Fund, currently worth about $30 million. The board of the Retirement Fund was composed of senior executives of the bank, who were aware of the group's good recent performance but unaware of the details of its operation. Janet had requested the opportunity to make a presentation to propose changes in the management of the account, and a meeting was set for November 19, three days from now. She intended to use this opportunity to recommend not only the use of the International Index but also the use of options, another of the division's successful innovations.

From her office in the Transamerica Building, Janet watched the evening fog flow in from the bay and enshroud the bank's namesake and symbol. Ron Meyer, her chief investment manager, came into the office with what she hoped was a final version of the report to the Retirement Fund board on which her presentation would be based. Much of it consisted of standard extracts which were usual in reports of this type but she and Ron had agreed that they should take more care than usual to make their recommended use of the International Index and of fiduciary puts seem routine.

Ron had phrased it accurately if not diplomatically when he said, "We are going to have to be dead sure they understand that international investments and options are not wildly speculative but, on the contrary, are extremely conservative given the kind of return that they are wanting. These guys are practically retired themselves and do not want to see two young kids playing Monopoly with their pension. You have to see their point of view. They have spent 40 years living up to the image of bank investments as a benchmark for conservatism and now we are asking them to let a computer play the options market for them."

Janet read through the following report before going to work on her presentation.

Golden Gate Bank
Retirement Fund Asset Allocation Analysis
Retirement Committee Meeting
November 18, 1981

Summary

The purpose of this study is to determine an appropriate investment policy for the Golden Gate Bank Retirement Fund expressed as an allocation of asset categories over a long-term (ten-year) time horizon. At present, there are three major asset classes in which the fund is invested—common stocks, the Standard & Poor's 500 Index Fund, and bonds. To reduce the volatility or risk of the portfolio as well as to provide the possibility of enhanced returns, we recommend that a portion of existing assets be reallocated to the Golden Gate Bank International Index Fund and to a modified equity investment strategy which employs security options to dampen the volatility of investment returns.

The analysis employs information in a February, 1980 presentation to the committee in which it was determined that an investment return of 6.33% per annum was necessary to maintain company contributions as a constant proportion of payroll covered by the plan.

In this study, long-term expected return risk and the interrelationship (correlation coefficient) between each asset type or strategy were entered into an analytical program. The probability of not achieving the target 6.3% rate of return for a family of portfolios with varying asset mixes was obtained. The likelihood of achieving an exceptionally good return of 8% or better, of losing money (0% return), or of incurring a fairly significant loss of 10% or more was also examined. The investment policy selected was that asset mix which minimized the probability of not achieving the 6.3% target return and at the same time allowed both a good chance of obtaining an 8% return over a 10-year time horizon and a low chance of incurring a loss of 10% or more.

The analysis performed in February, 1980 for the three basic asset vehicles currently used in the plan (bonds, common stocks, and the S&P 500 Index Fund) has been compared with that of the extended universe, which incorporates additional asset categories of an international index fund and low volatility options/equity investments.

As might be expected, the results demonstrate that the use of more investment vehicles with low co-movement and volatility leads to greater diversification of the plan, less volatility in expected outcomes, and hence less risk in terms of company pension contributions.

On the basis of this analysis, it is recommended that the following November, 1981 analysis asset allocation investment policy be adopted:

Table 1.10

	FEBRUARY, 1980 ANALYSIS	NOVEMBER, 1981 ANALYSIS
MANAGED COMMON EQUITIES	40% – 60%	20% – 40%
INDEX FUND	—	10%
BONDS	60% – 40%	45% – 25%
INTERNATIONAL INDEX FUND	—	15%
FIDUCIARY PUTS	—	10%
	100%	100%

Such a redeployment of assets will reduce the volatility of plan investment results, increase the probability of attaining both the 6.3% target and the 8% rate of return, and even reduce the likelihood that sizable losses might be incurred. The net effect of this strategy, therefore, is less risk and the likelihood that a lower level of contributions to the Golden Gate Bank Retirement Fund can be achieved than under the present investment policy.

Discussion

In this analysis, portfolios which provide the greatest return per unit of risk (i.e., which are "efficient") are calculated using assumptions as to the possible level of return for each asset category, its risk or uncertainty of return, and the known interrelationships (correlations) among returns from the different investment vehicles. From the risk and return of these optimal portfolios, the probability of not achieving a desired rate of return can be computed.

The long-term return assumptions which have been made in this analysis are consistent with empirical market studies. The expected return from bonds is assumed to be slightly lower than current yields on bonds owing to our assumption of lower reinvestment rates for future coupon income. The expected return from equities is assumed to be greater than the expected bond return by a margin consistent with its historical superiority. Based upon data from our tests of multiple valuation models, we have also estimated that the managed portion of domestic equities will provide a return of at least 50 basis points more than the Standard & Poor's Index (Exhibit 1).

Assumptions with regard to the two new investment alternatives are purposely conservative. Thus, it has been assumed that the International Index Fund return will equal that of the Standard & Poor's 500 Index even though it has exceeded the return of the Composite Index by a significant margin in nine out of the past ten years. The rationale for use of the Golden Gate Bank International Index Fund is summarized in Appendix A.

The return assumed for the fiduciary put strategy is based upon an extensive study of this subject by Professors Merton (MIT) and Scholes (University of Chicago), and Mr. Matthew Gladstein of Donaldson, Lufkin, Jenrette & Co. This study, which covered a lengthy period from 1963 to 1977, demonstrated that the fiduciary put strategy could produce returns equal to that of a pure equity strategy but with much less risk. We have revised these return estimates downward to reflect our belief that in the future a fiduciary put strategy may provide a lower level of return owing to a possible change in the pricing of puts. Finally, an unusually conservative assumption is embedded in the return distribution provided by the analytical program, which estimates downside risk approximately equivalent to the upside potential. In fact, downside risk is limited as is shown in Exhibit 2.

The interrelationship among returns in this analysis is expressed as a correlation matrix. The values of this correlation matrix reflect the last 10 years of investment history. The correlation coefficients for the fiduciary put strategy have been calculated from available data by Golden Gate Bank. These assumptions are summarized in Exhibit 1.

The most appropriate asset allocation investment policy incorporating international and fiduciary put strategies to meet the requirements previously outlined is delineated by a box in Exhibit 3A. The probabilities of attaining various target returns, using the changing composition of an expanded universe of asset types, is shown in Exhibit 3. Similarly, the optimal asset mix selected in the February, 1980 analysis is delineated by a box in Exhibit 4A. The relationship between the probability of attaining the various target rates of return and various asset mixes is shown in Exhibit 4. By comparison of Exhibits 3 and 4, it can be seen that the risk of not achieving the various threshold levels of return discussed previously is reduced by employing additional investment alternatives in the fund. It should be noted that the two new asset categories are so attractive that it has been necessary to constrain their proportions to the arbitrary maximums shown. Thus, risk can be reduced without sacrificing potential returns. This observation is consistent with the basic principle of investment diversification, which states that the more types of investment alternatives employed, the less will be the risk of a portfolio but without necessarily sacrificing return.

Exhibit 1

CORRELATION MATRIX FOR FIVE INVESTMENT TYPES

	BONDS	S&P	STOCKS	INDEX	OPTIONS[*]
Bonds	100				
Standard & Poor's 500 Index	51	100			
Common Stocks	49	98	100		
Golden Gate International Index	27	50	48	100	
Options (at the money)	47	94	90	46	100
Expected Annual Yield	8.5	13.0	13.5	13.0	11.0
Annual Standard Deviation	9.1	20.6	21.2	19.0	12.0
Maximum Portfolio Percentage	100	20	100	15	10
Minimum Portfolio Percentage	0	10	0	0	0

[*]The options consist of ownership of both a put option and the underlying stock.

Exhibit 2

MARKET RETURN VS. OPTIONED EQUITY PORTFOLIO RETURN

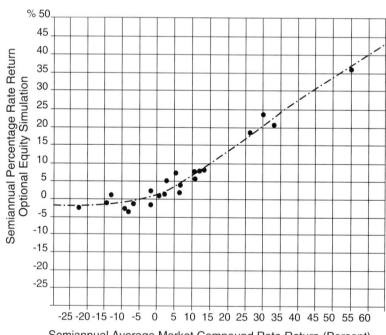

Exhibit 3

NOVEMBER, 1981 STOCKS, BONDS, INTERNATIONAL INDEX, OPTIONS PORTFOLIO

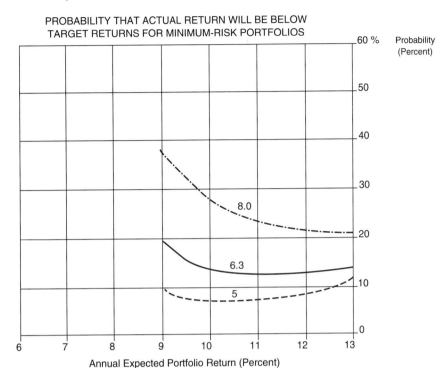

PROBABILITY THAT ACTUAL RETURN WILL BE BELOW
TARGET RETURNS FOR MINIMUM-RISK PORTFOLIOS

Exhibit 3A

RISK OF LOSS ANALYSIS — NOVEMBER, 1981

PORTFOLIOS ON EFFICIENT FRONTIER, MINIMUM RISK FOR GIVEN RETURN

120-MONTH HORIZON

Annual Exp. Return	Annual Standard Deviation	Probability of Annual Return of Less Than:					Minimum Risk Asset Mix:				
		−10.0%	0.0%	5.0%	6.3%	8.0%	BONDS	S&P	STOCKS	GGIF	OPTIONS
9.00*	9.3	0.0	0.2	10.1	19.7	37.7	87.7	10.0	0.0	0.0	2.3
9.34	9.2	0.0	0.1	8.2	16.6	33.5	77.1	10.0	0.0	4.1	8.9
9.50	9.2	0.0	0.1	7.5	15.4	31.8	73.1	10.0	0.0	6.9	10.0
10.00	9.7	0.0	0.1	6.4	13.2	27.5	62.2	10.0	2.8	15.0	10.0
10.50	10.8	0.0	0.2	6.6	12.7	25.0	52.1	10.0	12.9	15.0	10.0
11.00	12.0	0.0	0.3	7.1	12.6	23.4	42.1	10.0	22.9	15.0	10.0
11.50	13.4	0.0	0.5	7.7	12.8	22.5	32.1	10.0	32.9	15.0	10.0
12.00	14.9	0.0	0.8	8.4	13.2	21.8	22.2	10.0	42.8	15.0	10.0
12.50	16.4	0.0	1.1	9.0	13.6	21.4	12.3	10.0	52.7	15.0	10.0
13.00	18.0	0.0	1.5	9.7	14.0	21.2	2.4	10.0	62.6	15.0	10.0

*For example, with this portfolio the return each year is 9% ± 9.3%. There is a 10.1% chance that the 10-year average return is less than 5%. This information can also be read off the graph in Exhibit 3.

Exhibit 4

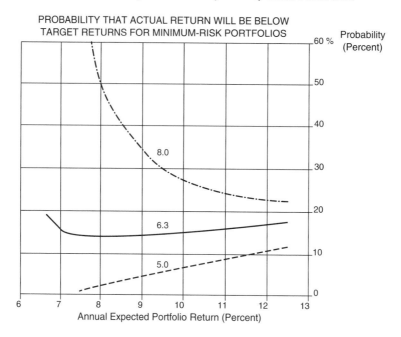

FEBRUARY, 1980 STOCKS, BONDS, CASH PORTFOLIO

Exhibit 4A

RISK OF LOSS ANALYSIS — FEBRUARY, 1980
PORTFOLIOS ON EFFICIENT FRONTIER — MINIMUM RISK FOR GIVEN RETURN
120-MONTH HORIZON

Annual Exp. Return	Annual Standard Deviation	Probability of Annual Return of Less Than:					Minimum Risk Asset Mix:			
		−10.0%	0.0%	5.0%	6.3%	8.0%	S&P	*KL1	*KL2	·T. BILLS
6.47	0.5	0.0	0.0	0.0	20.7	100.0	0.3	0.0	3.5	96.2
6.50	0.5	0.0	0.0	0.0	18.7	100.0	0.5	0.0	4.5	95.0
7.00	1.6	0.0	0.0	0.0	12.0	94.4	4.8	0.0	20.9	74.4
7.50	2.9	0.0	0.0	0.7	11.8	67.7	9.0	0.0	37.2	53.8
8.00	4.3	0.0	0.0	1.8	11.8	49.3	13.2	0.0	53.4	33.4
8.50	5.8	0.0	0.0	3.0	11.8	39.0	17.4	0.0	69.6	13.1
9.00	7.2	0.0	0.0	4.0	12.0	33.0	23.7	1.5	74.8	0.0
9.50	8.8	0.0	0.0	5.3	12.7	29.5	32.6	15.8	51.6	0.0
10.00	10.4	0.0	0.1	6.7	13.4	27.5	41.5	30.1	28.4	0.0
10.50	12.2	0.0	0.3	7.9	14.1	26.2	50.4	44.3	5.3	0.0
11.00	14.0	0.0	0.6	9.0	14.8	25.3	61.9	38.1	0.0	0.0
11.50	16.0	0.0	1.1	10.3	15.7	25.0	74.1	25.9	0.0	0.0
12.00	18.1	0.0	1.7	11.5	16.5	24.8	86.3	13.7	0.0	0.0
12.50	20.3	0.0	2.5	12.6	17.3	24.8	98.4	1.6	0.0	0.0

*KL1 and KL2 are bond indexes of Kuhn-Loeb.

▼   ▼   ▼

WHY INVEST INTERNATIONALLY?

A careful analysis of available evidence indicates that a properly conceived and executed program of international equity investing offers U.S. institutional investors an important means of increasing the probability of attaining superior long-term results. The increased diversification possible through an international investment strategy provides one of the most significant opportunities for reducing investment risk available to U.S. investors. The essence of the argument for international investing is simple, yet powerful. Not all world equity markets move together in a synchronized fashion. In varying degrees, each market has its own performance cycle because different national economies are subject to varying socioeconomic and political forces. Since the returns on common stocks in different markets do not move in lockstep, the opportunity exists to reduce the uncertainty of portfolio returns materially by diversifying across stock markets as well as within them.

The desirability of an international investment strategy is dependent upon expected returns in foreign equity markets as well as the risk reduction potential from additional diversification. Both financial history and fundamental economic factors suggest that for a number of countries of practical investment interest, future rates of return will at least be competitive with the U.S. equity market. Indeed, if history is at all suggestive of the future, returns from an international investing strategy are likely to improve the performance of a U.S. portfolio.

Why Index When Investing Internationally?

There is a very strong if not compelling rationale for the use of an index matching strategy when investing internationally. The arguments which favor an international index matching strategy are very similar to evidence supporting use of domestic index funds as summarized below:

▸ The efficiency of the U.S. equity market has been well documented by numerous investigations.

▸ The average U.S. equity manager has not been able to provide a risk-adjusted return as great as that of a buy-and-hold benchmark portfolio. The magnitude of this performance shortfall approximates the costs of management and trading.

▸ A domestic index fund is designed to essentially eliminate active management costs.

▸ U.S. index funds have been quite successful following this strategy. Index fund performance has consistently ranked among the first quartile of actively managed equity portfolios over an extended period of time.

The rationale for an international index fund is stronger than that for a domestic fund. The low negotiated commission rate structure of the United States does not exist in foreign countries. Not only are foreign commission costs measurably greater than in the United States, but in some countries, so are certain other related investment-management expenses such as taxes and custody. The stronger parallel argument for an international index matching strategy, then, is based upon the following facts:

▸ The efficiency of international currency and securities markets has been documented.

▸ Active international management trading and other costs are relatively high.

- Published studies indicate that the average international manager is unable to provide risk-adjusted returns greater than appropriate buy-and-hold benchmark portfolios.

- Performance of the majority of active international managers, taken from public and other data sources, reveals a general inability to provide returns as great as a benchmark portfolio such as the Capital International Europe, Far East and Australia (CIEFA) index.

- An index fund complements active management by providing an assured base of broad diversification upon which to build an aggressive active strategy. The advantages of active/passive strategies and their growing use domestically can be realized in an international investment program by use of a properly diversified international index fund.

WHY SELECT THE GOLDEN GATE BANK INTERNATIONAL INDEX FUND?

The Golden Gate Bank International Index Fund provides significant benefits as summarized below:

Unique

- Capital International Index-matching in nine countries via separate modular funds.

- The first, and still one of only a few, IRS-approved, international index funds available.

Flexible

- Appropriate weighting of country indexes allows matching of the Capital International Europe, Far East, and Australia (CIEFA) index.

- Other investment strategies may be utilized by varying country weights to meet specific client needs.

- Precious metal or commodity-related investment vehicles may be employed as alternative assets.

- Other country indexes than those provided may be added rapidly.

- Active country selection strategies can be used owing to the modular fund structure.

- U.S. corporations can index to local markets of their foreign subsidiary employee benefit plans.

Broadly Diversified

- Investments are held in approximately 600 companies representing 92% of the CIEFA index and 55% of the aggregate equity market outside North America.

- Broad diversification eliminates risks which drive from typical fund biases toward multinational, large, high-yield or low-growth companies.

Low Cost

▶ An aggressive continuing effort is directed toward reduction of brokerage, commission, custody, and other costs to the lowest possible level.

▶ Index fund trading techniques, including guaranteed closing prices, are employed.

Single Source For All Fiduciary Services

▶ Golden Gate Bank directly provides and controls all services necessary for an international investment program. A single manager is responsible for all aspects of international investing, and a client therefore need only deal directly with one individual and one organization with regard to such considerations as:

  • portfolio investment management
  • foreign currency transactions
  • foreign dividend withholding tax negotiations
  • short-term investment fund for handling cash flow and dividend payments
  • dividend collections
  • corporate actions
  • securities custodian status
  • performance measurement

Operational Expertise

▶ The Golden Gate Bank International Index Fund has been in operation since August 1979 — longer than any other IRS-approved fund.

▶ An operational system specially designed to deal with and protect you from the many diverse security practices of foreign markets provides assurance of a high level of quality, trouble-free service on an ongoing basis.

FIDUCIARY PUT OPTIONS

The advent of exchange traded options on the Chicago Board Options Exchange has led to an increased public awareness of options as investment vehicles. The traditional belief prior to exchange traded options held that options were speculative in nature and possessed only speculative attributes. There is a growing awareness of the various legitimate investment uses to which options can be put. Institutional investors' use of options has been increasing in recent years, and their usage in pension plan management has expanded dramatically. Options are a vehicle whereby the investment risks and returns associated with equity investments can be transferred among participants in the options transactions. Options enable the investor to obtain different returns at different levels of risk than from pure equity investments. While certain uses of options are surely speculative, other uses of options are conservative in nature, and involve the prudent investment practice of limiting investment risk.

Fiduciary Puts

The put option is one type of option which is currently traded on the public option exchanges. The owner of securities who purchases a put option obtains, for a limited period of time, the right to sell his security position at a specified price. (In option terminology, the time period of the option is called the term to expiration; the purchase price of the option is called the premium; and the price at which the purchaser of the put option obtains the right to sell the securities is called the strike price.) A simple analogy with which to compare the holder of equity securities who purchases a put option is that of a homeowner who purchases fire insurance for his property. The purchase of insurance guards the homeowner against an unanticipated catastrophe which would impair his financial well-being. Viewed in this light, the purchase of a put option is the purchase of insurance on equity holdings. The purchase of put options guards the security holder against unanticipated downside movements in the price of the equity securities, since he has obtained the right to sell these securities at the strike price. The holder of equity securities who has purchased put options has limited the downside possibility on return for his portfolio, while maintaining an essentially unlimited upside potential in terms of investment return.

While the holder of equities has obtained a different pattern of returns than he would have received from just holding equities, and while he has limited his downside risk, he has in no sense obtained something for nothing. The periodic purchase of put options entails an outflow of funds which are not recovered, much as the homeowner who purchases fire insurance has an outflow of premium on a periodic basis. Thus, while the investor has limited his volatility, he has also reduced the amount of return which he should receive through his fiduciary put option purchase strategy. By skillful investment management, however, the investor employing these strategies should be able to earn superior returns to those obtainable by an average investor following the same investment strategy. The employment of the fiduciary put strategy does not abandon the traditional investment principle of trying to obtain extra returns through management skill. Decisions which the user of put options must make include the attractiveness of option premiums, the strike price at which he wishes to protect himself, the term of the option which he wishes to purchase, and the outlook for the stock being protected. Investment skill is called for in the employment of the put option strategy.

Much of the work that we have done in terms of defining the risk and returns available from a fiduciary put option strategy rests on a rather lengthy empirical set of studies performed by academic options experts and options professionals. The studies which we have utilized performed computer simulations of various option equity strategies over a period ranging from 1963 through 1977. For the put option-strategy examination, various portfolios were constructed, and the returns and risks available from a pure equity strategy were compared to the returns and risks available from an optioned equity strategy. The major point of difference which some of our projections make from the return and risk results obtained by the studies cited are conservative. We have assumed a less favorable return experience from the fiduciary put strategy than was produced by the studies. It is interesting to note in the mixed simulations done in the attached analysis for the Retirement Fund, that even with vastly inferior returns to those produced by the option simulations, there is a clear place for the fiduciary put strategy within the Retirement Fund portfolio as a means for improving the risk/reward trade-off.

PUT OPTION VIEWED AS A TERM INSURANCE POLICY

Table 1.11

	GENERAL	EXAMPLE (6/19/81)
Asset Insured	Stock	IBM
Asset's Current Value	Stock Price, $S	$57.5
Term of Policy	Time until expiration of the put	6 months (Dec. 81)
Maximum Insurance Coverage [Face Value of Policy] (maximum loss to the insurer)	Exercise Price of Put, $E	$50.00
Amount of Deductible (maximum loss to the insured)	$[S - E]	$ 7.50
Insurance Premium	Put Price/per share	$ 0.875

*If an investor holds a risky security and reduces his risk by the purchase of a put option on that risky security, then such an investment strategy is called a "Protective Put," "Insured Equity," or "Fiduciary Put" strategy.

RETIREMENT FUND REQUIRED RATE OF RETURN RESULT, ASSUMPTIONS, AND SENSITIVITY ANALYSIS

RESULT

Required rate of return on assets assuming contributions as percent of payroll remain constant   6.33% per year

ASSUMPTIONS

Growth rate in benefit payments	8.00%	per year
Growth rate in normal costs	7.50%	per year
Amortization of unfunded past service costs	$398,000	per year
Actuarial rate of return	5.00%	per year
Growth rate in covered payroll	4.00%	per year
Ratio of contributions as percent of payroll (1979)	8.80%	

Table 1.12

CORPORATE CONTRIBUTION SENSITIVITY TABLE	
CONTRIBUTION/PAYROLL (PERCENT)	REQUIRED/RETURN (PERCENT/YEAR)
0.0	14.64
1.0	13.63
2.0	12.65
3.0	11.68
4.0	10.72
5.0	9.78
6.0	8.86
7.0	7.94
8.0	7.04
9.0	6.16
10.0	5.28
11.0	4.42
12.0	3.58
13.0	2.74
14.0	1.92
15.0	1.11
16.0	0.31

▼   ▼   ▼

EXERCISES ON DIVERSIFICATION

Use Figure 1.11 to help you answer questions 1, 2, 3 and 4.

1. The returns from two investments I_1 and I_2 have been estimated as follows:

   Figure 1.11 shows a graph of the mean and standard deviation for all possible portfolios involving I_1 and I_2. (It is advisable to check some of the computations directly. If you do, bear in mind that the standard deviations given by calculators usually presume historical data is being used and will give, in

Table 1.13

PROBABILITY	I_1	I_2
.2	15%	3%
.2	–3%	7%
.2	22%	4%
.2	9%	5%
.2	7%	11%

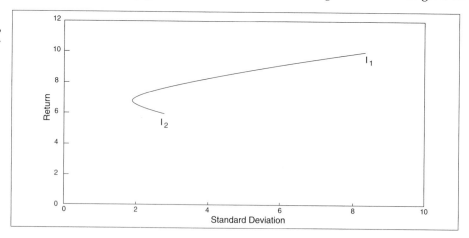

Figure 1.11

Harvard Business School note 9-184-115. Professor David E. Bell prepared these exercises as the basis for class discussion. Copyright © 1984 by the President and Fellows of Harvard College.

this case, values that are too big by a factor of 1.12.) What is the lowest standard deviation achievable from a portfolio of I1 and I2? What is the expected return on this portfolio? What proportion of the portfolio is in I1?

2. If a risk-free investment, I_0 , returning 6% is also available, in what proportion will investors hold I_1 and I_2?

3. When I_0 is available, why would anyone ever want to hold any of I_2 (which also gives a mean return of 6%, yet is risky)?

4. Assuming I_0, I_1, and I_2 are just three of many possible investments and that they are fairly priced, and if the market portfolio has a mean return of 13% with a standard deviation of 12%, calculate the betas of I_1 and I_2 and their correlations with the market portfolio.

5. Figure 1.11 shows the mean and standard deviation of return for six hypothetical investments, the market portfolio, and a risk-free asset.

   a. Investment 1 is definitely mispriced. How can you tell this from the graph?

   b. There is no reason to suppose the other five investments are mispriced. Explain why.

   c. Assume the five Investments 2 through 6 are fairly priced. Which investment has a higher beta? 4 or 2? 2 or 5? 5 or 6?

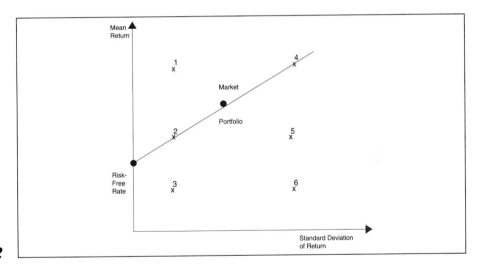

Figure 1.12

6. Call an event unsystematic if it has a correlation of 0 with the market portfolio. A (completely) systematic risk is one having a correlation of 1 with the market. Which of the following risks are unsystematic?

   a. A plane crash kills the entire board of directors of a company on their way to a retreat in Bermuda.

   b. The government eliminates the corporate income tax.

   c. The Bosnian conflict is resolved.

   d. The Occupational Safety and Health Administration (OSHA) determines that a form of wall insulation causes cancer and must be replaced. This kind of wall insulation is used in 25% of factories and offices.

7. Assume that the market portfolio has a mean return of 13%, a standard deviation of 20%, and that the risk-free rate is 6%. I_1 is an investment whose value in 12 months' time is expected to be $10,000 with a standard deviation of $5,000. The variation in value of the asset has a 0.8 correlation with the market. I_1 will open for trading tomorrow. Show that it should open at a price of $8,113.21.

8. Returning to Figure 1.11, suppose I_0, I_1 and I_2 are the only possible investments. Suppose that the market portfolio is $\frac{3}{8}I_1 + \frac{5}{8}I_2$. If there are one million shares outstanding for each of I_1 and I_2, and if I_1 currently trades at $15 per share, what is the price of I_2 shares? What is the correlation between I_2 and $\frac{3}{8}I_1 + \frac{5}{8}I_2$?

▼ 2 HEDGING

Diversification relies on risks "averaging out." The idea of a hedge is to find a second risk that, as closely as possible, offsets one you already hold. Insurance companies are in the business of constructing such offsetting risks (that's what insurance policies are). The futures markets are also useful as a source of offsetting risks. However, the first step is to determine exactly what risk you face. What *is* your current exposure? The chapter begins with a section that explains exposure and hedging, followed by two cases that will challenge your thinking about exposure. It also contains an introduction to futures contracts and explores the complexities of cross-hedging, the practice whereby one tries to hedge with risks that are *not* perfectly offsetting.

EXPOSURE AND HEDGING

Many things are uncertain, but only those uncertainties whose outcomes affect you are risks. You are uncertain what the exchange rate between francs and dollars will be by the end of this year (indeed you may be uncertain about its current level) but this may not represent a risk to you. A risk is an uncertainty that matters. If you have no assets or liabilities denominated in francs, if you do not intend to import a Peugeot or go to France for a vacation, chances are you do not care what the exchange rate is or will be. If you do have reason to be concerned about the exchange rate, you have a franc *exposure*.

The next question is, how serious is that exposure? If the franc were to drop from six to the dollar to five to the dollar, what would be the impact on your finances? Exposure analysis is not always straightforward. Different aspects of your position may be influenced by the uncertainty. For example, if you decided to "short" the S&P 500, do you want the market to go up or down? Down would improve the value of your short position, but suppose you also have a personal pension fund that is permanently invested (long) in the stock market? You'd be right to feel good about shorting the market if it goes down, but even so, you'd have been better off if the market had gone up (assuming the pension fund position exceeded the short position). One way to get exposure straight is to ask yourself, "If I hear the stock market (French franc, interest rates) has gone up, am I better or worse off?"

Another difficulty comes when the relationship between the uncertainty and your position is unclear. For example, you may think that your finances will be greatly influenced by a change in the price of oil and thus you keep a close eye on developments at OPEC meetings. But can you decide whether you

Harvard Business School note 9-186-036. Professor David E. Bell prepared this section. Copyright © 1985 by the President and Fellows of Harvard College.

will be better or worse off if oil prices go up? If you hold oil stocks, or oil and gas tax shelters, you may be better off. Even if you do not use oil you may be affected adversely over time due to the impact of oil increases on other energy prices and on the U.S. economy.

Your exposure may also depend on *when* an increase occurs. Therefore it is useful, in defining exposure, to make clear what assumptions are being made. For example, you might say, "Our cashflow for the remainder of this year will fall by $1,000 per day for each additional dollar per barrel on the price of oil."

Example

In June 1981, Madison Wire[1] had the following loans outstanding:

$2.5 million at 70% of the prime rate

$1.6 million at one point above prime

$1 million at 65% of the prime rate.

Interest was paid quarterly, based on the prime rate set by the First National Bank of Boston at the end of the quarter in question. The below-prime loans had been granted by the Industrial Revenue Board, which additionally had dictated that the effective interest rate on the $1 million loan could not fall below 8% or above 11%. What is Madison's exposure to the prime?

To avoid complication, we will ignore any effects that changes in the prime rate might have on the rest of Madison's business and concentrate solely on its loan payments. We must also be quite clear about whether we are referring to exposure on a quarterly payment, annual payment, or the total additional payments over the life of the loans. Again, let us take the easy course by measuring the exposure of one quarterly payment.

A 1% increase in the prime rate will increase the payments on the $2.5 million loan by:

$$\frac{1}{4} \times 0.01 \times 0.70 \times \$2,500,000 = \$4,375 \quad,$$

and on the $1.6 million loan by:

$$\frac{1}{4} \times 0.01 \times 1.0 \times \$1,600,000 = \$4,000 \quad.$$

The exposure of the $1 million loan depends on the current prime rate. If the prime is below $8 \div 0.65$ or 12.35%, then a small increase in the prime will not increase Madison's payments at all. Nor will it if current rates are above $11 \div 0.65$ or 16.9%. Between these rates Madison's exposure is:

$$\frac{1}{4} \times 0.01 \times 0.65 \times \$1,000,000 = \$1,625 \quad.$$

In fact the prime rate in June 1981 was 19%, so the exposure on Madison's quarterly interest payments to a 1% jump in the prime was $8,375.

Hedging

Having analyzed your exposure to an uncertainty, it is possible to think more objectively about the merits of the following risk management alternatives:

---

[1] Based on Madison Wire and Cable Corporation (B), Harvard Business School case 9-183-118.

1. **Collect more information.** If the outcome of the uncertainty is very important to you it may be worth trying to predict (forecast) the value of the uncertain quantity with greater precision. Unfortunately, this doesn't actually *change* the outcome, it merely tells you earlier what that outcome will be.

2. **Influence the outcome.** If you have any way to affect how the uncertainty turns out, the exposure analysis will tell you if it's worth doing. Driving slowly to avoid accidents is a clear example. However, if you are capable of influencing oil prices, there may be better uses for your talents than in managing risk.

The principal risk management device after an exposure analysis is thus to:

3. **Hedge.** A *hedge* is simply an action in which you undertake an additional cashflow that has equal but opposite exposure to your existing position. In this way, of course, the combined exposure is nil. For example, if you stand to lose $1,000 for every $1 per ounce increase in the price of gold, buy 1,000 ounces of gold. (This costs money of course, but it does eliminate the exposure.) If you stand to lose $10,000 if your car is a write-off, buy an insurance policy that pays off $10,000 if the car is damaged beyond repair.

How should Madison hedge its exposure to the prime? In the unlikely event that they have $4.1 million of capital sitting in the bank, invested at a fixed rate of return, they could use it to pay off the variable loans. Since the loans are at below market rates it might be more advantageous to lend out $3.35 million of that money at the prime. The right amount is $3.35 million because a one-point jump in the prime would then bring in $0.01 \times 1/4 \times 3,350,000 = \$8,375$. Even without available capital, Madison could have hedged its next few quarterly payments if there were forward markets (or futures markets) in the prime. However, there are none.

Cross-Hedging

If a perfect hedge is not possible, it may be possible to reduce exposure by taking offsetting positions that *tend* to move in the opposite direction to your status quo position. For example, if you find yourself long in Austrian schillings, but with no easy hedge, you might decide to short German marks in the belief that these two currencies, while not tied to each other in any formal way, nevertheless can be expected to move more or less in harmony.

Let Y be the variable whose value concerns you (asset position, cashflow, being alive) and X the uncertain quantity that might be a useful cross-hedge (the price of oil, the level of interest rates). Suppose you take a position in X such that you lose k dollars for every unit increase in X. Then your net position is $Y - kX$. You should choose the value k so that the risk in your net position is as low as possible. One could compare the spread in the risk profiles for different values of k, or, more formally, maximize the expected preference value.

For Madison Wire, a possible cross-hedge is in T-bills. We will continue to suppose, somewhat unrealistically, that Madison has extra cash that could be invested in T-bills. We have already calculated that they should invest $3.35 million if the return is tied to the prime, but how much do they need to invest if the return is tied to the T-bill rate? Table 2.1 shows a table of quarterly interest rates from March '76 to September '84. (This table would have been invaluable in June 1981 of course.) Table 2.2 shows the difference between the prime and T-bill rates ($P - T$), the difference between the prime and $1.25 \times$ T-bill rate ($P - 1.25T$), and the difference between the prime and $1.50 \times$ T-bill rate ($P - 1.50T$).

Table 2.1

QUARTERLY INTEREST RATE DATA (%)

Month	Prime Rate	Treasury Bill Discount Rate
1. March 1976	6.5	4.89
2. June 1976	7.0	5.51
3. September 1976	7.0	5.07
4. December 1976	6.25	4.41
5. March 1977	6.25	4.70
6. June 1977	6.5	5.01
7. September 1977	7.0	5.55
8. December 1977	7.75	6.03
9. March 1978	8.0	6.40
10. June 1978	8.25	6.63
11. September 1978	9.0	7.52
12. December 1978	11.25	9.166
13. March 1979	11.5	9.451
14. June 1979	11.75	9.526
15. September 1979	12.25	9.855
16. December 1979	15.25	11.018
17. March 1980	16.75	13.7
18. June 1980	14.0	7.675
19. September 1980	11.5	10.124
20. December 1980	17.75	14.384
21. March 1981	18.51	4.103
22. June 1981	20	15.675
23. September 1981	20	15.583
24. December 1981	15.5	10.4
25. March 1982	16.5	12.43
26. June 1982	16	11.52
27. September 1982	13.5	8.604
28. December 1982	11.5	8.28
29. March 1983	10.5	7.944
30. June 1983	10.5	8.65
31. September 1983	11	9.28
32. December 1983	11	8.9
33. March 1984	11	9.2
34. June 1984	12.5	9.83
35. September 1984	13	10.6

Table 2.2

	P – T	P – 1.25T	P – 1.50T
1	1.6	0.4	–0.8
2	1.5	0.1	–1.3
3	1.9	0.7	–0.6
4	1.8	0.7	–0.4
5	1.6	0.4	–0.8
6	1.5	0.2	–1.0
7	1.5	0.1	–1.3
8	1.7	0.2	–1.3
9	1.6	0.0	–1.6
10	1.6	0.0	–1.7
11	1.5	–0.4	–2.3
12	2.1	–0.2	–2.5
13	2.0	–0.3	–2.7
14	2.2	–0.2	–2.5
15	2.4	–0.1	–2.5
16	4.2	1.5	–1.3
17	3.1	–0.4	–3.8
18	6.3	4.4	2.5
19	1.4	–1.2	–3.7
20	3.4	–0.2	–3.8
21	4.4	0.9	–2.7
22	4.3	0.4	–3.5
23	4.4	0.5	–3.4
24	5.1	2.5	–0.1
25	4.1	1.0	–2.1
26	4.5	1.6	–1.3
27	4.9	2.7	0.6
28	3.2	1.2	–0.9
29	2.6	0.6	–1.4
30	1.9	–0.3	–2.5
31	1.7	–0.6	–2.9
32	2.1	–0.1	–2.4
33	1.8	–0.5	–2.8
34	2.7	0.2	–2.2
35	2.4	–0.2	–2.9

Which of these time series involves the least risk?

The Hedge Ratio

A particularly neat solution to the cross-hedging problem arises if we are prepared to say that the *standard deviation*[2] of the risk profile is an appropriate measure of the risk of that distribution. Certainly for normal (bell-shaped) curves this is true. It might not be a good measure for insurance problems where the payoffs are rarely S-shaped. In our example, the standard deviation

---

[2] For definitions of standard deviation, variance, and correlation, see the appendix to this section.

of the $P - T$ time series is 1.3, for $P - 1.25T$ it is 1.1, and for $P - 1.50T$ again 1.3. With this criterion, and among these three alternatives, a hedge of 3.35 million × 1.25 = \$4.188 million in T-bills appears to be the best strategy for Madison.

The *variance* is simply the standard deviation squared. The variance has some very nice properties:

▸   Variance $(kX) = k^2$ variance X (Hence variance $(-X)$ = variance X);

▸   Variance $(X + Y)$ = variance X + variance Y + 2 covariance $(X$ and $Y)$;

▸   Covariance $(aX$ and $bY)$ = ab covariance $(X$ and $Y)$.

From these expressions we can deduce that the variance of $Y - kX$ is equal to:

$$\text{variance } Y + k^2 \text{ variance } X - 2k \text{ covariance } (X \text{ and } Y).$$

What value of k minimizes this quantity? You can use calculus or high-school algebra to "complete the square":

$$\text{variance } Y + \text{variance } X \left[k - \frac{\text{covariance } (X \text{ and } Y)}{\text{variance } X} \right]^2 - \frac{[\text{covariance } (X \text{ and } Y)]^2}{\text{variance } X} .$$

This is minimized when:

$$k = \frac{\text{covariance } (X \text{ and } Y)}{\text{variance } X} .$$

This expression is equivalent to:

$$k = \text{correlation } (X \text{ and } Y) \times \frac{\text{standard deviation } (Y)}{\text{standard deviation } (X)}$$

and is known as the *hedge ratio* (for Y on X). More importantly (and suggestively) the hedge ratio is also the formula for the regression coefficent of Y on X, i.e., if:

$$Y = b_0 + b_1 X + \text{residual error} ,$$

then b_1 is the hedge ratio. Using the data in Exhibit 1 we may calculate the regression of P on T. It is $P = 0.473 + 1.247T$, with an R^2 of 0.93.

The Role of Regression Analysis

While regression analysis may not always be possible for an exposure analysis (if there's no data available you are immediately stuck), it is useful in explaining some of the ideas. Again, let's call your measure of performance Y. Let's call the uncertain quantity X. For exposure analysis we seek a relation of the form:

$$Y = b_0 + b_1 X + \text{residual uncertainty} .$$

This equation says: if X turns out to have a value 5, then Y will be equal to $b_0 + 5b_1$, plus a random element (the residual uncertainty) that is completely independent of the value of X. The random element incorporates all other uncertainties that may affect you. Thus the uncertainty in Y is represented as an uncertain quantity completely dependent on the (unknown) value of X, plus an uncertain amount completely independent of X.

$$\text{uncertainty in } Y = \text{uncertainty due to } X + \text{uncertainty unrelated to } X .$$

To see that b_1 is the right hedge ratio, note that if we hedge by taking a separate position $-b_1 X$ then your combined net position will be equal to:

$$Y - b_1 X = b_0 + b_1 X - b_1 X + \text{residual uncertainty}$$

$$= b_0 + \text{residual uncertainty,}$$

so that you are no longer exposed to X. The R^2 of the regression tells us the proportion of the variance in Y that can be eliminated by hedging with X.

The connection with regression also helps us to understand a few more issues:

▸ **Picking between various possible hedges.** Suppose you could hedge with either X_1 or X_2 or X_3: which should you choose? Leaving aside the cost of any hedge, you want to find the hedge that minimizes the uncertainty in your net position. Hence, you regress Y against each of X_1, X_2 and X_3 and hedge with the variable that gives you the highest R^2.

▸ **Multiple exposure analysis.** There really is no reason why you should restrict yourself to hedging with only one X at a time. How should you act if you may use any or all of X_1, X_2, and X_3 to hedge? The answer is to run the regression:

$$Y = b_0 + b_1 X_1 + b_2 X_2 + b_3 X_3 + \text{residual uncertainty}$$

and hedge with b_1 units of X_1, b_2 units of X_2 and b_3 units of X_3.

One difficulty normally occurring with regression is not a problem here, *causality*. We do not care whether a change in X causes a change in Y or if Y and X happen to move together due to a common relationship with a third variable.

Variability vs. Uncertainty

So far, the algebra of hedging has been based on the assumption that we want to minimize the long-term variability of $Y - kX$. This would make sense in Madison's case if it really were going to take excess cash and invest it repeatedly in T-bills. The more common situation is that Madison simply wants to eliminate the variability in its *next* payment. The difference in these two views of the problem is substantial and of crucial importance. To see the problem, imagine that Y is a variable that increases by two every year. A variable that increases by either one or two based on the toss of a coin is X. Consider the following historical data that might result (Table 2.3):

Table 2.3

Year	1	2	3	4	5	6	7	8	9
Y	10	12	14	16	18	20	22	24	26
X	10	11	13	15	16	18	19	20	22

A regression of Y on X would show a strong connection between the two and a hedge might be needed. Yet that is clearly nonsensical since Y is completely determined in advance: there is no uncertainty! More revealing would be the table of forecast errors in Y and X (Table 2.4):

Table 2.4

Year	1	2	3	4	5	6	7	8	9
Y	–	0	0	0	0	0	0	0	0
X	–	$-\frac{1}{2}$	$+\frac{1}{2}$	$+\frac{1}{2}$	$-\frac{1}{2}$	$+\frac{1}{2}$	$-\frac{1}{2}$	$-\frac{1}{2}$	$+\frac{1}{2}$

A more satisfactory definition of the appropriate regression to run in order to identify the right exposure is to regress Y (the actual value of the variable of concern) on:

▸ all variables known at the time of the hedge ,

and

▸ all variables that could be used as a hedge.

For example, if Madison is only worried about the next quarter's interest payment, it is exaggerating the uncertainty to look at the *historical* variation in the prime. Although the prime varies greatly over several years it rarely moves much from one quarter to the next. How uncertain is next quarter's prime rate given what we know today? From this perspective we want to choose the hedge ratio k in order to make the *uncertainty* of $P - kT$ as low as possible. How uncertain are we about the value of $P - kT$? Let's restrict our forecasting variables to this quarter's prime and this quarter's T-bill. We will run the following regression for any given k:

$$P - kT = b_0 + b_1 \text{Lag } P + b_2 \text{Lag } T + \text{residual uncertainty} \ ,$$

where the values of the coefficients will vary as we change k. The standard error of this regression will tell us how much uncertainty we do have about $P - kT$. We want to choose the k that has the smallest possible standard error. One way to do this would be to run the regression for various values of k and choose the one with the smallest standard error. But there's a quicker way!

Consider the regression:

$$P = b_0 + b_1 \text{Lag } P + b_2 \text{ Lag } T + b_3 T + \text{residual uncertainty} \ .$$

By virtue of the way regression works, the precise values of b_0, b_1, b_2, and b_3 minimize the standard deviation of the residual uncertainty in P. But by rewriting the regression as

$$P - b_3 T = b_0 + b_1 \text{Lag } P + b_2 \text{ Lag } T + \text{residual uncertainty}$$

we see that the multiple regression has also found the value of k (namely $k = b_3$) that allows $P - kT$ to be predicted with the smallest residual uncertainty.

The actual regression using Table 2.1 data is

$$P = -0.22 + 0.09 \text{ Lag } P + 0.39 \text{ Lag } T + 0.83 T$$

with a standard error of 0.62.

The Effect on Variability of Hedging Uncertainty

As we have seen, variability and uncertainty may be quite different things. A time series can be variable without being uncertain. For example, an ice cream store may have highly seasonal but predictable sales. A time series can be uncertain without being variable. For example, you have never died but you are unsure whether this will be true next year. We know now that the best hedge of uncertainty for Madison is to use a hedge ratio of 0.83. Let F_{t-1} be the forward interest rate at time $t-1$. Then Madison's actual payment in period t is

$$P_t + 0.83 \, (F_{t-1} - T_t) \quad .$$

We know that this hedge reduces Madison's uncertainty about its next quarter's payments. But what does it do for the variability of its payments over time? Suppose, for the sake of illustration, that the forward rate F_{t-1} is equal to the actual rate T_{t-1}. From the data we find that the standard deviation of $P_t + 0.83 \, (T_{t-1} - T_t)$ is 4.2 which *exceeds* the standard deviation of P_t alone (which is 4.0). Thus, acting to decrease one kind of exposure (short term uncertainty) can lead to an increase in a related kind of exposure (long term variability).

Summary of Example

There are two ways for Madison to tackle its exposure to the prime. One is to try and reduce the variability of its payments from quarter to quarter. This can only be done by lending out cash, $3.35 million at the prime, or $4.19 million at the T-bill rate. Since Madison is undoubtedly strapped for cash, this is impossible.

The second concern is to reduce the uncertainty it has about the size of its *next* payment. By lending out 0.83×3.35 million $=$ $2.78 million at the T-bill rate (or by buying $2.78 million of T-bills forward which does not cost any up-front cash) Madison can reduce its uncertainty to a distribution with a standard deviation of 6/10 of one percentage point.

APPENDIX

Consider the following two time series of data for variables X and Y (Table 2.5)

Table 2.5

Period	1	2	3	4	5	6	7	8	9	10
X	10	4	2	9	15	11	7	10	8	14
Y	5	2	3	4	10	7	5	3	4	7

The mean of X is:
$$\frac{10 + 4 + 2 + 9 + 15 + 11 + 7 + 10 + 8 + 14}{10} = 9$$

The mean of Y is:
$$\frac{5 + 2 + 3 + 4 + 10 + 7 + 5 + 3 + 4 + 7}{10} = 5$$

By removing the means (Table 2.6) we can look at the variability associated with each time stream in terms of deviations:

Table 2.6

Period	1	2	3	4	5	6	7	8	9	10
X	1	−5	−7	0	6	2	−2	1	−1	5
Y	0	−3	−2	−1	5	2	0	−2	−1	2
$X \times X$	1	25	49	0	36	4	4	1	1	25
$Y \times Y$	0	9	4	1	25	4	0	4	1	4
$X \times Y$	0	15	14	0	30	4	0	−2	1	10

The variance of X is: $\dfrac{1 + 25 + 49 + 0 + 36 + 4 + 4 + 1 + 1 + 25}{10} = 14.6$

The standard deviation of X is : $\sqrt{14.6} = 3.82$.

The variance of Y is: $\dfrac{0 + 9 + 4 + 1 + 25 + 4 + 0 + 4 + 1 + 4}{10} = 5.2$

The standard deviation of Y is : $\sqrt{5.2} = 2.28$.

The covariance of X and Y is:

$\dfrac{0 + 15 + 14 + 0 + 30 + 4 + 0 - 2 + 1 + 10}{10} = 7.2$

The correlation of X and Y is:

$\dfrac{\text{Covariance}}{\text{Product of Standard Deviations}} = \dfrac{7.2}{3.82 \times 2.28} = 0.83$

The correlation can range in value from –1 to 1.

A value of 0.83 means the variables are highly correlated. A visual inspection of Table 2.5 or Table 2.6 shows that X and Y tend to be high or low in synchronization.

MADISON WIRE AND CABLE CORPORATION (A)

In the summer of 1980 Harold Cotton and Bob Bretholtz, co-owners of Madison Wire and Cable Corporation, were reviewing their approach to copper inventory and procurement. Copper prices had recently been fluctuating wildly, increasing from $1.00 per pound to over $1.40 per pound and then falling back to $1.00 per pound. Copper demand was currently slack, but prices were rising due to a copper industry strike.

Background

Harold Cotton and Bob Bretholtz purchased Madison Wire and Cable Corporation of South Lancaster, Massachusetts for approximately $600,000 in April 1976. Madison was a manufacturer of multiconductor, low-voltage signal cables used in the electronics industry. Signal cables were used to transmit electronic information and should be distinguished from electric cables used to supply power to machines or appliances. The company produced custom-made cables to a wide variety of specifications. Signal cables made by Madison Wire could be found in computer peripherals and the central processing units of many mainframe computers.

Bob and Harold were both engineers with expertise in copper and plastics technologies. They also had experience in the manufacture of printed circuit boards, which combined copper, plastics, and other chemicals. In addition to his engineering degree, Harold had received an MBA from Harvard Business School in 1958.

After leaving Lewcott Chemicals and Plastics Corporation, a firm which they had founded and later sold to a European-based conglomerate, the two men purchased Madison in 1976. Soon after, they executed a leveraged buyout of Wil-Tec Wire Corporation, a Worcester, Massachusetts business which had recently filed a Chapter XI bankruptcy.

At first, Bob and Harold thought their acquisitions were making money; however, after instituting a new control system, they realized that poor labor utilization and excessive scrap materials were causing them to lose about $10,000 per week. Corrective measures were taken by early 1977. The decision to move the Madison Wire production facility to the Wil-Tec plant in Worcester to avoid duplication of overhead resulted in large write-offs and caused Madison to suffer huge losses in 1977. The following year, however, the company showed a profit of $420,000 on sales of $6.6 million. During 1978 and 1979, sales grew 127% while profits leaped 322%. Harold and Bob expected Madison's recent performance to continue for the foreseeable future.

Making Wire

The company business cycle started with the quarterly sales forecast. Harold used this forecast to estimate raw copper requirements in terms of specific sizes of commonly used copper wire. He then translated these requirements into a more or less level pattern of orders for each size. Madison purchased close to 1/2 million pounds of copper per quarter in over 100 sizes of wire, although 10 to 15 sizes accounted for most of the business.

Since all products were custom made, actual orders of raw materials differed occasionally from the forecast as the quarter unfolded. If demand was higher for some particular wire, Harold could increase the order so that inventories did not become uncomfortably low. Special raw materials purchases were also made when Madison received a large unanticipated order. On the other hand, no special measures were taken to reduce raw materials orders as inventories built up. The company held close to 400,000 pounds of copper in inventory, over and above work-in-progress. Harold viewed raw materials inventories as a hedge against increases in copper prices.

Once an order was received, Madison produced the specified product. Lead times were typically between 8 and 12 weeks but depended on the availability of copper and the complexity of the cable ordered. The production process involved coating raw copper wire with extruded plastic resins, usually PVC. Cables composed of more than one wire were produced by wrapping insulated wires in various configurations and with a variety of materials. Signal cables were generally differentiated by their insulation materials. Each insulator had a unique combination of electrical, thermal, and chemical properties.

Contracts with Customers

Madison Wire sold its products under both fixed- and variable-price contracts.

Fixed-price

This form of contract accounted for about 25% of Madison's sales volume. In a fixed-price contract, the company contracted to deliver a certain length of a specific type of copper cable at a specific price over a specific period of time. For example, the company recently contracted to sell 5 million feet of ten different types of cable to a computer accessories distribution house for $710,000. The cable was to be delivered over a 12-month period beginning September 25,

1980, with subsequent delivery dates to be agreed upon later and based on customer needs. This contract would use 104,000 pounds of copper and was estimated using a copper price of $1.02 per pound.

Variable-price

In this form of contract, the price of the delivered cable was adjusted to reflect the cost of raw copper at the time of delivery. As with fixed-price contracts, delivery took place in many installments over the life of the contract. The precise delivery dates were agreed upon later and depended on the customer's timetable. Madison adjusted the agreed bid price by calculating the difference between the price of copper on the delivery date and the price when the contract was bid. For example, if Madison contracted to deliver cable containing 10,000 pounds of raw copper and if copper prices were $1.00 per pound on the day Madison bid for the contract but had risen to $1.20 per pound on the delivery date, the amount paid for the delivered cable would be ($1.20 − $1.00) × 10,000 = $2,000 higher than the bid price. Had copper prices fallen to $0.80 per pound instead, the price paid for the delivered cable would have been ($0.80 − $1.00) × 10,000 = $2,000 *less* than the bid price. These adjustments could greatly affect profits since copper constituted roughly 21% of the Madison cost-of-goods sold.

Contracts with Suppliers

Madison received a delivery of copper wire each Thursday from at least one of its three suppliers. The suppliers calculated their price each week by adding a fabrication "adder" to the current spot price of raw copper. While raw copper prices changed each week, fabrication adders were generally changed only once each year. The adder for each type of wire was a function of that wire's complexity. Wires with more strands were considered more complex as were thinner wires.

Hedging

Harold estimated that Madison's sales dollar could be broken down approximately as 38% copper wire (of which 42% was raw copper and 58% was adder), 17% other materials, 20% manufacturing, 12% overhead, and 11% profit. Copper wire was the largest cost category and he wanted to review the company's policy on copper. Madison Wire had lost about $10,000 the previous year speculating with copper futures. Both Bob and he were wary of further involvement in the futures markets. The two of them wondered, however, whether they had just been unlucky or if a hedging policy involving copper futures made sense. They also wondered whether any other techniques could be used, alone or in conjunction with futures, to avoid the risks associated with copper price movements. Finally, they wondered whether fixed- and variable-price contracts warranted separate hedging strategies or if they could formulate one hedging policy to be used for all contracts.

▼   ▼   ▼

FOREIGN EXCHANGE

Whenever you have assets or liabilities in a foreign currency there is the potential for unexpected gains or losses as the relative value of the dollar and that currency fluctuates.

Companies typically have three concerns about their foreign exchange exposure:

1. **Transaction Risk.** The company has agreed to sell a piece of machinery to a French company for a price of one million francs. Payment will not be received for three months. If the franc drops in value in the interim, the company could find itself shipping the machinery at a loss.

    It is a simple matter to hedge this position with a sale of francs in the forward market. Suppose the current exchange rate is 3.80 francs to the dollar. The forward rate might be 4.00 francs to the dollar. By selling one million francs forward at 4.00/$ the company is guaranteed to receive $250,000 for the machinery. When payment in francs is received, it is delivered to fulfill the forward commitment. The company is completely indifferent to the actual exchange rate at that time.

2. **Translation Risk.** If a company has a foreign subsidiary, the end-of-year income statement and balance sheet for the parent can be greatly influenced by the exchange rate that prevails on the last day of the year. At the moment the relevant accounting rule is FASB 52, which says simply that the parent income statement is the sum of the subsidiary income statements, translated in the case of foreign based subsidiaries, at the current rates. The same is true for the balance sheets, with one exception. If income and balance sheets were simply translated at current rates, the company might find that last year's net assets plus this year's net income does not equal this year's assets. Hence shareholders' equity is used as a plug number. A line item under shareholder's equity reports the required change as a foreign exchange gain or loss.

    Suppose that the French subsidiary is anticipating earnings of one million francs on net assets of 10 million francs. The parent is very pleased with the state of affairs and would like to lock it in. How can it go about it? If they sell one million francs forward then the earnings will maintain their value but this won't help the assets. If they sell 10 million francs forward the assets will be hedged but they'll also have huge earnings if the value of the franc drops. FASB 52 allows a way out of this dilemma. It is possible to choose whether to attach a forward contract to the earnings statement, in which case profits and losses on it are included in earnings, or not to in which case profits or losses bypass the earnings and go straight to shareholders equity. Thus they should sell one million francs forward attached and 9 million francs unattached.

    The infamous FASB 8, the old accounting rule, followed U.S. domestic practice of listing some items at historical value (and translating them at historical exchange rates!) and others at current values (translating these at current rates). The plug number was the earnings figure: Thus the earnings figures were often whipsawed due to the leverage effect of foreign currency fluctuations on net assets. Since different categories of assets were translated differently, there was considerable effort devoted to manipulating the translation exposure by transferring assets between categories. For example, if the subsidiary were net long it could use cash (an exposed item) to build up inventory (a nonexposed item).

3. **Economic Risk**. The only measure of exposure that "ought" to be relevant is the dollar valuation of the company. This measure is also the hardest to calculate. A subsidiary whose costs and revenues are each in the same currency will suffer very little from exchange risk. A devaluation can actually be of benefit if the price of its product is set in the world market for then company revenues will remain constant, but expenses will be reduced.

One way to reduce economic exposure is to leverage the subsidiary as much as possible in its home currency and repatriate as much of the value as possible.

Properties of Forward Prices

Suppose that today one dollar is worth exactly one pound and that the one year forward rate is $1.06 per pound. What explains this differential? Here are some theories:

Purchasing Power Parity

If a Sony Walkman costs $50 in the United States and £50 in the United Kingdom, if the exchange rate is other than £1:$1 people could make money by shipping the items from one country to the other. If inflation is running at 10% in the United States and 4% in the United Kingdom, the Sony Walkman should be retailing for $55 and £52 respectively in one year's time. Hence the exchange rate in one year should be $55/$52 =1.06$/£.

Interest Rate Parity

Suppose interest rates are 11% in the United States and 5% in the United Kingdom. If I own $100, one thing I can do is deposit it in the United States and collect $111 at the end of the year. I could also use the $100 to buy £100 and deposit them in the United Kingdom. This would net me £105. Unless $111 is expected to be equal to £105 at the end of the year one of these options will be more attractive than the other. If £105 > $111 there will be a tendency for people to buy pounds now with the intention of selling pounds in one year. This pressure acts to bring the current and forward rates into line to eliminate this misalignment. Hence the forward exchange rate is $111/$105 =1.06$/£.

CASE

INTERNATIONAL FOODSTUFFS

International Foodstuffs is the disguised name of a U.S.-based multinational enterprise involved primarily in the processing and international trading of agricultural commodities. Its worldwide processing operations include activities such as animal feed manufacturing, soybean crushing (into meal and oil), and grain milling. Trading operations involve nearly all internationally traded commodities.

Prices of internationally traded commodities, continually fluctuating in response to global supply and demand, are almost always expressed in U.S. dollars. Each foreign-based division of IF normally writes contracts that fix payment in U.S. dollars or in its own currency. (Exceptions are made for customers in a handful of countries, mostly in Western Europe, with whom contracts are written in their currencies.) Trading commodities is a high-volume, low-margin business with pretax profits reaching as low as $0.50 per ton in a weak market. Therefore, even a small adverse move of exchange rates can turn profits into losses on a transaction.

Harvard Business School case 9-181-049. Professor David E. Bell prepared this case. Copyright © 1980 by the President and Fellows of Harvard College.

Jerry Grossman, International Foodstuffs' (IF) financial officer in charge of foreign exchange operations arrived at work late on July 17, 1980. As he sorted the papers in his "in-box" he found three matters requiring his immediate attention.

The first was a sale by IF of 10,000 tons of wheat to a British grain processor at £88.3467 CAD[3] per ton. IF currently planned to ship the grain on or about October 15 to meet the delivery "window" of October 18–November 12 specified in the contract.[4]

Jerry punched several buttons on his computer terminal, which immediately displayed the current spot and forward rates for the pound (Exhibit 1). He noted that the pound was trading at a forward discount. The previous day, Richard Koss, one of Jerry's analysts, had told him that the pound should strengthen in the very near future. Rich felt very strongly that forward rates were too low.

In addition to a transaction in the forward market, Jerry also considered a money market hedge. This would involve borrowing pounds in the Euromarket and buying dollars. The dollars would then be invested in Eurodollar notes. Once payment for the wheat was received, Jerry would repay his Europound loan. With the press of a few more buttons, Jerry checked the current Euromarket rates on dollars and pounds (Exhibit 1).

As Jerry was considering his options, Rich stopped by his office to talk about acquisition negotiations in London, which would be completed in a few days. When Jerry asked Rich what he recommended for the British grain deal, Rich suggested that it not be covered since the pound would surely not take the beating implicit in the forward exchange rates. Rich suggested Jerry should wait at least a week or two before hedging.

Jerry had three options to consider: a forward market hedge, a money market hedge, and no hedge at this time. The money market hedge implied slightly higher transaction costs than the forward market contract, which would be arranged through a bank. The forward contract, however, would be written for a specific maturity date and altering that date at a later stage to ensure continued coverage would involve some additional charges. This could be an issue since he would not know the exact shipping date until after the fact. For example, port facilities at the shipping docks might be congested on October 15, causing the grain to be shipped late. On the other hand, grain might also be shipped one or two days earlier than expected. Another difficulty Jerry faced was deciding how many pounds to hedge. He could not know for certain how much grain would eventually be shipped to London in advance of the actual shipment date. Because ships' holds vary in size, contracts are written with some flexibility in the amount to be shipped. Therefore, Jerry knew that the grain actually sent to London could vary as much as 10% in either direction from the contracted sale.

The second problem on Jerry's desk required him to review the foreign exchange strategy of IF's Brazilian subsidiary. The subsidiary treasurer was informing him via his monthly telex report to Jerry that a "maxi-devaluation," perhaps on the order of 20%, was imminent. While the Brazilian government

---

[3] C.A.D. is the abbreviation for "cash against documents." In other words, IF contracted to receive payment upon presentation of the shipping documents to the British grain buyer.

[4] Payment would thus be received on or about October 16 since it would take one day for a courier acting on IF's behalf to fly to London and present the shipping documents to the buyer.

steadfastly denied the devaluation rumors, pointing to its established policy of frequent publicly-announced mini-devaluations, several other sources agreed with the general thrust of the treasurer's analysis.

IF Brasilia's business includes soybean processing, animal feed manufacturing, and international trading in wheat, corn, and soybeans, along with several other agricultural commodities. The processed soybean products (i.e., soybean meal and oil) and animal feed are only being sold domestically at present, though exports could resume if international prices improved. While domestic prices are controlled for agricultural commodities, export prices are determined by the international economy and world events. Although Brazil's influence is growing in the world supply and demand of agricultural commodities, IF Brasilia's export prices are determined outside of the country, generally by the U.S. markets.[5]

With these facts in mind, Jerry reviewed IF Brasilia's current balance sheet and income statement as well as the budgeted statement for the end of the current year (Exhibit 2). Among the major issues Jerry wanted to resolve was how to measure IF's foreign exchange exposure in Brazil. IF's accountants calculated exposure as the difference between current assets and current liabilities. Noncurrent assets and liabilities were translated at historical exchange rates and thus were not considered exposed.[6] While this measure was relevant, Jerry wondered whether future transactions should somehow be considered. Another complicating aspect was the fact that IF Brasilia had not planned to remit any dividends to the U.S. parent for at least three or four years. Jerry was not sure how this should affect his analysis of IF's exposure and his decision about how to manage it. Finally, Jerry's potential hedging tactics were limited since there was no forward market in cruzeiros.[7]

The third matter requiring attention was the £2,500,000 purchase of A.J. Thomas & Sons, Ltd., a poultry processor in London. The acquisition negotiations were expected to be completed within the next week with the requisite contracts signed the week after.

IF's Poultry Division, headquartered in the U.S., had decided to acquire A.J. Thomas six months earlier. During its analysis of A.J. Thomas, IF's financial staff decided that the purchase should be made by Pickerings Ltd., a British subsidiary engaged in grain milling. Pickerings had suffered large tax losses in recent years prior to its acquisition by IF, and the tax loss carryforward prevented it from taking advantage of the tax deductibility of interest payments in the near future. Therefore, IF's financial staff instructed IF Bahamas, IF's profitable and cash-rich Bahamian subsidiary, to finance the deal for Pickerings as an investment. IF Bahamas was taxable by the U.S., allowing the firm as a whole to enjoy a net gain as cash providing otherwise highly taxed interest income was used in England as a substitute for additional high-cost debt.

Jerry needed to decide when and how IF Bahamas should shift funds to England to effect the transaction, which was to take place around the middle of January 1981 (the start of Pickerings' next fiscal year). He also had to decide

---

[5] Soybeans were trading at about $7/bushel. The exchange rate on July 17 was $0.0188 per cruzeiro which represented a 24% devaluation against the dollar since January 1. Domestic interest rates were about 60%. Agricultural loans could be obtained at substantially lower rates.

[6] If Brasilia's long-term debt was raised in $U.S. However, the company has made an arrangement with the Brazilian central bank whereby IF Brasilia deposited the dollars with the bank and the bank guaranteed to convert the cruzeiros back into dollars at the same exchange rate. The Brazilian government needs this device to encourage foreign firms to invest in Brazil. Accounting rules, however, require long-term debt to be translated at current rates.

7 Given the unstable economic conditions in Brazil and the government's policy of frequent mini-devaluations, no financial institutions were willing to trade forward cruzeiros.

whether to buy pounds forward either now or at some other date or hedge in the money market. Since IF had other potential uses for the Bahamian subsidiary's extra cash until A.J. Thomas was paid for, Jerry also considered waiting to buy pounds until the day before the cash was to change hands. However, he feared that Rich would prove correct and the pound would appreciate in terms of dollars.

Exhibit 1

	$/£	EURO-DOLLARS (% PER ANNUM) Borrow	Lend	EURO-POUNDS (% PER ANNUM) Borrow	Lend
Spot	2.3770				
1 Month	2.3615	$9\frac{1}{8}$	9	$16\frac{5}{8}$	$16\frac{3}{8}$
2 Months	2.3500	$9\frac{1}{4}$	$9\frac{1}{8}$	NA	NA
3 Months	2.3395	$9\frac{5}{16}$	$9\frac{3}{16}$	$15\frac{3}{4}$	$15\frac{1}{2}$
6 Months	2.3225	$9\frac{1}{2}$	$9\frac{3}{8}$	$14\frac{3}{8}$	$14\frac{1}{8}$

NA = Not Available

Exhibit 2

BRASILIA DIVISION

Balance Sheet ($000s)	Current	December 31, 1980 (Projected)
ASSETS		
Cash	$1,057	$ 1,160
Accounts Receivable	4,950	4,102
Inventory	13,300	9,885
Property	9,226	9,400
Total Assets	$28,533	$24,547
LIABILITIES		
Short-term Debt	$ 7,008	$ 3,021
Long-term Debt	2,320	2,200
Accounts Payable	7,925	5,382
Net Worth	11,280	13,944
Total Liabilities	$28,533	$24,547

PROFIT AND LOSS STATEMENT ($000S)		
Sales	$51,318	$86,792
Cost of Sales	41,940	70,561
Other Expenses	5,415	7,620
Depreciation	2,092	2,889
Tax	1,147	2,231
Earnings After Tax	$ 724	$ 3,491

▼   ▼   ▼

FUTURES CONTRACTS

A farmer is growing 100,000 bushels of wheat. He is concerned about the price that will prevail at harvest time. At the same time, a flour miller, who normally buys 100,000 bushels of wheat at harvest time, is also worried about the harvest price. What can they do? Both the farmer and the miller would be happy to settle for today's cash price but the farmer's wheat hasn't grown yet and the miller doesn't want to pay holding costs. If they know of each other they could write a forward contract in which the farmer agrees to deliver his wheat to the miller at a price to be determined now, but paid at the time of delivery. In practice the farmer would not usually be able to find such a perfect match; even if he finds a miller needing at least 100,000 bushels, the miller may want a slightly different variety of wheat, may be geographically distant, which increases transportation costs, and whose reputation is unknown, thereby introducing legal costs and administrative effort.

The futures market is a location which brings together buyers and sellers so that the farmer can find the miller. To make trading easier there are only a few possible contracts that can be agreed upon through the exchange. (Buyer and seller may always write a forward contract without going through the market.) The advantage of a small number of contracts is that there is more trading on each one, which provides stability of prices since high volume helps to create market efficiency.

To avoid distrust, the farmer sells a contract to the exchange, the miller buys an equal and opposite contract from the exchange. The exchange is responsible for the finances and reliability of the individual parties. Since buyers and sellers are always balanced (not only in numbers but also in price), the default risk is the only risk the exchange bears. To reduce this, the exchange "clears the market" every day. At the end of each business day no one owes anyone anything: all buyers must settle up *as if* they had sold their positions at the close of the day's trading. All sellers must settle up *as if* they had bought back all their contracts at the close of trading.

In fact, the exchange doesn't run the risk of default due to fluctuations in price even during a single day. It requires each buyer and seller to post a 10% margin as security. If the price of a commodity moves by more than 10% (the limit on price change is actually set in terms of cents rather than percentages), the exchange halts trading until the next business day. At the end of each day a margin that has been depleted must be made up. A margin account that has grown during the day may be drawn down.

So if our miller buys 100,000 bushels of wheat at $3.00 he must immediately pay $30,000 in cash or securities to the exchange. If the price of this futures contract grows over time to $5.00 the exchange will have paid $200,000 into the miller's account. Therefore, whenever the miller chooses to buy back his contract ("clearing his position"), no additional money needs to change hands. The miller then buys wheat on the open market at about $5.00. Since he made a cash gain of $2.00 a bushel on the futures market, the effective price he pays is only $3.00, the amount he "locked in" originally. This is how the hedge works.

Of course the farmer is less fortunate. He must pay a total of $200,000 to meet the margin calls and must do so before being able to sell any of the crop,

Harvard Business School note 9-183-126. Professor David E. Bell prepared this note. Copyright © 1982 by the President and Fellows of Harvard College.

which is still growing. For this reason, farmers who wish to make use of the futures market usually write a forward contract with a bank. The bank can hedge its own position in the futures market if it wishes.

The Standard Contract

Exhibit 1 lists some of the commodities currently traded in various exchanges. An exchange will trade contracts for a specific quantity of a commodity (e.g., 5,000 bushels) for a few delivery dates (e.g., May, September, and January), which vary by commodity.

The contract that is traded is very specific. When the farmer sells a contract he is agreeing to deliver exactly 5,000 bushels of a particular grade and variety of wheat, with moisture content in a specified range, at a specific time (e.g., a three-day period at the end of May), at a specific place (e.g., a particular location in Kansas City), delivered in an acceptable form (e.g., railroad box car). Certain deviations with respect to grade and variety are permitted with pre-specified penalties. This latitude is necessary for commodities such as live cattle where the exact composition of the delivery (in particular, weight) cannot reasonably be guaranteed. Because of the standardization, everyone knows what they are getting or selling and all they need agree on is price.

The small number of contracts, and this standardization of them, encourages speculators to enter the market. A speculator need not have a knowledge of the intricate varieties of wheat when trading. Since the contract is with the exchange he need not worry about default or liquidity. (With a forward contract the other party may choose not to cancel at any price.) The speculators help the farmers and millers because the day the farmer wishes to sell the miller may not be there to buy. The speculator, sensing more sellers than buyers buys cheaply and waits for there to be more buyers than sellers. (The time frame is minutes, not days.) The speculators also have the incentive to be well informed on value so that farmers can be reasonably sure of getting a fair price for their crop. Of course that price may not reflect the true price at harvest time, but it was fair at the time of the contract.

Less than 1% of contracts result in delivery. The remainder are closed out (reversed) before the expiry date. This is because most buyers do not want the particular grade and amount of wheat (say) specified in the contract and almost certainly don't want it at the regulated delivery point. This disincentive is equally true for sellers.

Example

A miller needs 10,000 bushels of wheat in 100 days' time. She is worried about the price that will prevail at that time. The current cash price is $2.60. The futures price is $2.70 for delivery in 150 days time. She could buy the wheat now but holding costs would exceed the 10¢ a bushel premium she would pay with a futures contract.

Day 1	Miller buys two futures contracts.
Day 100	The cash price is now $3.50. The futures price for delivery in 50 days is $3.54. The miller has received a net of $10,000 \times (3.54 - 2.70) = \$8,400$ in margin payments during the course of the 100 days.
	The miller sells two futures contracts thus cancelling out her earlier position. She buys 10,000 bushels of wheat in the usual way from a local supplier.

To summarize the miller's cash flow:

Day 1
She puts up 10% of 10,000 × 2.70 or $2,700 in a margin account. She is paid interest on this. Alternatively she could have put up securities worth at least $2,700.

Day 2–99
She pays or is paid amounts that reflect the profit or loss she has made on her contract since buying it. In this case she receives $8,400.

Day 100
She sells her two contracts. No money changes hands except that she receives her margin money back. She pays $35,000 for 10,000 bushels of wheat. Thus her true price paid is ($35,000 − $8,400)/10,000 or $2.66.

Note that the effective price paid was not exactly the original cash price ($2.60) nor the original futures price ($2.70). This is because the difference or *basis* between the futures and cash price changed during the 100 days and was reduced to 4¢ from 10¢ by the time the miller got out. Hedgers in the futures market are still exposed to basis risk.

Price Movements

On the last day of an open contract a buyer has the option of taking delivery or of closing out his position. If the futures price is less than the cash price, the buyer will prefer to take delivery. If the futures price is more than the cash price, the buyer will prefer to sell the contract and buy cash wheat directly. For the seller of a contract the reverse is true. If the cash price is higher than the futures price, the seller would prefer to buy back his contract and sell his wheat directly. Since there are exactly the same number of buyers and sellers, the futures price on the last day of the contract equals the cash price. (In fact, due to the transaction costs of delivery, this may not hold exactly.)

At any time prior to the last day, the value of a futures contract will be approximately its expected value at maturity. If the expected spot price in 3 months time is $3.20 and the current futures price is $3.10, one could buy a three-month futures contract and expect to profit by selling the wheat on the spot market when the contract matures. Since this is not riskless arbitrage, the Capital Asset Pricing Model indicates that the correlation between changes in forward rates and the stock market affects the current futures price. Though such a correlation may be significant for financial commodities (not least the stock index futures) and precious metals, this is unlikely to be an important issue for agricultural commodities. Hence, a social bonus comes out of the market in that the futures prices provide a consensus forecast of future commodity prices.

Maturity Curves

At any time there are several contracts on a given commodity but with different expiry dates. Typically they are spread out every two or three months over the next couple of years. A graph of the prices plotted against the expiry dates is called the maturity curve.

You are about to sell 5,000 bushels of wheat for $3.00/bushel when you notice that the futures price for delivery in three months is $3.35. Allowing for financing and holding charges this, for you, is still a good deal. So you sell one contract and hold on to the wheat. Simultaneously you have withheld your wheat from the current market, encouraging cash prices to rise, and have bid down the futures price. In this way the two prices will adjust until the futures price is at most today's cash price plus holding costs. (See Figure 2.1.)

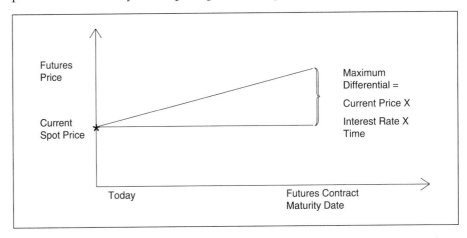

Figure 2.1

Suppose instead you are about to buy 5,000 bushels of wheat for $3.00 and see that the futures price for delivery in three months is $1.50. What can you do? If you need the wheat now, there is no way to take advantage of this situation. Certainly anyone that could wait three months will already have decided to do so. There is no bounding of futures prices on the downside. This situation occurs frequently when a harvest is due between the current date and the contract maturity.

The maturity curve can be any line starting from the asterisk whose slope never exceeds the interest rate. Note that since the interest rate could itself be predicted to change, the slope might vary accordingly. For a commodity like gold which *must* be held, the maturity curve will always look like that in Figure 2.1.

Basis Risk

A basis is the price differential between a futures price and a cash price. Its importance in hedging may be recognized from its role in the following example. Suppose at time 0 the maturity curve looks like that in Figure 2.2. You require 5,000 bushels of wheat in six months. There is no contract exactly six months out, so you buy one eight months out.

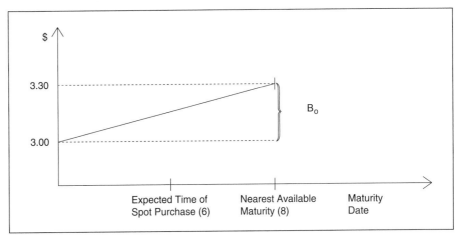

Figure 2.2

The current cash (spot) price is \$3.00. Today's price of the futures contract is \$3.30. The current basis is 30¢.

In six months the maturity curve may look like that in Figure 2.3.

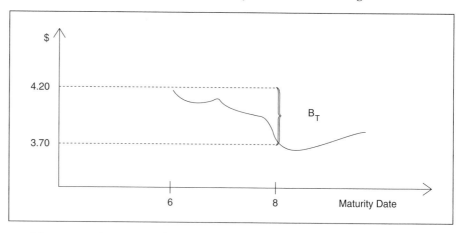

Figure 2.3

The spot price is now \$4.20. The price of the nearest futures contract (the one you bought) is now \$3.70. The difference between the price of the contract you wish you'd bought and the one you have bought is negative 50¢. Your cash-flow for the entire deal is:

$$\underset{\substack{\text{Futures Contract} \\ \text{Bought}}}{-3.30} + \underset{\substack{\text{Futures Contract} \\ \text{Sold}}}{3.70} - \underset{\substack{\text{Spot} \\ \text{Purchase}}}{4.20} = -3.80$$

The question is, how does this compare with what you hoped you'd bought? If the maturity curve had not shifted the way it did the basis would have narrowed[8] to $7\frac{1}{2}$¢ and you would have had a cashflow of:

$$-3.30 + 4.27\frac{1}{2} - 4.20 = -3.22\frac{1}{2} \quad .$$

You pay a total of $57\frac{1}{2}$¢ more than you had anticipated. This fluctuation is your basis risk. However, the observed variability of the basis is much less than the variability of the price. This basis risk is one of the side effects of futures contracts. (Some dealers trade contracts on basis risk, but we won't discuss that here.)

Note that this *temporal* basis risk was created by buying a contract that did not mature at exactly the time you wanted. Any difference between the futures contract you buy (or sell) and the precise contract you would have liked introduces a basis risk. A second type of basis risk is *geographical*. Supply and demand for a particular kind of wheat may vary in different parts of the country due to local conditions. Prices can't get too far apart or else it becomes profitable to transport wheat from one place to the other. If you are in Kansas City and are trading Chicago futures, it doesn't matter to you if the KC-Chicago *basis* is constant at 10¢, say. You will pay 10¢ too much when you buy a contract but you'll get it back when you sell. However, if the basis alters while you hold the contract you may lose. If there is a 10¢ premium on the futures contract when you buy, but a 10¢ premium on the Kansas City cash market when you sell, your

---

[8] See Figure 2.2 for an example. If the cash price moves exactly along the maturity curve, then in six months it will be three-quarters of the way to eight months and will have closed the gap from 30¢ to 7 $\frac{1}{2}$¢.

hedge has cost you 20¢ per bushel. Fortunately there is an upper bound on the amount you can lose this way (namely a round trip fare KC-Chicago-KC) unless some tragedy like a rail strike or a severe winter removes the possibility of geographical arbitrage. In this case the basis risk could be unlimited.

A third type of basis risk is *cross-product*. The farmer may not have the kind of wheat traded in the contract. If demand for his own variety drops for some reason, his futures contract will not fall in price to match it. When the contract matures or when he wishes to sell, he must buy back his contract for a much higher price than he is able to get for his own wheat. Nor can he force delivery since he has the wrong wheat. (In the case of wheat, it is possible to deliver different varieties; there is an agreed-upon table of premiums/discounts for the different varieties. In other commodities this is not always the case.)

Market Cornering

When the delivery month arrives, most people try to close out their positions. If someone insists on taking delivery (which they are allowed to do), the unfortunate seller who is last to close out his position has two alternatives:

▶ Ship his own wheat to the delivery point (at great expense).

▶ Locate someone nearer to the delivery point who can sell him wheat which is then shipped (a shorter distance) to the delivery point. (Enterprising people locate themselves at the delivery point for just this purpose. They act as a bank: the physicals don't move, only the labels on them.)

Now suppose the seller doesn't have enough wheat to cover the contract. He is then at the mercy of whoever has the wheat. If the only person who has wheat to sell is also the person to whom you are supposed to deliver, you have been *cornered*. It was alleged that the Hunt brothers deliberately bought spot silver and silver futures so that they could force delivery. The poor sellers would have had to buy silver from the brothers (at great expense) only to return it to them under the terms of the futures contract. The Commodity Futures Trading Commission is a federal regulatory watchdog agency (akin to the SEC) that tries to prevent such occurrences.

As the number of open contracts falls as maturity approaches, the (temporal) basis which has been narrowing starts to fluctuate because of the low trading volume, which reduces efficiency. There is also the fear that someone may get "stuck" with having to deliver or take delivery against his will. Thus most people who intend to reverse their positions do so two weeks or so before the maturity date.

Properties of an Item to be Traded in a Futures Market

The following is a list of properties widely agreed upon as necessary for a successful market.

1. The item must have a price that varies.

2. There must be enough trading volume to ensure orderly price movements and liquidity. In particular:

    a. It must not be too similar to an existing contract.

    b. It must not be too far out in the future (risk is usually a short-term issue, not many people are interested in long-term contracts).

    c. The contract sizes must be large enough to be worth transaction costs including possible delivery, but small enough to allow people holding actuals to trade.

3. Some people must be naturally long or short. Otherwise it's just a gambling house. (Gold is an exception for historical reasons.)

4. The commodity must be deliverable. The threat of delivery keeps prices in line with spot prices, which preserves the hedge value. If delivery were not required, the final price could be manipulated by the last few buyers holding out on the sellers. (What is actually required is some objectively determined method of defining a settlement price. Stock Index Futures are settled in cash; no portfolio is delivered.)

5. The commodity must be fairly standard or at the very worst, such that differences in quality can easily be offset by side payments. You couldn't trade second-hand cars on the futures market because the differences in quality would be hard to judge. Wheat is fairly uniform, as is oil and gold. Live cattle are more variable, but the buyer typically will be satisfied with variations if he is recompensed.

Exhibit 1 _____

Metals	Meat	Money	Grain
Aluminum	Boneless Beef	British Pounds	Barley
Copper	Broilers	Canadian Dollars	Corn
Gold	Live Cattle	Dutch Guilders	Flaxseed
Lead	Feeder Cattle	French Francs	Oats
Nickel	Hogs	German Marks	Ryeseed
Palladium	Pork Bellies	Japanese Yen	Rye
Platinum		Mexican Pesos	Wheat
Silver		Swiss Francs	
Silver Coins		Eurodollars	
Tin			
Zinc			

Financials	Other Materials	Other Foods
Commercial Paper	Cotton	Cocoa
Commercial Paper (30 days)	Heating Oil #2	Coffee
GNMA	Industrial Fuel Oil #6	Fresh Eggs
U.S. Treasury Bills	Lumber	Orange Juice
U.S. Treasury Bonds	Plywood	Potatoes
U.S. Treasury Notes	Propane	Soybeans
S&P 500	Rubber	Soybean Meal
Value Line	Gasoline	Soybean Oil
NYSE		Sugar
NYFE		

EXERCISES ON FUTURES

1. On Tuesday, March 23, 1993 David Stirzaker agreed to provide a customer with 200 troy ounces of gold on June 11, 1993, at a price of $70,000. Stirzaker had no inventory of gold and was concerned that the price might far exceed $350 per ounce by June. Use Table 2.7 to determine an appropriate hedging strategy for him.

Table 2.7

	Open	High	Low	Settle Change	Lifetime High	Low	Open Interest
Gold (CMX) – 100 troy oz.; $ per troy oz.							
Mar 93	331.60	332.00	331.60	331.90 – 1.00	334.50	326.00	0
Apr	332.10	332.80	332.00	332.30 – 1.00	410.00	325.80	30,920
June	333.50	334.10	333.40	333.70 – .90	418.50	327.10	30,659
Aug	335.00	335.30	334.80	335.00 – .90	395.50	328.50	13,654
Oct	336.50	336.80	336.50	336.50 – .80	395.00	330.80	2,056
Dec	337.60	338.30	337.60	338.00 – .80	402.80	331.70	14,103
Feb 94	339.80	339.80	339.30	339.50 – .80	376.80	333.80	5,874
Apr		–	–	341.00 – .80	360.00	335.20	3,795
June		–	–	342.50 – .80	383.50	339.40	2,667
Aug		–	–	344.20 – .80	351.80	341.50	3,215
Oct		–	–	346.00 – .80	346.00	344.00	1,219
Dec	348.30	348.30	347.70	348.00 – .80	383.00	343.00	2,552
June 95		–	–	354.50 – .80	352.00	351.00	744
Dec		–	–	362.20 – .80	403.00	358.00	752
June 96		–	–	370.70 – .80	482.70	446.20	362
Dec	379.60	380.00	379.60	379.90 – .80	380.00	379.60	389

Est vol. 38,000; vol Mon 35,817; open int 113,001, –215.

Cash Prices

Gold, troy oz.			
Englehard indus bullion	333.11	333.82	339.63
Engelhard fabric prods	349.77	350.51	356.61
Handy & Harman base price	331.90	332.60	338.40
London fixing AM 331.90 PM	331.90	332.60	338.40
Krugerrand, whol	a333.50	334.50	341.25
Maple Leaf, troy oz.	a343.50	344.50	350.75
American Eagle, troy oz.	a343.50	344.50	351.00

Wall Street Journal, Wednesday, 24 March 1993.

2. Assuming Stirzaker closed out his position on June 11, 1993, use Tables 2.7 and 2.8 to calculate his net cash flow (ignoring margin calls and transaction costs) for the deal.

Table 2.8

	Open	High	Low	Settle Change	Lifetime High	Low	Open Interest
Gold (CMX) – 100 troy oz.; $ per troy oz.							
June	370.50	371.20	363.00	366.10 – 3.50	418.50	327.10	2,586
Aug	371.50	373.50	364.50	367.50 – 3.50	395.50	328.50	87,245
Oct	373.10	374.80	366.00	369.20 – 3.60	395.00	330.80	4,811
Dec	375.00	376.50	367.50	370.80 – 3.70	402.80	331.70	33,058
Feb94	376.30	378.10	369.50	372.30 – 3.80	390.00	333.80	9,040
Apr	379.90	379.90	375.00	373.90 – 3.90	393.00	335.20	5,741
June	381.00	381.00	371.50	375.50 – 4.00	392.50	339.40	4,447
Aug	382.60	382.60	377.50	377.30 – 4.00	394.00	341.50	3,218
Oct	–	–		379.20 – 4.10	391.30	344.00	2,093
Dec	387.20	387.80	377.00	381.30 – 4.20	400.00	343.00	11,274
Feb 95	384.00	384.00	384.00	383.60 – 4.30	400.00	368.00	1,100
June	–	–		388.60 – 4.30	401.50	351.00	1,819
Dec	394.00	394.00	394.00	396.60 – 4.40	415.00	358.00	1,155
June 96	–	–		405.20 – 4.40	422.00	370.90	453
Dec	417.00	417.00	417.00	414.30 – 4.40	440.00	379.60	488
Dec 97	–	–		435.30 – 4.40	453.00	406.00	384

Est vol 50,000; vol Thur 31,663; open int 168,949, –4,034.

	Cash Prices		
Gold, troy oz.			
Englehard indus bullion	371.63	372.08	340.83
Engelhard fabric prods	390.21	390.68	357.87
Handy & Harman base price	370.35	370.80	339.60
London fixing AM 370.20 PM	370.35	370.80	339.60
Krugerrand, whol	a368.00	371.00	344.50
Maple Leaf, troy oz	a379.00	382.50	354.00
American Eagle, troy oz	a379.00	382.50	354.00

Wall Street Journal, Monday, 14 June 1993.

3. Repeat questions 1 and 2 for the case where the fixed price contract was for 27 August 1993. (Use Table 2.9.) Why did Stirzaker's profit go down, delivering in August rather than June?

Table 2.9

	Open	High	Low	Settle Change	Lifetime High	Low	Open Interest
Gold (CMX) – 100 troy oz.; $ per troy oz.							
Aug	368.10	368.10	368.10	369.30 + 1.30	409.00	328.50	194
Oct	370.40	371.20	369.40	370.30 + 1.30	411.50	330.80	10,572
Dec	372.20	373.00	370.80	372.10 + 1.30	414.00	331.70	108,915
Feb 94	373.50	373.60	373.20	373.80 + 1.30	415.70	333.80	15,769
Apr	375.10	376.20	375.00	375.50 + 1.40	418.50	335.20	5,726
June		–	–	377.10 + 1.40	417.20	339.40	7,601
Aug		–	–	378.80 + 1.40	415.00	341.50	3,853
Oct		–	–	380.60 + 1.40	417.00	344.00	2,592
Dec	380.30	382.00	380.30	382.50 + 1.50	426.50	343.00	9,455
Feb 95		–	–	384.40 + 1.50	411.00	368.00	2,865
Apr	386.20	386.20	386.20	386.40 + 1.60	425.00	386.20	1,337
June		–	–	388.50 + 1.60	430.00	351.00	2,409
Dec		–	–	395.30 + 1.60	439.50	358.00	1,468
June 96		–	–	402.70 + 1.60	447.00	370.90	694
Dec		–	–	411.00 + 1.60	443.00	379.60	577
Dec 97	429.50	429.50	429.50	430.70 + 1.60	477.00	406.00	465

Est vol 19,000; vol Thur 42,982; open int 174,495, +1,941.

Cash Prices

Gold, troy oz.			
Englehard indus bullion	370.53	372.53	341.23
Engelhard fabric prods	389.06	391.16	358.29
Handy & Harman base price	369.25	371.25	340.00
London fixing AM 370.05 PM	369.25	371.25	340.00
Krugerrand, whol	a372.00	371.00	342.50
Maple Leaf, troy oz	a382.00	381.00	351.50
American Eagle, troy oz	a382.00	381.00	351.50

Wall Street Journal, Monday, 30 August, 1993.

4. Explain the simple pattern of forward prices for gold evident in all three tables. What is the annualized rate of price appreciation? Now explain the pattern of forward prices for corn shown in Table 2.10.

Table 2.10

Grains and Oilseeds

	Open	High	Low	Settle	Change	Lifetime High	Lifetime Low	Open Interest
Corn (CBT) 5,000 bu.; cents per bu.								
Sept	233	234 1/2	230 3/4	234	+ 1	271 1/2	217 3/4	29,182
Dec	238 1/2	241 1/2	237 1/4	241 1/4	+ 2 1/4	268 1/2	225 1/4	173,441
Mar 94	247 1/4	249 3/4	245 3/4	249 1/2	+ 1 3/4	266 1/2	232 3/4	28,790
May	252 1/2	254 3/4	250 1/2	254 1/2	+ 1 3/4	270 1/2	238 1/2	9,198
July	255	257 3/4	253 1/2	257 1/2	+ 2	270 1/2	241	10,247
Sept	248 1/2	250 1/4	248 1/2	250 1/4	+ 1 1/4	259	240 1/2	957
Dec	243	244	241 1/4	243 3/4	+ 1/2	255	236 1/2	9,262

Est vol 40,000; vol Thur 63,394; open int 261,077, –2,432.
Wall Street Journal, Monday 30 August 1993.

5. A copper wire manufacturer has arranged his business so that he is not exposed to copper price risk so long as he buys copper in the cash market at the time it is needed for work-in-progress. Because of the threat of a transportation strike he is ordering four months' supply to be delivered next week. How can he use the futures market to maintain his usual neutral exposure despite the large temporary inventory he is acquiring?

EXERCISES ON HEDGING

In this exercise, ignore the effects of transaction costs, taxes, the time value of money, etc. Assume throughout that it is possible to buy or sell wheat with a forward contract that matures in six months' time.

1. A farmer is growing a crop that will be harvested six months from now. He is uncertain about the spot price at harvest time and about the eventual size of his crop. Which of the following, if any, are true advice for a risk averse farmer?

   (a) Always sell forward the average (expected) total crop yield.

   (b) Never sell forward any more than the minimum possible total harvest.

   (c) Never sell forward more than the maximum or less than the minimum total harvest.

2. A farmer is growing a crop which, due to vagaries of weather, disease and so on, will produce 10,000, 15,000, or 20,000 bushels with equal likelihood. The cash price at harvest time could be $3, $5, or $10 per bushel with equal probability. He could sell all or part of his crop forward now at $6 making up any shortfall in the spot market. Assume he can make transactions only now or at harvest time. By looking at the relevant risk profiles, use your own judgement to decide how much he should sell forward in each case.

   (a) Price and yield are independent.

   (b) The price is high when the yield is high and low when the yield is low.

   (c) The price is high when the yield is low and low when the yield is high.

3. ABC millers compete directly with XYZ millers in the same geographical area. Both millers have traditionally added a 50% surcharge to their buying price of wheat when selling the flour. Neither would change this policy except when a competitor's costs are lower, in which case they must offer a corresponding price or lose most of their customers. Currently the six-month forward price of wheat is $4 and ABC believes that the cash price six months from now is equally likely to be $2 or $6. If ABC is prepared to make decisions *using an expected value criterion*, what proportion of their wheat needs should they hedge if:

(a) XYZ are known to be buying all of their wheat forward.

(b) XYZ are known to be buying none of their wheat forward.

(c) XYZ are buying a fraction *f* of their requirements forward.

(d) ABC judges that XYZ will either buy all its wheat forward (with probability *p*) or none of it (with probability 1–*p*).

SOUTHWEST LUMBER DISTRIBUTORS

Late in September 1979, George Simpson, sales manager of Southwest Lumber Distributors, was reviewing the terms of a major potential sale. Dave Butler, head buyer for Plainview Homes, a major Dallas-area homebuilder, had recently approached George with a unique offer. Plainview proposed to buy one million board feet (BF) of framing lumber, at a price to be negotiated at present, for delivery six months later, in March. Mr. Butler explained that Plainview was planning to start next spring the construction of approximately 100 units in a subdivision northeast of Dallas. Plainview would be willing to purchase all of its framing requirements from Southwest if Mr. Simpson could quote an acceptable firm price in September. Because of recent soaring prices of building materials Plainview was very cost conscious and desirous of fixing in advance as large a portion of its construction costs as possible.

Southwest Lumber followed industry practice by only committing to selling prices three to four weeks ahead of delivery. Whenever possible it utilized **PTS** pricing, that is *Price* in effect at *Time* of *Shipment*. Neither wholesaler nor retail buyer were thus exposed to the risk of substantial price fluctuation between the time an order was placed at the mill and its eventual delivery. Mr. Butler, however, appeared to be asking Southwest to assume this price risk by quoting in September for March delivery. He did indicate, though, that Plainview would be willing to pay more than the 3% margin which Southwest usually commanded from its direct sales. At the same time, he hinted that Plainview expected a competitive price considering the size of the purchase.

George Simpson began to consider his alternatives. He first consulted his records to familiarize himself with the magnitude of the price risk he might be assuming. He compared the mill price of the requested item, Southern Pine #2, 2 × 4, during September of the last eight years with the mill price which prevailed during the following March. His worst fears were confirmed.

Harvard Business School case 9-180-134. Robert L. Vaughan prepared this case under the supervision of Professor David E. Bell. Copyright © 1980 by the President and Fellows of Harvard College.

Table 2.11

	SEPTEMBER	MARCH	$	%
1971	135	147	12	9
1972	153	175	22	14
1973	201	166	(35)	(17)
1974	118	125	7	6
1975	134	180	46	34
1976	197	193	(4)	(2)
1977	278	238	(40)	(14)
1978	237	247	10	4
1979	319	?		

The potential for large speculative gains or losses was apparent. Assuming the price quoted to Plainview would be close to the September level, it was evident that in five of the past eight years he would have had to deliver wood in the spring at higher price levels. Because of the small margins allowed, any significant price appreciation could wipe out his profit. The 1975–1976 scenario was an example of the disaster that could happen. Still, there was the potential for extraordinary profit, as shown in 1973–1974 and 1977–1978. During these years, Southwest could have honored its short commitment with substantially cheaper wood than originally foreseen.

Simpson realized there were alternatives to waiting until the following spring to make the necessary purchase. Southwest could buy the lumber now and store it until time for delivery. However, such a large purchase threatened to strain Southwest's storage and delivery capabilities. Simpson had also heard of wholesalers who used the futures market to hedge their transactions. Although Southwest had never previously utilized futures he wondered if the Plainview project might not be a good application. He asked his assistant, Bob Webster, to look into futures hedging techniques as well as the economics of buying the lumber for storage. The Plainview deal looked risky on the surface, but Mr. Simpson believed that it might preview key developments in the industry and present an opportunity which his company in particular could ill afford to miss.

Company Background

Southwest Lumber Distributors is a closely-held corporation founded in 1952 by brothers Greg and Bill Simpson. Southwest originally serviced the retail lumber market of north and central Texas and most of Oklahoma, acting as an interface to the mills supplying these dealers. Headquartered in downtown Dallas, the company had a travelling salesforce, ranging from six to ten, and a small office staff. Salesmen, under the direction of Bill, called on lumber dealers in assigned territories, becoming acquainted with their particular needs and calling in their orders to the Dallas office.

Greg headed a three-man buying team which placed the dealers' orders through an extensive network of mill contracts. About half of the orders were placed with mills in Texas, Louisiana, and Arkansas, while the remainder were referred to mills in the western United States or Canada. In constant communication with these mills, Greg was able to channel his orders to producers with available stock, or even surpluses which they were especially anxious to move. The Southwest buyers became aware of which mill manufactured the highest quality items in each product category. These quality variations were due to different timber sources and manufacturing practices.

The concern for quality was important because Southwest attempted to differentiate its services through the quality of the products it delivered. The salesforce was instructed to concentrate on those dealers stocking premium products and to persuade others to upgrade their product offerings. Because of this quality association, Southwest was able to command slightly higher margins for its services, but the average never moved much above 5%. Although sales volume was obviously critical because of this low profitability, this goal sometimes contradicted the quality orientation. Nevertheless, Southwest was able to prosper and grow throughout the 1950s and 1960s because of the competence of the sales and buying groups and the steady rate of residential construction in the trade area.

The Plainview Deal

George Simpson, Bill's son, recently promoted to sales manager, considered the Plainview proposal in light of the present competitive environment. He was not aware of any other Dallas-area wholesalers who were making six-month commitments. He wondered if such a service might not enable Southwest to develop its contractor sales efforts into the profitable business he felt was possible. At the same time he was well aware of the price risks which such a policy entailed. He decided to review the information his assistant had prepared regarding the storage option as well as futures hedging.

Buy and Hold

Southwest had never undertaken a systematic analysis of its inventory carrying costs, but Bob Webster had prepared some figures using company records and his own best estimates. The largest component of inventory carrying costs was the cost of the working capital investment. Southwest normally paid two points over the prime lending rate for its short-term funds requirements. Although prime had recently topped 15%, Bob believed the rate was bound to fall over the next few months and was reluctant to use a 17% money cost. He decided that 15% was an adequate estimate for the cost of working capital on an annualized basis. He then considered those other costs associated with holding inventory: various taxes and insurance, and an allocation of annual fixed asset depreciation. Based on historic inventory turnover rates, he arrived at the following estimates of all carrying costs as a percentage of inventory value:

taxes	$\frac{1}{2}$%
insurance	$\frac{3}{4}$%
depreciation	2%
capital costs	<u>15%</u>
	18% per year or 1.5% per month .

George Simpson was now able to develop a price quotation for Plainview based on the six-month's storage of the lumber. The cost to Plainview, before any profit for Southwest, was composed of three elements: Southwest's delivered material cost, the related six month carrying cost, and Southwest's own delivery charge. Southwest's present delivered material cost was \$325/M (thousand board feet). This consisted of a \$320/M FOB mill price, less 5% wholesaler commission, plus \$21/M freight charge. To the \$325/M cost Simpson added approximately \$30/M for carrying costs and the \$5/M charge it normally assessed for its jobsite delivery service. The result of these calculations was a delivered cost to Plainview in the spring of about \$360/M before Southwest profit. Southwest usually earned a margin of 5% – 7% for delivered orders of this type.

George next compared this price quotation to one he might offer for current delivery. For an order of this size the normal procedure would be to arrange for direct shipment from the mill to Plainview's own yard or jobsites. In this case George would quote a delivered cost of \$325/M (same as to Southwest's yard) plus a 3% – 5% margin. George doubted that Plainview would be willing to pay the \$35M premium for the firm price in the spring. The builder did not have the facilities to store the lumber himself through the winter; that explained his offer to Southwest. But if the \$35/M premium for a firm spring price was unacceptable, Southwest's only recourse was to reject the offer or to speculate on spring prices. Given recent price performance (see Table 2.11) Simpson was extremely reluctant to commit now based on a cost to be determined in six months. At the same time he viewed the Plainview offer as a chance to pioneer with the marketing technique which could give Southwest the competitive boost it needed. He wondered if the futures market might provide a solution to his quandary.

Futures Hedging

George Simpson's optimism was buoyed after his reading of hedging materials assembled by his assistant. He could see a definite application of the so-called "long hedge" to the Plainview deal. In theory, any price fluctuations imperilling his short cash commitment between September and the following March would be dampened by offsetting movements in his long futures position. This effect was predicated, of course, on the convergence of cash and futures prices at the expiration of the March contract. He was able to confirm this event by a look at the relevant price histories:

Table 2.12

	1971	1972	1973	1974	1975	1976	1977	1978
March futures, closing	115	182	168	118	151	180	223	213
Net wholesale price	114	179	169	114	151	179	217	220

The similarity was not surprising since he expected that astute traders would take advantage of appreciable differences through arbitraging activities. Simpson was still bothered by the problem of hedging a non-contract species. He wondered if the vital price convergence between southern pine and futures prices would operate.

The Decision

George Simpson felt he had as much information as he was going to be able to collect. He now had to decide whether or not to commit to the Plainview offer. Actually, he was faced with two decisions. First he had to quote a delivered price to the Plainview buyer. (The relevant costs are summarized below.) Simpson knew that competitive factors would constrain his price determination. Given the current delivered market price of \$325/M (plus profit) he was confident that

Plainview would balk at the price associated with the buy and hold strategy. Whatever price he quoted, Simpson would then have to decide whether or not to hedge the commitment. He was uncertain how to factor in Southwest's risk posture. Simpson regarded the entire proposition as a marketing experiment which might point the way to a re-establishment of competitive advantage. At the same time he realized that the company's competitive position had not slipped sufficiently to warrant substantial risk-taking.

Costs Summary

Delivered Cost: (to Southwest warehouse or Plainview jobsites)

$320/M current FOB mill price

($16/M) less 5% distributor commission

$21/M plus freight into Dallas area

$325/M

Plainview price quotes:

Deliver in spring	Deliver now
$325/M (from above)	
$ 30/M carrying cost	
$ 5/M delivery charge	
$360/M	$325/M from above
Margin 5%–7%, $18–$25	Margin 3%–5%, $11–$18

Futures Facts

100,000BF contract approximately equals four southern pine truckloads

Transaction costs: (per thousand board feet)

commission	.55	about $55 per contract
margin funds	—	no opportunity cost
admin. expense	.45	rough approximation
	1.00	

Price Series

Exhibit 1 tracks yearly price histories and September to March fluctuations for southern pine, northern futures, and the northwest species underlying the futures contract.

Exhibit 1

	CASH AND FUTURES PRICE HISTORIES			
	September	March	$	%
Southern cash fluctuations* – September and following March FOB mill price per MBF				
1971	135	147	12	8.9
1972	153	175	22	14.4
1973	201	166	(35)	(17.4)
1974	118	125	7	5.9
1975	134	180	46	34.3
1976	197	193	(4)	(2.0)
1977	278	238	(40)	(14.4)
1978	237	247	10	4.2
1979	319	?	—	—
Futures fluctuation** – Price of March contract during September and at contract expiration				
1971	95	115	20	21.1
1972	132	182	50	37.9
1973	117	168	51	43.6
1974	111	118	7	6.3
1975	129	151	22	17.1
1976	168	180	12	7.1
1977	192	223	31	16.1
1978	204	213	9	4.4
1979	234	?	—	—
Northern cash fluctuation* – September and following March FOB mill price				
1971	113	120	7	6.2
1972	149	188	39	26.2
1973	176	178	2	1.1
1974	121	120	(1)	(.8)
1975	134	159	25	19.0
1976	174	188	14	8.1
1977	211	228	17	8.1
1978	239	232	(7)	(2.9)
1979	285	?	—	—

*Reported in *Random Lengths Yearbook*, 1978
**Reported in *Wall Street Journal*, 1971–79

3 Risk versus Return

So far, in this book, we have tacitly assumed that risk reduction is costless: that the only challenge is to figure out how best to reduce the risk. Often risk can be reduced only at a cost. Clearly, if the price gets too high it may be better to stick with the risk. These risk-return tradeoff decisions are among the most difficult in risk management. In this chapter we show how to think through these dilemmas. There are three cases, in each of which the protagonist wrestles with these issues. Thinking through these cases will teach you a lot about the complexity of such problems. Thoroughly understanding the probability distribution of likely payoffs is only the beginning.

LIFE INSURANCE

At one time it was the practice for a deceased worker's colleagues to take up a collection on behalf of the bereaved family, thus providing a limited form of social insurance. Mine workers practiced an arrangement that encouraged larger contributions: they contributed a fixed sum each time a worker died, with the money going to a fund for the family of the *next* victim.

Americans hold nearly 70% of all life insurance policies. This statistic, though surprising at first glance, is less so when you stop to consider who else is likely to buy such insurance. The socialist economies believe that providing for the needs of survivors is the responsibility of the state, not the deceased. The inhabitants of developing countries are usually too poor to afford the premiums, even if the mechanism were available. This leaves only Western Europe, Japan, Australia, and North America. The United States is unusual with its vast middle class, who are the major purchasers of life insurance. The poor rely on social security to support their families, and the rich have no need for insurance. It is only those families whose standard of living and aspirations hinge exclusively on the future income of a single breadwinner that may require insurance against the loss of that income.

The most common reasons for purchasing life insurance are:

1. **Provisions for death expenses.** Dying can be expensive, not just the direct costs such as medical bills (which might be insured separately) and funeral expenses, but also indirect costs such as flying college-age children home, unpaid time off work for other working members of the household, overseas phone calls, and so on. Lawyers typically charge 5% of the value of any estate they process.

Harvard Business School note 9-182-139. Professor David E. Bell prepared this note. Copyright © 1981 by the President and Fellows of Harvard College.

2. **Provision for clearance of debts.** Two typical debts that become important on the death of a principal wage-earner are a mortgage on the home and the state and federal taxes on the estate. Fortunately, these are somewhat offsetting since large estates typically arise because of property owned. The larger the mortgage debt, the lower the value of the estate and therefore the lower the taxes.

3. **Provision for liquidity at death.** The expenses mentioned in items 1 and 2 may be well within the means of the family, but the assets may be largely illiquid. A time of bereavement is not the moment to go out seeking a good price for the family silver. Even if insurance companies do not pay out promptly, a bank loan against the policy is usually a simple matter.

4. **Replacement of earned income of deceased.** This is the single greatest financial blow to most families. Exceptions are where the proportion of income that is earned is low. For example, retired people often have little or no earned income, so life insurance may be needed for this purpose only to the extent that income from a pension may be sharply decreased on the death of one spouse. Another exception is when the surviving spouse is able to replace the lost income by going out to work.

5. **As a method of saving.** Some life insurance policies have provisions by which the policyholder accumulates a cash figure that may be borrowed during the life of the policy. If it is not repaid the principal and interest are deducted from the death benefit paid out. Such policies also have a surrender value which after 30 years or so may be of the same size as the death benefit. An advantage of this form of saving is that interest earned accumulates tax free. Taxes are paid on the interest only if the policy is surrendered for its cash value.

It is not necessary to buy life insurance directly to have one's life insured. Many companies have group loans whereby the employees' lives are insured, typically for a small multiple of their annual salary.

Life Insurance Companies

There are two common structures for life insurance companies. A mutual life insurance company regards itself as a pool in which policyholders become, in effect, shareholders. Profits from underwriting (insurance) are either retained or paid out in dividends to the policyholders, usually in proportion to premiums paid. The other structure is that of a normal corporation. Dividends are paid to equity holders who may or may not be policyholders.

The companies are closely supervised by the government to ensure that their reserves are substantial enough to meet future benefits that have been guaranteed. This reserve is rarely a problem because insurance premiums are paid at the beginning of the insured period whereas benefits are paid sometime after any death that occurs, and these deaths are scattered evenly over the period.

Hence a company makes money in two ways: from the underwriting business itself, and from the returns on investments made using the float and retained earnings. It is no coincidence that the tallest buildings in the United States belong to insurance companies, the most recent being the New York PanAm building, acquired by Metropolitan Life for $400 million in cash, a small fraction of their liquid assets.

Broadly speaking, if the investment returns are separated out, life insurance companies break even on underwriting. What the company gains is the time value of the money held in their reserves.

Types of Insurance

The two most prevalent types of insurance are term and whole life insurance.

Term insurance

This class of policy insures a life in exactly the same way as fire insurance covers a home. A premium sum, paid in advance, gives insurance protection against a person's life for a specified period (term), usually one year. At the end of the period, if the insured has not died, a mutual company will often pay a dividend to the insured. The size of this dividend is not guaranteed in advance but varies with the loss experience of the company for term policies during that period. The dividends are treated as taxable income by the IRS.

Since each renewal constitutes a separate contract, someone who used term insurance repeatedly would pay rapidly increasing premiums as a result of increasing age. Exhibit 1 shows the rates offered by a leading mutual life insurance company to a 35-year-old male in a preferred health category as of January 1981. The $972 premium at age 55 is that which would be charged to a 55-year-old male in a preferred health category or to any 55-year-old male who had been taking out term insurance repeatedly since age 35.

Whole-life insurance

In return for annual payment of a premium which is fixed in size at the time of the initial contract, the company will pay a fixed sum to the appropriate beneficiary upon the insured's death. Thus whole-life insurance has the distinctive feature of insuring an event which is sure to happen.

This policy also produces annual dividends, which are usually retained by the company either to offset premium payments or to enlarge the size of the death benefit. Paid-up whole-life is a variant in which a higher constant premium is paid, but only to some predetermined age such as 65. Dividends are not taxed if they are applied to the purchase of additional coverage.

Exhibit 2 shows that an annual payment of $1,792 would secure whole-life insurance for the same 35-year-old male covered by Exhibit 1.

The level premium feature of whole-life insurance means that much more is paid in early years of the policy than is actuarially necessary, this being necessary to make up for later years when it is too low. There arises the question of what to do about a policyholder who wants to terminate the policy before death. Possible options are:

▶ To pay the policy holder the amount accrued in excess of administrative expenses and life insurance coverage already consumed by the insured. This is called the cash value of the policy.

▶ To recalculate the amount of whole-life insurance that could have been bought with the premiums paid. The insured no longer pays premiums but does receive the guaranteed paid-up insurance (see Exhibit 2) at death and the stream of dividends associated with this lower coverage.

The illustrative paid-up insurance (Exhibit 2) is the amount of paid-up insurance that is held if dividends are used to buy additional coverage.

Surrender values were first introduced in the 1850s in Massachusetts as a result of the action of Elizur Wright, the Commissioner of Insurance. Companies were concerned about this practice because of problems of adverse selection (people with poor health are less likely to cancel the policy) and because of the possibility of a sudden rush of cancellations during a national financial crisis, just when the company itself might have liquidity problems. This latter effect was mitigated by introducing a six-month waiting period for payment upon cancellation, to deter cancellation for short-term liquidity purposes.

Term vs. whole-life

Although there is no reason to confine oneself to only one of these forms of insurance—and many people do hold both—a common question is to decide which is better to hold.

Term is evidently better for someone with only temporary coverage needs. Term is also preferable for someone with cash flow problems since the initial payments are much lower. Term is also advantageous for a somewhat limited group who, although healthy, anticipate early death. Suicide used to be grounds for non-payment of life insurance but this exclusion is now only valid within two years of an initial policy contract. The perception persists, however, that there is adverse selection by higher-risk people towards term insurance, which, if true, would cause higher rates. A more convincing reason for term to have higher underlying rates is turnover, since this increases administrative costs. Precisely because many people buy only temporary coverage, administrative costs are high which penalizes someone wishing to use term coverage over a longer period. Administrative costs are also higher for term because it's typical that 25% of the first year's premium is paid as commission to the selling agent. For whole-life this figure is 50% but because of the higher payment the company still gains even if whole-life is not renewed. The agent receives 11% of the premium paid for each of the next four years so long as the policy is renewed. Note, however, that the policy in Exhibit 1 guarantees renewal to the policyholder even if his health deteriorates, so long as his coverage is held continuously.

The disadvantage of term insurance is that premiums rise dramatically for older people such that coverage becomes prohibitive "just when you're most likely to collect." Whole life offers the complementary advantage that, due to inflation, the cost of coverage decreases in real terms over the life of the policy (and individual). The fact that the policy has a cash value also provides a source of collateral should the insured require a loan at a later time. A loan will be issued by the insurance company at an interest rate determined at the date of issue of the policy. In the 1980's, this feature created a windfall for policyholders who were able to borrow money at rates such as 4%. It is this feature that makes many purchasers of whole-life insurance regard it as a method of enforced saving. Others assert that the enforced savings could just as well be invested by the individual (with the implication that this could be done with better returns) and the accrued value used to pay the higher term premiums that occur later in life.

It is argued that underwriting rates are lower for whole-life customers because the high up-front payments mean that people who do die early have paid more in premiums than have those who buy term. Lastly, a repeat buyer of term insurance bears the risk that deteriorating health before death will eliminate financially feasible coverage just prior to death. Whole-life insurance thus "ensures insurability."

How Rates Are Set

Four components affect rate calculations:

‣ Mortality predictions
‣ Investment return
‣ Profit requirements
‣ Administrative costs

Substantial data provide companies with reliable probabilities of death for average U.S. citizens by ages and gender. Although longevity has been increasing, and can be expected to continue, companies tend to be retrospective in their analyses. Were age and gender the only discriminants used in determining rates for a given type of policy, adverse selection would lead to bad loss experience and then higher rates; this would tend to drive out the healthier people. Hence insurance companies try to predict more closely the risk class of each applicant.

The following data are among those used to determine risk class: age, gender, build, weight, girth, medical examination, family health history, habits (such as drugs including tobacco and alcohol), morals,[1] residence, nationality, and occupation.[2]

Clearly, with a greater number of risk categories, the reliability of the data is poorer for each class. There is also a higher risk that an applicant will be incorrectly assigned, which may cause the individual to decide against insurance or to seek evaluation from another company. This raises problems of adverse selection and administrative expense.

Investment return is typically quite low relative to the general field of available opportunities. One reason for this is that long-term bonds provide an appealing form of investment for insurance companies since the terms of the bonds can be matched with the maturities of the life policies outstanding, thus eliminating inflation and investment risk to the company. A further cause of low investment return being guaranteed on whole-life policies is that if actual returns were to drop below guaranteed returns, this loss to the company would occur simultaneously across all policies. This is one reason for the unguaranteed nature of the dividends.

Profit demands obviously vary with competitive forces. Life insurance is never regarded as a loss-leader. Administrative costs are almost purely a function of renewal rates in the case of term insurance and cancellations in the case of whole-life. This is partly due to the cost of form processing, medical exams and such, and partly due to the agents' incentive system mentioned earlier.

Moral Hazard

Apart from the normal difficulties of adverse selection, moral hazard is created when the fact of insurance affects an insured's probability of death.

The extreme case is, of course, suicide. The two-year non-payment clause is considered sufficient to deter those who might take out insurance with intent to defraud in this manner. Murder of an insured by a beneficiary is still a possibility insurers face, although a convicted murderer is not paid. To reduce the possibility of this kind of temptation the beneficiary must (at the time the policy is taken out) have reason to prefer the insured alive rather than dead. In England in the 18th century it was a common practice for individuals to speculate on the health of public figures by taking out life insurance upon them; in fact, newspapers carried a list summarizing the health of public figures as a service!

Moral hazard can influence company profitability in less dramatic ways. Just as a homeowner with fire insurance may feel less inclined to expend a lot of effort on fire prevention than an uninsured neighbor, so at one time it was argued that a breadwinner with life insurance may feel less responsibility to stay alive for the sake of his family. Life insurance was opposed by some groups on these grounds.

---

[1] The author confesses ignorance as to how this is assessed.

[2] Airline pilots are not charged a premium.

Exhibit 1

SAMPLE POLICY—TERM INSURANCE

PLAN OF INSURANCE: ONE YEAR TERM LIFE INSURANCE RENEWABLE-CONVERTIBLE[a]

CLASSIFICATION: PREFERRED   AGE: 35-MALE   AMOUNT OF INSURANCE: **$100,000**

ANNUAL PREMIUM: SEE BELOW

Policy Year	Annual Premium Basic Plan	Disability Waiver Benefit	Total Annual Premium	Dividend End of Year	Net Premium For Year
1	$242	$13	$255	None	$255
2	250	14	264	76	188
3	260	15	275	79	196
4	269	16	285	82	203
5	282	18	300	85	215
6	299	20	319	89	230
7	319	23	342	94	248
8	340	27	367	99	268
9	365	32	397	104	293
10	393	39	432	109	323
11	426	47	473	116	357
12	464	56	520	124	396
13	503	66	569	125	444
14	549	78	627	126	501
15	606	91	697	128	569
16	683	108	791	130	661
17	748	129	877	134	743
18	816	154	970	139	831
19	891	184	1,075	145	930
20	972	218	1,190	151	1,039

	End of 10 Years	End of 20 years
Summary for period shown:		
Total annual premiums	3,236	11,025
Total annual dividends	817	2,135
When dividends are applied to premiums or paid in cash		
Total premiums less total dividends	2,419	8,890
When dividends accumulate at interest[b]		
Accumulated dividends at interest	1,052	3,769
Total premiums less accumulated dividends		
at interest	2,184	7,256

	10 years	20 years
Interest-adjusted 5% indexes (basic policy)		
Life insurance net payment cost index	$2.21	$3.33
Equivalent level annual dividend	$0.75	$0.94

[a]Renewable to the policy anniversary at attained age 70, and convertible prior to the policy anniversary at attained age 60.

[b]Three percent guaranteed: 6.65% current; interest subject to federal income tax.

Exhibit 2

SAMPLE POLICY—WHOLE LIFE INSURANCE

PLAN OF INSURANCE: WHOLE LIFE

CLASSIFICATION: PREFERRED   AGE: 35-MALE   AMOUNT OF INSURANCE: $100,000

	ANNUAL PREMIUM	YEARS PAYABLE
BASIC POLICY	$ 1,792.00	LIFETIME
DISABILITY WAIVER	71.00	29
TOTAL ANNUAL PREMIUM	1,863.00	

ANNUAL DIVIDENDS USED TO BUY PAID-UP ADDITIONAL INSURANCE

End of Policy Year	Annual Dividend	Guaranteed Cash Value	Illustrative Cash Value[a]	Guaranteed Paid-up Insurance[b]	Guaranteed Paid-up Insurance[b]	Illustrative Death Benefit[c]
1	None	None	None	None	None	$100,000
2	$117	$100	$217	$400	$788	100,388
3	189	1,100	1,412	3,600	4,602	101,002
4	228	2,500	3,057	7,800	9,531	101,731
5	282	4,000	4,870	12,100	14,715	102,615
6	343	5,500	6,760	16,100	19,769	103,669
7	404	7,100	9,032	20,600	24,986	105,086
8	461	8,700	11,386	23,800	30,049	106,649
9	522	10,300	13,930	27,300	35,063	108,463
10	588	12,000	16,574	30,900	40,337	110,337
11	649	13,700	19,416	34,200	45,452	112,452
12	723	15,400	22,376	37,300	50,535	114,735
13	795	17,200	25,456	40,400	55,778	117,078
14	867	19,000	28,763	43,300	60,975	119,675
15	945	20,800	32,206	46,000	66,136	122,436
16	1,116	22,700	35,886	48,800	71,756	125,456
17	1,192	24,600	39,718	51,400	77,327	128,627
18	1,263	26,500	43,603	53,800	82,835	131,835
19	1,340	28,400	47,754	56,100	88,391	135,291
20	1,419	30,300	52,080	58,300	93,995	138,895
Age 60	1,993	40,400	77,208	68,200	124,351	159,651
Age 65	2,402	50,700	108,118	75,800	156,350	184,050

[a]Guaranteed cash value, cash value of additional insurance and any terminal dividend.

[b]Paid-up insurance available if you stop paying premiums and reduced paid-up insurance option is chosen. Illustrative paid-up insurance includes paid-up insurance bought by dividends. Any remaining optional benefits end when paid-up option takes effect.

[c]Basic insurance, additional insurance and any terminal dividend.

LOUISE SIMPSON

Louise Simpson is looking forward to finishing her M.B.A. soon and beginning a career in the financial community of Atlanta. Because her salary will not be needed for current family expenses, and her husband Philip expects to receive a major raise this year, Louise wants to devise a plan for investing their surplus funds. She also wants to check that the investments that she and Phil already have, fit their objectives in view of their changing financial situation and the current investment environment.

Phil, who (like Louise) is forty years old, is employed as director of site selection in the Southeastern United States regional office of Valu-Mart, a world-wide retailing firm. During the nineteen years that Phil has worked for Valu-Mart, he has progressed from stock man to his present position, which pays $40,000 a year. Furthermore, sometime this year he will receive a promotion that will result in a raise of at least $8,000.

The Simpsons have two children. Roger, who became seventeen this past December, is a senior in high school; William, who became fourteen last June, is a freshman.

After Roger and William graduate from high school, they want to go to college, preferably a private one. Tuition, fees, room, board, books, supplies, personal expenses, and transportation for three quarters are estimated to cost $2,889 at a public university like Georgia State University if a student is a state resident, lives at home, and commutes by bus, and to cost $7,001 at a private university like Emory University if a student lives on campus. Because of the boys' school records, the Simpsons believe some scholarship help based on merit will be available. However, if no aid is available, the Simpsons plan to finance their children's college educations through current income.

Phil is also partially responsible for the support of his 78 year-old mother. At present these expenses total about $1,200 a year and can be met out of current income. But, looking ahead, the Simpsons have decided that to handle any emergency Phil's mother might have and to take care of their other responsibilities, they should maintain a reserve fund equal to one half of their "bare bones" annual expense budget.

The Simpsons want to obtain large enough returns from their investments to offset inflation and increase their real (or inflation adjusted) value. Yet the Simpsons would not feel comfortable in taking a large amount of risk, an attitude they realize will limit their returns.

To help them to devise and execute an appropriate investment strategy, the Simpsons have consulted an investment counselor at the brokerage firm of Morgan, Lodge, Paine, Felton and Straus. In response to his inquiries, the Simpsons have supplied him with the following additional information about their financial circumstances and needs.

Financial statements

The Simpsons' income, taxes, expenses, and savings during the past year and their balance sheet as of the end of last year are shown in Exhibit 1. Louise is initially projecting her and Phil's income, taxes, expenses, and savings for this year on the basis of the following assumptions. She will start to work on April 1 at an annual salary of $18,000. Phil will receive an $8,000 annual raise on July 1.

Investment income will be at least $1,050. Thus, her and Phil's income for the year will total $58,550. Accordingly, their social security, state income, and federal income tax will amount to $20,700. Although their incremental Georgia income tax remains at 6% (the maximum), their incremental U.S. income tax will rise from 39% last year to 50% this year. Those expenses that were in last year's budget and are not fixed will rise 12% because of inflation; in addition, on April 1 Louise will begin to incur incremental expenses for transportation, lunches, and clothes of $90 per month, while hiring a maid to clean the house one day a week will cost an extra $25 per week. As a result, the family expense budget this year will total $29,212, and $9,068 will be left for savings and investments.

Home ownership

The Simpsons own a ten year-old house having a current market value of $55,000 and a $7\frac{1}{2}$% mortgage with an unpaid balance of $19,000. Their monthly payments, including principal, interest, taxes, and insurance, are $226. Although the Simpsons could afford a more expensive home, they do not want to move in the near future. However, they are wondering if they should consider buying a second home for recreational purposes.

Insurance

Phil has $31,000 worth of life insurance that will be fully paid up when he reaches the age of 65; this insurance has a current cash value of about $4,500 and permits him to borrow up to this amount from the life insurance company at an annual interest rate of 5%. Through Valu-Mart Phil also has $76,000 in group term life insurance (which he can increase as his salary increases), $150,000 worth of business travel accident insurance (paid by his employer), and comprehensive medical, long-term disability, and accident insurance.

Social security benefits

If Phil should die, Louise will receive a lump-sum payment of $255 for burial expenses; in addition, each surviving member of the family will receive monthly benefits of $490, based on Phil's earnings record and subject to a maximum monthly family payment of $1,142. Each of the children will receive $490 monthly until he becomes eighteen, or if he remains a full-time student, until he becomes twenty-two; Louise will receive $162 monthly as long as she remains at home to care for a child under eighteen. Social security benefits are exempt from federal and state income taxes, and the monthly benefits (but not the lump-sum payment) increase as the cost of living rises. However, if Louise, Roger, or William earns more than $3,720 per year, her or his benefit will be reduced $1 for each $2 of earnings in excess of $3,720.

Other income for the surviving family

If Phil dies and Louise works outside the home, she will earn about $18,000 per year and receive $1,050 in interest and dividends from the family's current investments. If she is taxed as the head of a household and continues to live in her present home, she will pay $4,770 in federal income, Georgia income, and social security taxes on a gross annual income of $19,050. Any additional income from investing the proceeds from Phil's life insurance will be subject to incremental federal and state income taxes of 28% and 6% respectively.

On the other hand, if Louise dies, Phil will earn about $44,000 this year and receive $1,050 in interest and dividend income. If he is taxed as a head of household and continues to live in his present home, he will pay $15,489 annually in federal income, state income, and social security taxes on his gross annual income of $45,050. His incremental federal and state income taxes will be 50% and 6% respectively on personal service income such as salary, and 51% and 6% on other income such as interest and dividends.

Reserves

The Simpsons have $600 in a joint checking account at a commercial bank. In addition, they have $10,000 in a 5 1/2% ninety-day notice account and $4,000 in a 6 1/2% four-year savings certificate at a federally insured savings and loan association. If the Simpsons withdraw funds from the savings account without giving notice, they forfeit the interest accrued since the end of a quarter. Similarly, if the Simpsons withdraw the funds in the savings certificate before it matures next December 31, the interest rate falls to 5 1/4% and all interest for three months is forfeited. However, the Simpsons can borrow up to 90% of the face value of the savings certificate at 8 1/2% interest.

Investments

Over the years Phil has purchased 126 shares of Valu-Mart common stock through the employee purchase plan; currently the stock sells for $20 per share and pays a cash dividend of $1.20. In addition the company has given Phil an option to buy 200 shares at $30 per share at any time during the next three years. Finally, the Simpsons have deposited $4,000 at the geriatric care center that manages the apartment in which Phil's mother lives; this obligatory deposit earns 3% interest and will be returned to the Simpsons upon the death of Phil's mother.

Retirement plan

The Simpsons expect to receive pensions from three sources. First, Phil is fully vested in Valu-Mart's (noncontributing) pension plan. His annual pension will be about 50% of the average of the three largest yearly salaries he earns at Valu-Mart; thus Phil's pension appears to be protected from inflation until he retires, but not afterward. Second, when Louise becomes employed, she will also have some type of retirement plan. Third, when retired, the Simpsons will be eligible for social security benefits.

After analyzing these facts, the investment counselor recommended that Phil purchase $300,000 worth of term insurance and a 7.2%, six-year deferred annuity. The guaranteed rate on the annuity after the first year is 6% per annum, and 7% of the original principal may be withdrawn each year without a penalty. However, any amount withdrawn in excess of 7% is subject to a decreasing withdrawal penalty ranging from 7% in the first year to 1% in the last year.

Louise is wondering if this plan really meets their needs, and if not, what their investment strategy should be.

Exhibit 1 _____

FINANCIAL STATEMENTS

Income During Last Year

Salary	$40,000
Dividends and Interest	1,050
Total Income	$41,050

Taxes, Expenses, and Savings During Last Year

Social Security, Georgia Income, and U.S. Income Taxes	$10,920
Food and Clothing	6,000
Housing	2,712
Loan Payments	1,356
Auto Expenses	2,500
Utilities	1,500
Expenses for Mother	1,200
Insurance	2,574
Savings and Investments	5,000
Vacations and Recreation	2,000
Gifts and Contributions	1,500
Medical and Dental Expenses	500
Miscellaneous Expenses	3,288
Total Expenses	$41,050

Assets as of the End of Last Year

House	$ 55,000
Savings	14,000
Checking Account	600
Investments	6,520
Home Furnishings and Personal Effects	20,000
Two Automobiles and a Boat	8,000
Cash Value of Life Insurance	4,500
Total Assets	$108,620

Liabilities and Net Worth as of the End of Last Year

Mortgage	$ 19,000
Automobile Loan	2,150
Total Liabilities	$ 21,150
Net Worth	87,470
Total Liabilities and Net Worth	$108,620

▼   ▼   ▼

WHY PREFERENCE CURVES ARE USEFUL FOR RISKY DECISIONS

Act I

The act opens with a businessman (B) and a management consultant (C) lunching at their club.

B: Our business is quite unusual. Each day we are allowed to examine two lines of gold dust. The lines have equal amounts of dust per unit length. We are allowed to select one of the lines and keep all the gold dust in it. Usually it's fairly easy to tell which line is longer, but not always. It's hardest to tell when the lines are far apart or at an angle. Is there any way to help us consistently to pick the line that has more gold in it?

C: Let me ask you a few questions. In what situations do you feel absolutely sure that one line is longer than the other?

B: If both lines were parallel, close together, and such that each had an end in about the same place, then the line that sticks out further at the other end is longer. Like this.

———————————————— ← Shorter

———————————————————— ← Longer

C: Your mention of sticks gives me an idea. Do you agree with the following rule: "If line 1 is the same length as line 2, and line 3 is the same length as line 4, and if line 2 is longer than line 3, then it must be that line 1 is longer than line 4?" (I'll call this "rule R.")

B: (After a pause.) Yes, I suppose that must be true.

C: Then I know what you can do.

1. Find a stick that is at least as long as any of the lines you usually see. Paint one end of it white.

2. If you wish to compare the lengths of two lines, line 1 and line 4, start by laying the stick parallel and close to line 1. Be sure that the white end of the stick is very close to one end of line 1.

3. Make a mark on the stick next to the other end of line 1. Call the line that goes from the white end of the stick to the mark, line 2. Of course line 1 and line 2 are the same length.

4. Repeat Step 3 but with line 4. Call the new line on the stick line 3. Now line 4 and line 3 have the same length.

5. Compare line 2 and line 3. You can because they are parallel, close together and have an end in common (the white end of the stick). If line 2 is longer than line 3 then line 1 is longer than line 4. If line 3 is longer than line 2 then line 4 is longer than line 1. This works out because of "rule R."

Harvard Business School note 9-183-030. Professor David E. Bell wrote this drama. Copyright © 1982 by the President and Fellows of Harvard College.

B: You're right! (Pause). Mind you, one thing bothers me. It's a lot of messing around using that stick all the time.

C: You don't have to use it all the time, only when you don't trust your judgement and you think the effort of using the stick is worth the increase in accuracy. Actually it's like everything else, if you take the trouble to practice using it, you'll find you never want to be without it.

B: I've seen the light. From now on I'll never be without my "rule R" stick.

Act II—Several Years Later.
Scene I

B: You remember a few years ago you helped me devise our system of measuring lines with sticks. As you may know that gold opportunity didn't last long but my father did make a fortune selling these Rulers©. Sadly, he passed away recently but he's left me with a problem. You know how crazy he always was. His will was read yesterday and in it he left me two things. The first was the right to select one of two urns each containing 100 checks. The checks will be made out for different amounts. I will have one hour to examine the contents of the two urns, after which I will be allowed to select one urn, pick a check at random and cash it for my own benefit. The remaining checks will be burned. The difference between the value of his estate and my check will be given to charity.

C: Your father was certainly unusual.

B: And I'm scared to death about this urn business, those checks could be for as much as $10 million or as little as a penny. How can I be sure of picking the right urn?

C: Let me ask you a few questions. In what situations would you feel absolutely sure that you are picking the better urn?

B: Well, if all the checks in one urn are bigger than all the checks in the other urn, I'd know I was right to pick the urn with the bigger checks.

C: That's not much to go on. Incidentally, what was the other thing your father left you in his will?

B: A French Curve. I told you he was crazy.

C: Just a minute, that gives me an idea. Suppose we practiced choosing among urns now when you'd have all the time you'd want to make your choice?

B: How can we be sure we'll practice with the same distribution of checks my father has picked?

C: That's not the idea. I'm going to use your practice answers together with your French Curve to give you the equivalent of a Ruler© for urns.

B: That would be absolutely fantastic. I'd be forever grateful if you can do it.

C: I need to ask you a few questions first:

  1. Suppose you judge urn 1 and urn 2 to be equally preferred. Suppose you judge urn 3 and urn 4 to be equally preferred. Suppose you further judge urn 2 to be better than urn 3. Do you agree this means that urn 1 is better than urn 4?

B: Of course.

C: 2. Suppose urns A, B, C and D all contain the same number of checks and that you have decided A and B are equally valuable, and that C and D are equally valuable. For the sake of argument we'll say A and B are preferred to C and D.

B: That's fine.

C: Suppose I tip all the checks from urns A and C into a new urn, call it urn 1. Suppose I also tip all the checks from urns B and D into a new urn, call it urn 2. Would you agree that you should now be indifferent between drawing a check at random from urn 1 as from urn 2?

B: Yes, that seems right.

C: OK. Now look at these two urns. The first has 50 checks worth $10 million and 50 checks worth $0. The second contains 100 checks each saying $1 million. Which of these two urns would you pick?

B: (Long pause.) The $1 million urn.

C: How much would those checks in the second urn have to be worth in order that you would be just indifferent between the two urns?

B: (Very long pause.) That's a terribly hard question. Thank goodness I don't have only an hour for this kind of question. I'd say $800,000.

Scene II   Much Later

C: So that's that. I've plotted a graph giving your answers to the urn questions. From Figure 3.1 we can deduce, for any percentage composition of $10 million checks and $0 checks in an urn, what your equivalent check for sure would be worth. For example, an urn with 75% of its checks saying $10 million and 25% saying $0 would be equivalent to an urn all of whose checks said $2 million.

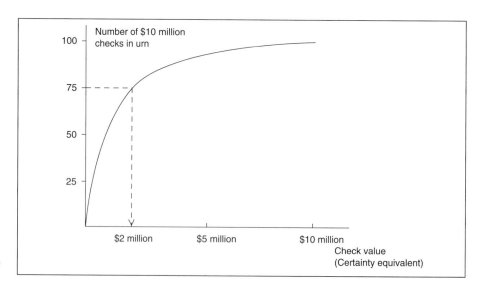

Figure 3.1

B: Yes, that French Curve really came in handy. But how is this going to help me tomorrow?

C: First I'll tell you what to do. Then I'll tell you why it's the right thing to do. Let's suppose that you have to choose between two urns, 1 and 2. Get two sheets of paper. Label one urn 1 and the other urn 2. Take each check out of urn 1 one by one and write on the paper the check's "percentage equivalent." This is the number you get by starting on the horizontal axis with the value of the check, go up to the curve and across and read off the percentage equivalent. When you've done this for all 100 checks, repeat the exercise for urn 2. Now add up the percentage equivalents for urn 1 and for urn 2. You want the urn with the higher total.

B: I can do that in an hour, but what's it got to do with anything? You've lost me, I'm afraid.

C: Imagine the following process:

- Line up four columns of 100 empty urns (that's 400 urns), and have four other empty urns available nearby. Let's call the four columns A, B, C, and D.

- Bring over urn 1, and take out one check from it. Make 100 copies of this check, and put those copies in the first empty urn in Column A. Put the original check on one side.

- Take the next check from urn 1, and repeat the process, using the next empty urn in Column A. Continue until all the checks in urn 1 have been copied. Then replace all the original checks back into urn 1.

- Go through the same procedure with urn 2, using the urns in Column C for the copied checks. Each of the urns in Column C now contains 100 copies of one of the original checks in urn 2, with each of Column C's urns corresponding to one of the checks in urn 2. Similarly, each of the urns in Column A contains 100 copies of one of the original checks in urn 1.

- Now go back to the first urn in Column A. Determine from your graph the number of $10 million checks that would be equivalent to the face value of the checks in this urn. For example, if the urn's checks are each for $2 million, then an equivalent urn would contain 75 checks saying $10 million and 25 checks saying $0. Take the first empty urn from Column B and fill it with this "percentage equivalent" of $10 million checks. Then add checks worth $0 to the urn until there are 100.

- Repeat this procedure for the remaining urns in Column A, matching each with an urn in Column B; and then continue through Column D, matching with the urns in Column C.

- You have now filled 400 urns, each with 100 checks.

- Finally, take four more empty urns, and call them urns A, B, C, and D. Tip all the checks from all 100 urns in Column A into urn A. (Urn A contains, therefore, 100 x 100 = 10,000 checks.) Tip all the checks from all the urns in Column B into urn B. Similarly, fill urns C and D with the checks in the urns of Column C and Column D respectively.

Now to use the rules you gave me. Clearly you are indifferent between drawing a check at random from urn 1 as from urn A.

B: Sure, urn A is just urn 1 replicated 100 times.

C: Good. Now by the second rule you gave me, you are indifferent between urn A and urn B.

B: That's because each time I tipped the contents of an urn into urn A, I tipped an equivalent urn into urn B.

C: Exactly. By similar reasoning, urn 2 is indifferent to urn C which is indifferent to urn D.

B: O.K.

C: Now, which urn do you prefer, urn B or urn D? Note that if you prefer B to D that means, by rule 1, that you prefer urn 1 to urn 2.

B: If I've followed all this, urns B and D contain only $10 million checks or $0 checks.

C: Correct.

B: So it seems to me I prefer the one that has the more $10 million checks.

C: Quite right. And how many $10 million checks **are** in urn B?

B: (Lengthy pause.) The sum of the percentage equivalents of the checks that were in urn 1!

C: How many $10 million checks are there in urn D?

B: The sum of the percentage equivalents of the checks that were in urn 2! Why, that is amazing. You've done it again!

C: Don't forget we couldn't have done it without your "Pa's French Curve©."

RISK ANALYTICS ASSOCIATES

Michael Warren and Chad Kent, consultants for Risk Analytics Associates (RAA), had been working for several weeks on a Monte Carlo computer simulation model of Hartford Steam Boiler's insurance loss experience. The model was intended to help Hartford Steam Boiler (HSB) with its reinsurance decisions. The two consultants were preparing to meet with Jerry Spila, the vice president of the insurance risk group of RAA.

Michael and Chad had encountered some difficulties in developing the simulation model because of the unavailability of certain data pertaining to HSB's historical claim and loss figures. Nonetheless, a simulation model which provided a first cut at the problem had been developed. Further refinements would surely be needed, however, if the model's output were to be a useful tool for HSB's reinsurance decisions.

A presentation to HSB's vice president for underwriting was scheduled for September 29, 1976, only two weeks away. Jerry Spila had emphasized the importance of this project to Michael and Chad. HSB was a large U.S. insurer of boilers and industrial machinery, and if RAA could make a convincing presentation of the value of their model, they would surely gain a new and profitable client.

Background for Risk Analytics Associates

RAA had been founded in 1970 by two business school graduates. The firm specialized in the analysis of risk relating to insurable losses. It helped their clients to answer such questions as to how much and what type of insurance to purchase. RAA had grown substantially during its first six years of existence and had expanded its analytical services into other types of business-related risk. The most promising of these had been the analysis of financial risk involved in investment and capital budgeting decisions, and the handling of risks related to currency fluctuations for international concerns.

Harvard Business School case 9-181-032. Doctoral candidate Keith B. Jarrett prepared this case under the supervision of Professor Warren Oksman. Copyright © 1980 by the President and Fellows of Harvard College.

Insurance-related risks had remained the central focus of RAA's business. Demand for this type of service had increased substantially in the 1970s as a result of a dramatic increase in both the need for and cost of insurance. Rates for many of the liability insurance coverages had skyrocketed. Enormous court awards, expansion of worker's compensation, and general broadening of the legal definition of pecuniary liability for damage and injury (e.g., manufacturers' product liability) were some of the primary causes for increased pressure on insurance rates. As a consequence, companies were much more attuned to the need and cost of insurance, and RAA's business had flourished.

The Hartford Steam Boiler Project

Hartford Steam Boiler Inspection and Insurance Company (HSB) was established in 1867 and had since grown into the nation's leading industrial insurer of boilers, pressure vessels, and machinery. Their policyholders included manufacturing firms, public utilities, and commercial and public buildings. HSB and their Canadian affiliate, the Boiler Inspection and Insurance Company of Canada (BI&I), claimed about 40% of the total boilers and machinery insurance industry in 1975. That year, they insured about 1.7 million objects under 119,000 different policies (Exhibit 1) and earned premiums of $82.7 million (see Exhibit 2 for consolidated financial statements for HSB and BI&I).

Boiler and machinery insurance differs from most other types of insurance in two important ways. First, HSB performs inspection services of the insured objects to reduce the number of accidents. Second, insurance claims are relatively infrequent, but can be quite large. Most of HSB's policies cover not only the equipment items themselves, but related damage and lost revenues as a result of damage. It is because of these large potential losses that HSB carries reinsurance.

Reinsurance is simply HSB's purchase of insurance from other insurance companies to cover any of its policyholders' losses in excess of a prespecified amount. The purpose of the reinsurance is both to shield HSB against extremely large losses and to generally dampen the potentially erratic effects that large losses could have on HSB's earnings.

Reinsurance is divided into "layers," with each layer covering a specified portion of any large loss. Each layer has its own rate structure and is insured by its own insurance underwriting syndicate.

For 1977, there were to be six layers of reinsurance. Recent negotiations with the reinsurance syndicates had tentatively established the next year's rate structure. The first reinsurance layer was to cover any loss up to $1 million in excess of $500,000 (i.e., from $500,000 to $1,500,000). This layer would be insured by an underwriting syndicate from Lloyd's of London. The premium rate for this layer was to be $^{100}/_{80}$ of all losses in the layer, subject to a 2.5% minimum and 7.5% maximum of HSB's total 1977 earned insurance premiums.

The second layer was to cover losses between $1.5 million and $5 million, for a maximum of $3.5 million net loss. It would be covered by the same syndicate as the first reinsurance layer. The rate structure for this layer was to be a flat rate of 5.5% of HSB's 1977 earned premiums. Premiums were forecast to be approximately $100 million in 1977.

The third through sixth layers were to have a flat rate structure, similar to the second layer, and covered losses from $5 million to $40 million.

HSB had a participation option in the underwriting syndicate covering the first two layers. This option required HSB to "retain" at least 10% of the insurance coverage in these layers, but allowed them to retain a larger percentage if they so wished. A 100% retention would be equivalent to no reinsurance at all. There was no participation option for the third through sixth reinsurance layers.

A similar participation option in the first two layers with a specified minimum percentage had been the standard arrangement in recent years between HSB and the reinsurance syndicates covering these layers. Reinsurance in past years had been relatively inexpensive, and, in the spirit of the reinsurance concept, HSB had traditionally opted for the minimum percentage participation in both layers. The situation for 1977, however, appeared to be different. Indeed, it was the level of HSB's reinsurance participation for 1977 which was the core issue of RAA's project.

Since 1973 HSB had experienced a significant increase in the number of "hits" which had penetrated the reinsurance layers (see Exhibit 3 for loss history). This, aggravated by inflation and rising costs of repairs and new equipment, had substantially increased the losses borne by reinsurers. As a result, the reinsurance syndicate significantly increased HSB's reinsurance premiums. The bounds on the first reinsurance layer were changed from their 1976 values of $300,000–$1.2 million to $500,000–$1.5 million for 1977. The minimum and maximum reinsurance premiums for this layer were raised from 1976 levels of 1.5% and 6% to 2.5% and 7.5% of HSB's 1977 earned premiums. The $^{100}/_{80}$ loss formula remained intact. The second layer bounds changed from their 1976 range of $1.2 million–$5.0 million to $1.5 million–$5.0 million for 1977. The cost of second layer reinsurance for 1977 was 5.5% of total earned premiums, up from 3.5% in 1976. This represented an increase of about $2.0 million just for second layer reinsurance, even though the coverage bounds (and hence the risk exposure of the reinsurers) of the second layer had narrowed.

In early 1976, as a result of the bad loss experience over the preceding three years, HSB conducted a thorough review of recent losses. Several problems were identified. For example, a disproportionate amount of losses had come from their Canadian affiliate, BI&I. HSB was not without blame, however. Outdated underwriting and pricing procedures, as well as a preponderance of new, risky accounts, had helped contribute to HSB's bad loss experience since 1973. Corrective action had been instituted which included new monitoring and pricing policies, a review of accounts, and dropping about $3 million worth of risky accounts. HSB management felt confident that these actions had alleviated most of the problems that had produced the unusually high number of recent, large losses.

Even with these corrective actions, the reinsurance underwriting syndicate had insisted upon the higher premiums for 1977. HSB felt that these premiums were higher than necessary given their aggressive program of correcting the problems which contributed to the losses. One way to offset the higher premium costs for reinsurance would be to increase their participation in the first two reinsurance layers. They were required to take at least 10% of each layer, but they now wondered if they should take more. The critical question was how much participation was appropriate, and what sort of loss exposure or potential impact on earnings and earnings variability would this increased participation represent?

The Model

In order to answer these questions, Michael and Chad felt that HSB must have a tangible means of comparing the potential cost impact of different reinsurance participation strategies. They decided that the only practical approach to this problem was through a Monte Carlo computer simulation model. They developed such a model to estimate a cumulative probability distribution, or risk profile, for all costs associated with the first two layers' reinsurance premiums and the direct payments to claimants due to HSB's participation in the first two layers. By varying the percentage participation "strategies," a variety of risk profiles could be produced, one corresponding to each strategy. These risk profiles should give a much clearer indication of the impact that increased participation might have on earnings.

The computer simulation model generated risk profiles for the first two reinsurance layers in the following way. First a random number representing the number of individual losses penetrating into the reinsurance layers was drawn. If, for example, that number turned out to be seven, then seven more random numbers were drawn (from a different distribution), representing the size of the total loss associated with each of these seven hits. By applying the reinsurance premium and participation structure to this particular loss history, the cost to HSB was calculated. By repeating this procedure many times, a cumulative frequency distribution of costs (or risk profile) to HSB was obtained. (Exhibit 4 shows a flow chart for the simulation model.)

The frequency of losses and severity of loss distributions to be used in the simulation were approximated using historical data. For the frequency of losses distribution, an estimate of p, the probability that any particular policy would result in a claim, was determined from available historical data by dividing the total number of hits penetrating the reinsurance layers in a particular period by the total number of policy years during that same period. Chad and Michael recognized that this estimate of p was indeed a rough estimate with many implicit assumptions. By assessing only one p for all policies, they were assuming that each policy was equally likely to produce a loss penetrating the reinsurance layers. In other words, they were assuming homogeneity of claim potential between HSB and BI&I policies as well as across all industries and types of policies. A further complication was that one policy may represent several insured "objects," some of which are in different locations. The number of objects for any particular policy certainly has an impact on the likelihood of that policy "initiating" a claim.

Incorporating these policy distinctions into an estimate of p for 1977, or estimates of several ps for different categories of policies, was dependent on the availability of the pertinent historical data. Unfortunately, much of these data were not readily available. Although HSB had recently installed an electronic data processing system, use of the system for informational purposes was in its infant stages. Additionally, the only pertinent summary data available for the 1966-1976 period are presented in Exhibits 3 and 5, data on reinsured losses and number of policies each year, by industry. There were no summary data on the number of insured objects per policy except for object profiles. (See Exhibit 1.) This object profile did not change much from year to year. More detailed data were available only in the manual files of each individual insurance policy, kept in the company archives. With hundreds of thousands of policies, and tens of thousands of losses over the past 10 years, the cost of aggregating additional summary figures from these individual files would be quite large.

Determining the severity of losses probability distribution was also based on historical data. The only data available for losses penetrating the reinsurance layers were from the period 1966 through July 1976. (See Exhibit 3.) The data were adjusted for inflation using the industrial commodity price index, so that all losses were in 1976 dollars. On this adjusted basis, data were available on all losses in excess of $465,000 for the period 1966-July 1976. (See Exhibit 6.) The frequency distribution for these data was used in the model to estimate the distribution for the loss size of each of the reinsurance hits. (See Exhibit 7.) The maximum loss value was selected to be $7.5 million, although the largest reported loss of the period had been $6.02 million. While the $7.5 million value seemed to fit well with the frequency distribution, its selection was somewhat arbitrary. It should also be noted that this approach of a single severity of loss distribution assumes homogeneity of the distribution of loss sizes for all of HSB's or BI&I's policies.

For the first run of the model, only two frequency of loss probabilities were used, one for all of HSB's policies, and one for BI&I's. Values of the average number of reinsurance hits per year per policy were determined from each of the HSB and BI&I historical records, and used to estimate the two p parameters for the model. The number of policies in force for 1977 for HSB and for BI&I were determined from Exhibit 5. Exhibits 8, 9, and 10 show the results from an 800-trial simulation of the 1977 situation for a range of possible retention strategies. Michael and Chad knew that the model was only a rough cut but felt that the results might give HSB valuable guidance even so. They hoped Jerry Spila could provide some direction.

Exhibit 1

OBJECT AND LOCATION PROFILES FOR HARTFORD STEAM BOILER POLICIES, NUMBER 1975

Number of Objects	Policies	%	Number of Locations	Policies	%
1	23,233	22.8	1	86,013	84.4
2	20,610	20.2	2	7,759	7.6
3	13,790	13.5	3	2,824	2.8
4	8,852	8.7	4	1,490	1.5
5	5,702	5.6	5	881	.9
6	4,389	4.3	6	597	.6
7	3,143	3.1	7	429	.4
8	2,575	2.5	8	324	.3
9	2,001	2.0	9	264	.3
10	1,646	1.3	10	215	.2
11	1,363	1.3	11	146	.1
12	1,228	1.2	12	123	.1
13	996	1.0	13	104	.1
14	861	.8	14	87	.1
15	752	.7	15	73	.1
16	684	.7	16	53	.1
17	626	.6	17	41	.0
18	562	.6	18	48	.0
19	541	.5	19	32	.0
20	503	.5	20	26	.0
21–25	1,840	1.8	21–25	119	.1
26–30	1,223	1.2	26–30	83	.1
31–35	897	.9	31–35	29	.0
36–40	658	.6	36–40	31	.0
41–45	491	.5	41–45	16	.0
46–50	393	.4	46–50	22	.0
51–60	595	.6	51–60	27	.0
61–70	392	.4	61–70	12	.0
71–80	299	.3	71–80	8	.0
81–90	224	.2	81–90	6	.0
91–100	151	.1	91–100	8	.0
101–125	249	.2	101–125	9	.0
126–150	125	.1	126–150	6	.0
151–200	124	.1	151–200	2	.0
201–300	114	.1	201–300	5	.0
301–400	31	.0	301–400	7	.0
401–500	21	.0	401–500	2	.0
Over 500	37	.0	Over 500	4	.0

Source: Company Records

Exhibit 2

1975 CONSOLIDATED FINANCIAL STATEMENTS – HARTFORD STEAM BOILER INSPECTION AND INSURANCE CO.

CONSOLIDATED INCOME STATEMENT

FOR THE YEARS ENDED DECEMBER 31	1975	1974
Operating revenues		
Premiums earned	$82,650,000	$70,581,000
Engineering services income	8,113,000	4,185,000
	90,763,000	74,766,000
Operating expenses		
Claims and adjustment	36,917,000	30,909,000
Underwriting & inspection	48,728,000	44,023,000
Engineering services	6,995,000	3,736,000
	92,640,000	78,668,000
Operating loss	(1,877,000)	(3,902,000)
Net investment income	6,854,000	6,827,000
Income before federal income taxes	4,977,000	2,925,000
Federal income taxes		
Current	(201,000)	(1,222,000)
Deferred	602,000	259,000
Total federal income taxes	401,000	(963,000)
Net income	$4,576,000	$3,888,000
Per share based on 1,800,000 shares outstanding	$2.54	$2.16

CONSOLIDATED STATEMENT OF CAPITAL GAINS AND LOSSES

FOR THE YEARS ENDED DECEMBER 31	1975	1974
Realized gains (losses)	$ (629,000)	$ (4,245,000)
Unrealized gains (losses)	11,809,000	(20,937,000)
	11,180,000	(25,182,000)
Capital gains taxes		
Current	(5,000)	(76,000)
Deferred	3,567,000	(6,330,000)
	3,562,000	(6,406,000)
Net gains (losses)		
Realized	(624,000)	(4,169,000)
Unrealized	8,242,000	(14,607,000)
	7,618,000	(18,776,000)

CONSOLIDATED STATEMENT OF RETAINED EARNINGS

FOR THE YEARS ENDED DECEMBER 31	1975	1974
Balance, beginning of year	$55,772,000	$73,954,000
Net income	4,576,000	3,888,000
Net capital gains (losses)	7,618,000	(18,776,000)
Cash dividends to stockholders	(3,384,000)	(3,294,000)
Balance, end of year	$64,582,000	$55,772,000

Exhibit 2 continued

1975 CONSOLIDATED FINANCIAL STATEMENTS – HARTFORD STEAM BOILER INSPECTION AND INSURANCE CO.

CONSOLIDATED BALANCE SHEET

December 31	1975	1974
ASSETS		
Cash	$ 3,202,000	$ 2,732,000
Short-term investments, at cost, which approximates market	15,260,000	15,759,000
Bonds, at amortized cost (market, $50,770,000 and $48,498,000)	57,684,000	57,839,000
Stocks at market (cost, $43,322,000 and $38,455,000)	65,619,000	48,714,000
Investment in unconsolidated subsidiary	6,070,000	0
Home office property, equipment and automobiles, at cost less accumulated depreciation of $5,155,000 and $4,659,000	5,091,000	4,812,000
Premiums receivable	10,833,000	8,347,000
Prepaid acquisition costs	9,914,000	9,184,000
Federal income taxes recoverable	453,000	1,653,000
Other assets	3,353,000	3,447,000
Total assets	$177,479,000	$152,511,000
LIABILITIES		
Unearned premiums	$55,705,000	$ 51,762,000
Claims and adjustment expense	33,375,000	27,634,000
Dividends payable	846,000	846,000
Deferred federal income taxes	11,724,000	7,466,000
Other liabilities	5,947,000	3,731,000
Total liabilities	$107,597,000	$ 91,439,000
STOCKHOLDERS' EQUITY	1975	1974
Capital stock, 55 par value, authorized 6,000,000 shares	$ 10,000,000	$ 10,000,000
Retained earnings	64,582,000	55,772,000
Less treasury stock, 200,000 shares at cost	(4,700,000)	(4,700,000)
Total stockholders' equity	69,882,000	61,072,000
Total liabilities and stockholders' equity	$177,479,000	$152,511,000
Stockholders' equity per share based on 1,800,000 shares outstanding	$38.32	$33.93

Exhibit 3

TEN-YEAR HISTORY OF LOSSES IN EXCESS OF HSB'S RETENTION LEVEL (ALL IN 1976 DOLLARS)

Year	HSB's Retention	Losses Which Exceeded HSB's Retention	Industry Category
1966	$231,000	$ 358,400	Chemical
		2,204,900	Chemical
		503,800	Chemical
		295,500	Chemical
		275,500	Chemical
		669,100	Chemical
		428,500	Utility
		1,531,900	Steel
		443,900	Chemical
		266,700	Chemical
		366,800	Paper
		1,210,300	Chemical
		251,000	Chemical
		409,200	Chemical
		637,200	Refinery
		623,900 (C)	Concrete
		350,900	Warehouse
		518,000 (C)	Chemical
		335,200	Chemical
		370,000	Chemical
1967	$465,000	$ 519,100	Chemical
		1,759,000	Utility
		574,600	Utility
		782,300 (C)	Paper
		474,700	Chemical
1968	$445,000	$1,276,500 (C)	Chemical
1969	$430,000	$1,089,800	Chemical
		1,238,900	Utility
1970	$415,000	$682,400	Paper
		908,400	Steel
		1,824,000	Utility
1971	$400,000	$2,930,900	Utility
1972	$387,500	$ 702,900	Concrete
		1,222,200	Utility
		626,600	Utility

Exhibit 3 continued

TEN-YEAR HISTORY OF LOSSES IN EXCESS OF HSB'S RETENTION LEVEL (ALL IN 1976 DOLLARS)

Year	HSB's Retention	Losses Which Exceeded HSB's Retention	Industry Category
1973	$435,000	$ 572,700	Paper
		519,500	Chemical
		709,900	Utility
		1,493,000	Chemical
		464,400	Chemical
		911,400	Chemical
		802,100 (C)	Mining
		1,549,500 (C)	Mining
		4,218,100 (C)	Mining
		1,341,000 (C)	Oil Refinery
1974	$357,000	$5,929,800	Utility
		1,222,600	Chemical
		1,748,200	Refinery
		967,600	Paper
		662,000	Utility
		451,200	Hotel
		509,900	Chemical
1975	$318,000	$4,271,000 (C)	Refinery
		866,800	Refinery
		607,100	Mining
		607,100	Mining
		370,900	Mining
		374,200	Utility
		441,200 (C)	Utility
		467,600	Chemical
		781,700	Chemical
		428,100 (C)	Paper
		1,040,400	Paper
1976	$300,000	$1,200,000	Utility
		1,700,000 (C)	Refinery
		950,000	Utility
		6,022,170 (C)	Utility
		525,734	Paper

Notes: 1) "(C)" refers to losses by the Canadian affiliate, BI&I.
2) All figures are inflation-adjusted to 1976 dollars.

Source: Company records

Exhibit 4

HSB MONTE CARLO COMPUTER SIMULATION MODEL FLOW DIAGRAM

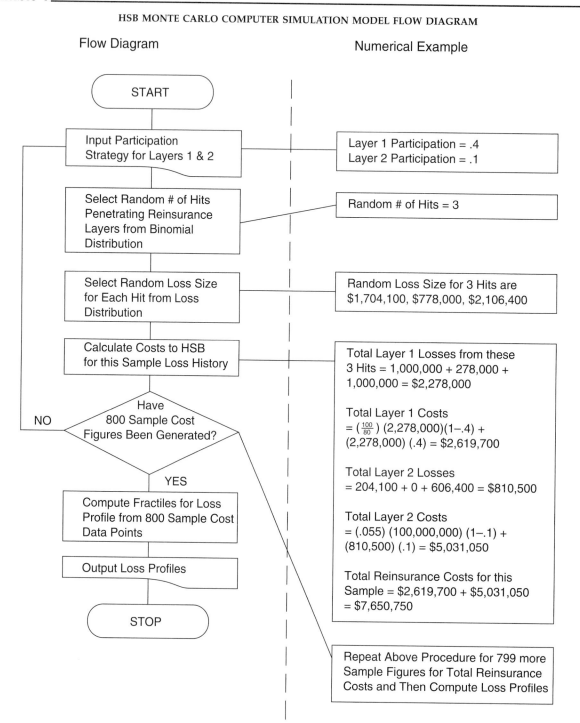

Exhibit 5

TOTAL NUMBER OF POLICIES IN FORCE BY INDUSTRY CATEGORY FOR BI&I

	Chemical	Mining	Refining	Pulp & Paper	Utilities	Other	Total
1966	49	85	41	76	44	9,998	10,293
1967	61	108	38	74	37	10,915	11,233
1968	69	115	35	73	27	11,709	12,028
1969	68	106	26	64	19	12,853	13,136
1970	61	77	26	65	15	13,632	13,876
1971	54	54	29	67	14	14,452	14,670
1972	55	40	40	70	15	15,277	15,497
1973	60	35	55	70	17	16,103	16,340
1974	72	25	70	67	18	17,024	17,276
1975	72	21	83	65	18	17,927	18,186
1976	72	19	95	61	17	18,688	18,952
1977[1]	79	17	111	58	17	19,651	19,933

[1]Values for 1977 represent forecasts

TOTAL NUMBER OF POLICIES IN FORCE BY INDUSTRY CATEGORY FOR HARTFORD STEAM BOILER

(U.S. POLICIES ONLY)

	Chemical	Mining	Refining	Pulp & Paper	Utilities	Other	Total
1966	765	78	227	354	529	82,874	84,827
1967	731	73	208	338	440	82,901	84,691
1968	744	69	228	331	394	84,560	86,326
1969	793	68	273	327	377	87,832	89,670
1970	902	73	281	362	510	98,620	100,748
1971	1,013	92	295	400	611	104,345	106,756
1972	1,053	104	275	396	681	107,366	109,857
1973	981	105	279	335	632	101,330	103,662
1974	861	88	280	330	619	99,813	101,991
1975	813	82	288	314	583	99,751	101,831
1976	752	78	269	305	587	101,424	103,415
1977[1]	692	71	258	293	572	101,391	103,277

[1]Values for 1977 represent forecasts
Source: Company records

Exhibit 6

DETERMINATION OF "P" PARAMETER FOR BINOMIAL PROBABILITY DISTRIBUTION

P = PROBABILITY OF ANY POLICY GENERATING A REINSURANCE "HIT" (> $465,000) DURING ANY ONE YEAR

EXAMPLE:

Two Categories

1. HSB (USA Only) 2. BI&I (Canada)

$$P_{HSB} = \frac{\text{Total \# Hits}(1/66\text{-}7/76)}{\text{Total \# Policies}(1/66\text{-}7/76)} = \frac{39}{1,030,702} = .00003784$$

$$P_{HSB} = \frac{\text{Total \# Hits}(1/66\text{-}7/76)}{\text{Total \# Policies}(1/66\text{-}7/76)} = \frac{11}{1,53,590} = .00007162$$

Twelve Categories

HSB (USA Only)

Chemical	Mining	Refinery	Paper	Utility	Other
$\frac{14}{9,095}$	$\frac{2}{877}$	$\frac{3}{2,791}$	$\frac{5}{3,665}$	$\frac{12}{5,718}$	$\frac{3}{1,008,556}$

BI&I

Chemical	Mining	Refinery	Paper	Utility	Other
$\frac{2}{663}$	$\frac{3}{677}$	$\frac{3}{498}$	$\frac{1}{727}$	$\frac{1}{234}$	$\frac{1}{150,791}$

Exhibit 7

CUMULATIVE PROBABILITY DISTRIBUTION OF ALL LOSSES GREATER THAN $465,000 (IN 1976 DOLLARS) FOR THE PERIOD 1966–JULY, 1976

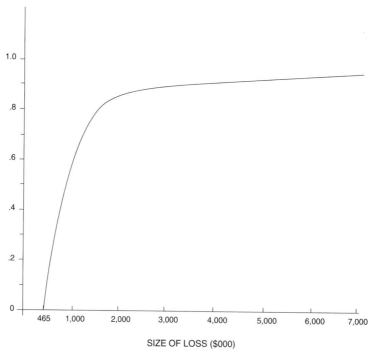

SIZE OF LOSS ($000)

Exhibit 8

COMPUTER RUN OF THE SIMULATION MODEL

*****HARTFORD STEAM BOILER SIMULATION MODEL*****

INPUT N(=NUMBER OF YEARS TO BE SIMULATED)(...MULTIPLE OF 20 PLEASE.)
800.

INPUT THE NUMBER OF INDUSTRY CATEGORIES
2

INPUT THE HISTORICAL VALUES FOR THE MEAN NUMBER OF HITS PER YEAR PER POLICY FOR THE 2
INDUSTRY CATEGORIES.
.00003784 .00007162

INPUT THE NUMBER OF POLICIES TO BE INSURED IN INDUSTRY CATEGORIES 1 THRU 2 FOR THE
UPCOMING YEAR
103277. 19933.

INPUT THE TOTAL DOLLAR AMOUNT OF PREMIUMS FOR THE SIMULATED YEAR(IN$000)
100000.

```
    ****************************************************************
    ********* RETENTION STRATEGY: 1ST LAYER = .10; 2ND LAYER = .10.*********
    ****************************************************************
FRACTILES:    0.01    0.05    0.10    0.25     0.50     0.75     0.90     0.95     0.99
TOTAL COST: 7494.3  8161.3  8389.5  9306.2  10730.6  12874.2  14799.9  16113.9  18247.9
LAYER 1:    2259.9  2309.6  2347.9  2417.2   3169.2   4470.6   5715.9   6538.4   7507.9
LAYER 2:    4950.0  4950.0  4950.0  4954.6   5069.8   5302.1   5526.7   5642.0   5951.8

TOTAL COST MEAN= 11255.6 STD DEV= 2488.0
```

```
    ****************************************************************
    ********* RETENTION STRATEGY: 1ST LAYER = .10; 2ND LAYER = 1.00.*********
    ****************************************************************
FRACTILES:    0.01    0.05    0.10    0.25     0.50     0.75     0.90     0.95     0.99
TOTAL COST: 2544.3  3263.8  3613.2  4802.3   7488.0  10727.4  14175.6  15950.4  21485.2
LAYER 1:    2259.9  2309.6  2347.9  2417.2   3169.2   4470.6   5715.9   6583.4   7507.9
LAYER 2:       0.0     0.0     0.0    45.6   1198.1   3521.3   5766.8   6920.2  10017.9

TOTAL COST MEAN= 8228.1 STD DEV= 4124.1
```

```
    ****************************************************************
    ********* RETENTION STRATEGY: 1ST LAYER = 1.00; 2ND LAYER = .10.*********
    ****************************************************************
FRACTILES:    0.01    0.05    0.10    0.25     0.50     0.75     0.90     0.95     0.99
TOTAL COST: 5369.7  6540.0  7185.3  8498.1  10128.3  12031.2  13772.2  14931.1  18328.9
LAYER 1:      98.5   569.0   978.8  1672.3   2587.1   3649.5   4666.1   5374.2   7605.5
LAYER 2:    4950.0  4950.0  4950.0  4954.6   5069.8   5302.1   5526.7   5642.0   5951.8

TOTAL COST MEAN= 10377.5 STD DEV= 2585.7
```

Exhibit 8 continued

COMPUTER RUN OF THE SIMULATION MODEL

```
* * * * * * * * * * * * * * * * * * * * * * * * * * * * * * * * * * * * * * * * * * * * * * * * * * * * * * * * * * *
********* RETENTION STRATEGY: 1ST LAYER = 1.00; 2ND LAYER = .50.*********
* * * * * * * * * * * * * * * * * * * * * * * * * * * * * * * * * * * * * * * * * * * * * * * * * * * * * * * * * * *
```

FRACTILES:	0.01	0.05	0.10	0.25	0.50	0.75	0.90	0.95	0.99
TOTAL COST:	3169.7	4367.1	5088.5	6618.1	8723.7	11028.6	13403.2	14645.0	19607.8
LAYER 1:	98.5	596.0	978.8	1672.3	2587.1	3649.5	4666.1	5374.2	7605.5
LAYER 2:	2750.0	2750.0	2750.0	2772.8	3349.1	4510.6	5633.4	6210.0	7759.0

TOTAL COST MEAN= 9031.9 STD DEV= 3240.2

```
* * * * * * * * * * * * * * * * * * * * * * * * * * * * * * * * * * * * * * * * * * * * * * * * * * * * * * * * * * *
********* RETENTION STRATEGY: 1ST LAYER = 1.00; 2ND LAYER = 1.00*********
* * * * * * * * * * * * * * * * * * * * * * * * * * * * * * * * * * * * * * * * * * * * * * * * * * * * * * * * * * *
```

FRACTILES:	0.01	0.05	0.10	0.25	0.50	0.75	0.90	0.95	0.99
TOTAL COST:	419.7	1637.4	2367.7	4101.8	6828.5	9933.5	13211.0	14886.8	21517.3
LAYER 1:	98.5	596.0	978.8	1672.3	2587.1	3649.5	4666.1	5374.2	7605.5
LAYER 2:	0.0	0.0	0.0	45.6	1198.1	3521.3	5766.8	6920.2	10017.9

TOTAL COST MEAN= 7349.9 STD DEV= 4226.9

Exhibit 9

RISK PROFILES OF SELECTED RETENTION STRATEGIES

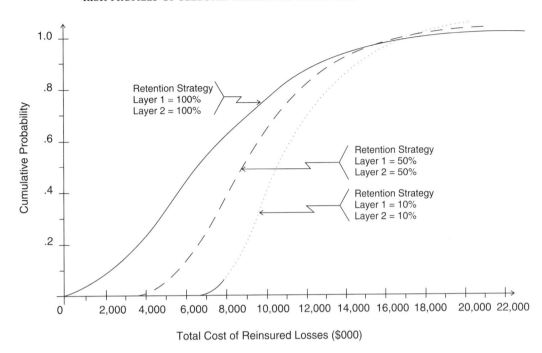

Exhibit 10

MEAN VS. STANDARD DEVIATION OF TOTAL LAYER 1 AND LAYER 2 COSTS FOR SELECTED RETENTION STRATEGIES

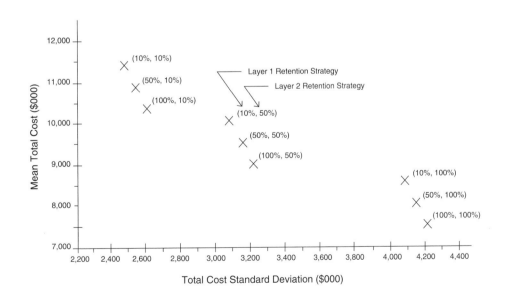

PROPERTY-CASUALTY INSURANCE

Property-Casualty (P-C) insurance is roughly the rest of the insurance industry, aside from life and health. It includes insurance for damage to personal property (houses, autos), personal liability because of injury to the person or property of someone else, and commercial counterparts including worker's compensation, which reimburses an employee for job-related health impairments. Some insurance companies concentrate exclusively in the P-C sector (e.g., Commercial Union), some are equally active in P-C and life (e.g., Travelers) and some focus more on life (e.g., Metropolitan). Some P-C companies are regular stock companies having private shareholders (Travelers), others are mutual companies, returning dividends to policyholders (Metropolitan). Total premiums (revenues) for stock companies alone were $63 billion in 1979 with underwriting losses (premiums minus claims minus expenses) of about $350 million. As with all insurance businesses, premiums are received well in advance of claims, allowing income to be earned on the float which supplements underwriting performance. Since underwriting in itself is more or less a breakeven proposition, the role played by investment income is a significant factor in earnings and growth.

Claim Patterns: Actuarial Rate Setting

The industry suffers from the difficulty of establishing its prices before it knows its costs. With each policy the company undertakes three risks:

▸ The likelihood of a claim against the policy

▸ The size of the claim, and

▸ The timing of the claim.

In the case of auto insurance the likelihood of a claim is a function of personal attributes of the driver, the type of car (not only its safety, but, as with a sports car, the implication about how it will be driven), the amount of driving anticipated, and the geographical location. The size of a claim is a function of the kind of driving to be done (highway or local, commuting or recreational) the value of the car, and the rate of inflation between the date the premium is set and the date of the claim. The timing of the claim is important because a claim on the first day of the policy rather than the last permits less investment return on the float. If accidents are more frequent in the winter months, insurance companies might prefer to have customers pay their premiums in the spring.

Of course the whole idea of an insurance company is that claims will average out over a large number of policyholders. This will be true so long as actuarial data continues to predict future claim patterns. Anything that systematically distorts the frequency or size of claims is a threat to the profitability of an insurance line.

For example, in 1965 Hurricane Betsy gave the entire industry what was then its worse year ever. The Arab oil embargo of 1973 caused a sudden jump in the inflation rate from 6% to over 12% (even higher for auto repair costs) which helped to give the P-C companies their worst year to date in 1975. The 55-mph speed limit, combined with increasing gasoline prices, caused accident rates to decrease, creating something of a windfall in 1976–1977. This then worked against the companies when states with insurance commissioners empowered to set rates took this ultimately short-lived phenomenon as a signal of things to come, and lowered rates. Two major hurricanes (David and Frederic) caused more than $1.6 billion of claims in 1979, contributing to major underwriting losses for that year.

In these and other ways, the P-C insurance business can be seen to be much more vulnerable to variation in earnings than the life insurance business, where death patterns change very slowly (usually for the better) and the benefit size is fixed in advance.

Nevertheless, the setting of premiums, or the arguments for allowed rates when regulated, follows the established actuarial pattern:

$$Premiums = Expected\ Claims\ Expenses + Administration\ Expenses$$
$$+ Underwriting\ Margin$$

Property-Casualty Lines

Property damage

About 37% of P-C business is the insuring of property against damage. This includes autos, homes and factories. Damage is fairly predictable in frequency except for major hazards such as severe weather or rioting. Claim size is also predictable because claims are usually settled within 18 months of payment of a one year premium.

Liability

Thirty-three percent of premiums are earned for protection against the claims of others, nearly two-thirds of them for auto insurance. Also included are product liability and professional malpractice. The liability area is particularly risky because claims are often made well after the period of protection and although these intervals can also be predicted, the unknown inflation rate affects all claims in parallel. There is another kind of inflation that has been rising faster than the CPI, the so-called social inflation. Juries are judging for the plaintiff with greater frequency and awarding larger sums when they do.

Worker's compensation

Worker's compensation comprises 15% of premiums, and is the line with the greatest uncertainty in underwriting margin. Insuring employees against any kind of job related health impairments, reimbursing both medical expenses and lost earnings, is a risky proposition in days of sharp inflation in hospital costs. Moreover, treatment (and expenses) can continue for many years. In addition, some claims such as those for asbestos-related diseases are not made for 30 to 40 years, at which time multiple claims are made. On top of all this, the company has unlimited liability which is not usually the case for the liability lines discussed above.

Assets and Liabilities

The assets of an insurance company must, at all times, be large enough to ensure payment of all future claims. The premiums received on a policy go into an *Unearned Premium Reserve*. The premiums become "earned" in proportion to the time that has elapsed on the policy. After six months of a one-year policy, half of the initial premiums will still be in the Unearned Premium Reserve. The company must not only have the reserves to pay for claims on events that have yet to occur, but also on those that have occurred but have not yet been paid.

These fall in three groups, those fully settled but for which payment is being spread out over many years, (worker's compensation, for example), those whose claims have been made but the size of payment has not yet been decided upon (because of processing delays, investigations or litigations), and those which have not yet been filed and are presently unknown to the company. The three divisions correspond to different degrees of uncertainty in the assessment of suitable reserves. The total anticipated claims in this category are called the *Loss Reserves*. The expenses to be incurred in processing these claims are in the *Loss Expense Reserve*.

The remaining assets form the shareholder (or policyholder) surplus. The true size of shareholder equity consists of the surplus plus about 30%–40% of the unearned premium reserve. The reason is that claims and related expenses usually only amount to about 60%–70% of premiums. This 30%–40% has, in a sense, already been earned since it consists of the initial cost of marketing and writing the policy.

A P-C company balance sheet thus looks something like Table 3.1. The proportions are approximate industry averages for 1979.

Table 3.1

Assets		Liabilities	
Municipal bonds	36	Unearned premiums	20
Industrial bonds	15	Loss reserve	40
Common stocks	20	Loss expense reserve	10
Preferred stocks	3	Other liabilities	10
Cash and Treasury notes	11	(taxes, declared dividends)	
Miscellaneous (real estate, mortgages)	15	Surplus	20
	100		100

Federal taxes are usually minimal since most of the interest earned is tax-free, much of the other investment return is in the form of capital gains, and the underwriting business, which is the only income to be taxed at the corporate rate, merely breaks even. States impose a tax on premiums of between 1% and 4%, usually about 2%.

By convention, and regulatory requirement, all bonds and other secured loans are accounted for at face value (the amount due at maturity). If the bonds were bought at a discount, amortization takes place so that they reach par at maturity. Stocks are accounted for at market value. Certain assets such as goodwill and general property such as furniture, fixtures and supplies are not included on the balance sheet. In a slight variation permitted for reporting to shareholders rather than to the regulators, the expenses of writing a policy are deferred to be coincident with the earning of the premiums. In this case the shareholders surplus does represent their equity.

Business Indicators

Although profitability for the company is determined by the sum of underwriting gains and investment income, the viability of the company depends upon its success as an underwriter. The standard performance measures applied to P-C companies are the expense ratio (expenses $\times$ 100 $\div$ premiums written) and the loss ratio (claims × 100 ÷ premiums earned). The combined ratio (expense ratio plus loss ratio) represents the total cost of underwriting as a percentage of premiums generated. Exhibit 1 shows 1979 industry averages for these ratios in the major product lines.

The ratios have been deteriorating (i.e., increasing) due to greater competitive pressure and tighter regulation. There is no completely analogous ratio similar to debt/equity since there is no formal debt. Closely related statistics are Loss Reserves/Surplus and Premiums Written/Surplus. Premium volume represents the company's ability to attract business and market share and is thus somewhat forward looking. The Loss Reserves reflect the loss history in the recent past and give an indication of the composition of the product line mix. Both ratios offer an indication of how secure the reserves are against a sudden increase in loss experience or a major loss in the value of assets held.

The experience of 1974, when surging inflation caused unexpectedly high claims and simultaneously caused severe declines in the stock market is a nightmare still etched in the memories of company executives. Many companies were particularly hard hit by being forced because of vanishing surpluses to bail out of the stock market just as it hit the bottom.

Regulations

The insurance industry is regulated by the states. Attempts to empower the Federal Government in this respect have never succeeded. Although regulations and standards are fairly uniform throughout the United States, national insurance companies occasionally find it beneficial to set up a subsidiary to operate in a particular state so that the whole company is not subject to the standards of that state. The state insurance commissioners have the power to require the companies to meet certain financial conditions, such as the various reserves, which are intended to ensure that the company will be able to meet its future commitments. In addition, in some states the commissioners have the power to set the pricing structure for various lines of insurance including, particularly, auto insurance. In doing so, they try to balance the reasonable desire of shareholders to obtain a satisfactory return on their equity and the needs of the customers for affordable insurance. This is particularly difficult in the case of auto insurance which is becoming increasingly expensive and yet is required of drivers. States have experimented with schemes to reduce the expenses of underwriting auto losses by such means as no-fault insurance. Many companies have come to regard their operations in certain particularly unprofitable states as loss leaders.

The commissioners may grant and revoke licenses to sell insurance in their state. Often a license is withdrawn only temporarily until the financial condition of the company returns to a condition acceptable to the commissioner. The threat of such disruption and bad publicity is sufficient to ensure vigorous self-policing on the part of the companies. For example, in 1976 the states of Wyoming and Arizona restrained GEICO from writing further policies until its financial condition (then extremely poor) was remedied.

The National Association of Insurance Commissioners monitors the financial condition of property-casualty companies. It has a screening procedure in which 11 ratios are calculated for each company and checked for unusual levels. The ratios and the levels considered unusual are summarized in Table 3.2:

Table 3.2

Ratio	UNUSUAL VALUES Equal to or	
	Over	Under
1. Premium to surplus	300	—
2. Change in writings	33	–33
3. Surplus aid to surplus	25	—
4. Two-year overall operating ratio	100	—
5. Investment yield	—	5.0
6. Change in surplus	50	–10
7. Liabilities to liquid assets	105	—
8. Agents' balances to surplus	40	—
9. One-year reserve development to surplus	25	—
10. Two-year reserve development to surplus	25	—
11. Estimated current reserve deficiency to surplus	25	—

If four or more ratios have unusual levels the company is subjected to closer scrutiny. The Premium/Surplus ratio has long been considered the primary statistic of interest although some companies now regard Loss Reserves/Surplus as being of nearly equal importance as an indicator of financial health. Since higher ratios typically mean higher returns on equity (surplus) because of the greater leverage, companies have to balance their concern for greater profitability with the desire to avoid attention from state commissioners.

Table 3.3 gives the P/S and L/S ratios for a number of P-C companies as of the end of 1979. Exhibit 2 shows a scatter diagram of these ratios.

Table 3.3

	Premiums/ Surplus	Loss Reserve/ Surplus
Aetna Life & Casualty (AET)	3.20	2.86
Allstate (S)	2.58	1.71
American Express (AXP)	3.52	3.60
American General (AGC)	2.68	2.35
American International Gp. (AIG)	1.73	1.71
Chubb Corp. (CHUB)	3.02	2.64
Connecticut General (CGN)	2.96	2.97
Continental Corp. (CIC)	2.49	2.38
Crum & Forster (CMF)	3.37	3.63
Hartford Fire (ITT)	2.36	2.61
INA Corp. (INA)	2.96	3.20
Lincoln National (LNC)	2.60	1.59
Ohio Casualty (OCAS)	3.08	1.70
SAFECO (SAFC)	1.70	1.23
St. Paul Companies (STPL)	2.69	2.91
Trans America (TA)	3.79	2.73
Travelers (TIC)	2.33	2.03
United States F&G (FG)	2.66	2.14

Still other regulatory limitations involve explicit constraints on the type of investments that may be made with the funds in the reserves. Some states require no more than 10% of general assets or 100% of the amount of the surplus to be held in common stocks. A hidden constraint is placed on premium growth by the statutory accounting procedure. Because the unearned premium reserve is overstated (it includes money that has already been spent on initial writing and marketing costs) a growth in premiums causes a drain on the surplus which increases the critical ratios. The effect is to constrain rapid growth unless a sufficient surplus is available.

Underwriting Cycle

For many years the P-C industry has repeated a profitability cycle of about six years. Starting the cycle at a peak of profitability (low combined ratio) the companies derive large surpluses which enable them to finance higher premium totals. For any individual company, these increases can be gained by an increase in market share and so price cutting ensues. The regulators also reduce rates because of the bright profit picture. Since the total market size remains constant, price cutting raises the combined ratio which reduces profits. Regulators are loath to increase rates and the industry moves into a decline. In the remainder of the cycle, premium rates creep back up until profitability is restored.

Investment Strategies

The foremost investment goal is that of safety of principal. Typically companies adopt a more conservative stand than even the regulators require. Naturally investment return is an objective and the more aggressive companIes, usually stock companies, put a high proportion of their surplus into common stocks. There is a greater incentive to find investments with an inflation hedge than in life insurance because the liabilities increase naturally with inflation. A third goal is that of liquidity. Whereas life insurance companies may buy an entire privately-placed bond issue and expect to hold it to maturity, P-C companies prefer to buy substantially more marketable publicly traded bonds to insure liquidity. Finally there is the goal of diversification. The P-C business has had long practice in diversifying its underwriting risks geographically and by lines (at one time many companies specialized in only one or two P-C lines).

External Competition

In recent years the P-C community has been "invaded" by competitors from other fields. Some of the large mutual life companies have been expanding their domain of interest. Many non-insurance companies have set up insurance subsidiaries to get around tax laws which disallow self insurance funds as a tax deduction. These captive insurance companies eventually branch out into insuring other businesses to reduce effective overhead. Thus profitability is not such an important consideration for them. Reinsurance companies are integrating forward into direct coverage. Finally, foreign insurance companies are entering the market with high combined ratios with a view to gaining a beachhead in the U.S. P-C business.

Exhibit 1 _____

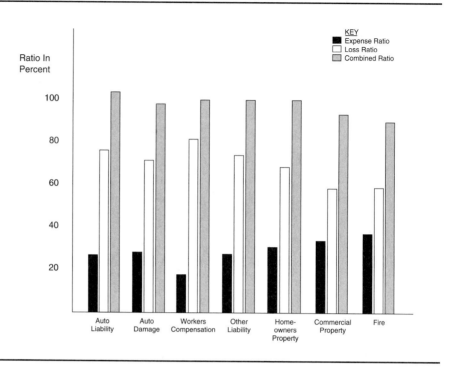

Exhibit 2 _____

KEY RATIOS FOR P-C COMPANIES IN DECEMBER **1979**

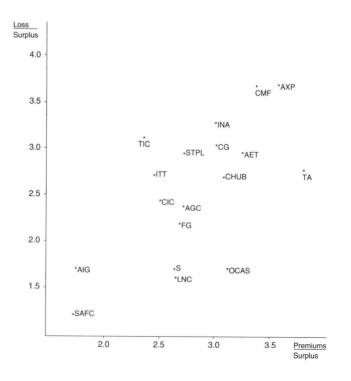

THE TRAVELERS INVESTMENT MANAGEMENT COMPANY

On June 2, 1980, Kevin Bradley, chairman of the board of the Travelers Investment Management Company (TIMCO) met with Eliot Williams, president of TIMCO, and David Dunford, senior vice president and director of portfolio construction, to discuss the presentation they would make to the Finance Committee of the Travelers Corporation, scheduled for the day after next. TIMCO had been asked to make a presentation that would be relevant to the committee's pending decision about the proportion of equities in the portfolio of the Travelers Casualty-Property Group (TCPG).

Kevin Bradley joined TIMCO in 1977 after periods as vice president and portfolio manager of the College Retirement Equities Fund and, most recently, as research director, senior vice president and member of the board of Bache Halsey Stuart, Inc. Eliot Williams brought 11 years of experience in TIMCO to the job when he became president of the company in early 1980. He had received an MBA from the University of Virginia and, most recently, had spent three years as director of research. David Dunford joined the company immediately after taking an MBA at New York University. He spent six years as an analyst before taking over as director of portfolio construction in 1978.

The Travelers Corporation

The Travelers Insurance Company began in 1864 by selling accident insurance. In 1906 The Travelers Indemnity Company began offering property and casualty insurance under the sponsorship of the Travelers Insurance Company. In 1965 The Travelers Corporation was set up as a vehicle for the acquisition of complete and direct ownership of the whole Travelers Group of companies, including such companies as the Phoenix Insurance Company and The Charter Oak Fire Insurance Company, whose names did not include the name Travelers.

By 1980 the Travelers Casualty-Property Group of Companies (TCPG) was the fifth largest multiple-line insurer in the United States in terms of net premium writings. Following a long period of expansion, the premium volume had leveled off over the previous several years. Although underwriting profitability had been restored in the most recent couple of years, performance in the period from 1974 through 1976 had been generally unfavorable. A three-year combined ratio for 1974–1976 of 109%, was the company's worst ever. The company's surplus was further eroded during this period by unfavorable returns on its investment portfolio. During 1974 the surplus dropped by nearly 20%, leading to a new investment policy in which the proportion of assets invested in common stocks was drastically reduced.

Steps were also taken to improve the profitability of company underwriting. These included more refined techniques to estimate loss reserves, particularly for worker's compensation lines, substantial rate increases on personal lines, and improved loss control programs for commercial customers.

TIMCO

TIMCO is a wholly-owned subsidiary of the Travelers Corporation. Its business is the professional investment management of clients' portfolios. With about 25 investment professionals they are responsible for some $1.5 billion in assets, of

Harvard Business School case 9-182-210. Professor David E. Bell prepared this case. Copyright © 1982 by the President and Fellows of Harvard College.

which about $500 million is in the stock portion of insurance company surplus portfolios, $250 million in variable annuities, and a mutual fund, and $700 million in pension and profit-sharing portfolios.

A pension fund, for example, might give TIMCO 20% of its assets to manage. Recognizing that the return on a portfolio is related to the risk taken, TIMCO establishes with the client a total risk objective for the portfolio. Risk is defined both in terms of "beta" or volatility relative to the Standard & Poor's 500 Index, and residual risk, which is a measure of portfolio diversification. At the end of an evaluation period, the client compares TIMCO's performance with other managed portfolios having the same risk objectives. The objective beta becomes the nominal risk level from which TIMCO may deviate according to its assessment of the relative opportunities or risks existing in the capital markets.

One of TIMCO's clients is the Travelers Casualty-Property Group of Companies. About $200 million of their stock portfolio was actively managed by TIMCO prior to this presentation.

Investment Strategy for the TCPG Portfolio

The principal investment vehicles for the assets of TCPG were bonds and common stocks. As with all investors, a tradeoff had to be made between the anticipated higher rate of return from common stocks and the relatively lesser risk associated with the return from bonds. Exhibit 1 gives the TCPG income statement, balance sheet and investment portfolio for the period 1972–1979. It shows that in 1979 common stocks represented only 4% of the total assets of the company and 19% of total equity. This latter percentage had varied over the years (see Exhibit 2) as a function, not only of fluctuations in stock values, but as a matter of policy. The stock market "crash" of 1973–1974 came at a time when the ratio of common stocks to surplus was over 90%. The result of the market decline and unfavorable underwriting experience was that the sensitive Premiums to Surplus ratio increased from slightly over 2:1 to well over 5:1 (see Exhibit 3). Although no property-casualty company was immune to this difficulty, those with higher common stocks/surplus ratios were hurt the most.

Like many insurance companies, TCPG was forced to reduce exposure to the stock market to avoid any further damage to their already weakened surplus. To make matters worse, when the stock market recovered in 1975–1976, they gained little benefit because of their small stock position. These events were traumatic for TCPG and led them to avoid exposure to such swings in the future.

By March 1978 the wounds had healed sufficiently for the Finance Committee of the Travelers to approve a slightly higher stock participation level than had prevailed since the "crash." The new investment guidelines for TCPG became:

1. Stocks should comprise at most 30% of the company's surplus.
2. The actual proportion of surplus invested in stocks as a proportion of the maximum shall be varied from time to time in accordance with market opportunities and company needs. (At the time of the March 1978 meeting this proportion was set at 75%, that is, $22\frac{1}{2}$% of surplus was to be invested in stocks.)

3. The stock portfolio should have the following characteristics:

Market risk (beta)	0.80 to 1.05
Residual risk	1% to 5%
Dividend yield	1.0 to 1.5 times the S&P 500 Index Yield

Residual Risk refers to the variation in returns not correlated with the market (unsystematic risk).

Two years later, in the spring of 1980, Roderick O'Neil, chairman of the Finance Committee, wondered whether this policy was unduly conservative. Among major stock property-casualty companies, TCPG was second only to Connecticut General with its low common stock to surplus ratio (see Exhibit 4). The climate of opinion concerning the attractiveness of investment in the stock market had improved, and continued high combined ratios increased the need for larger yields on investments. Therefore O'Neil asked Bradley to analyze the prospects available in the stock market and to recommend whether the common stocks/surplus limit of 30% should be raised, and if so, to what.

Information on Future Performance

David Dunford began by preparing a forecast of stock market performance for the next several years. It was a simple matter to calculate from historical data (as in Exhibit 5) the average annual return (11.3% and standard deviation of annual return (22%) given by the market over the past 50 years. However, there was some reason to be cautious in using data from the 1920s to say something about returns in the 1980s. Most particularly, inflation rates were currently considerably higher than during most of those 50 years. Dunford felt that a better way to look at those returns was to break up the actual return into components of inflation and real return:

$$Total\ Return = Inflation\ Rate + Real\ Return\ \ .$$

Exhibit 5 shows that annual stock returns and inflation were negatively correlated over the period 1948–1978. This was because of the effects of unanticipated inflation, which acted to depress stock returns in the short run. Even without this difficulty, there remained the problem of forecasting future inflation rates for use in the model. Dunford countered these problems by using five-year holding returns for stocks, which showed much lower volatility (annual return of 9.8% ± 9.1% compounded over five years) and comparing these with the return offered on a five-year U.S. Treasury Bond in the corresponding time period. His results suggested that stocks offered a 5% per year premium over the five-year bond, which was currently offering 9%. Thus he projected an expected five-year return of 14% per annum with a standard deviation of 9.1%. It is possible to demonstrate that an average annual return of 14% + 9.1% over five years is equivalent to an annual expectation of 15.7 + 20%. That is, a simulation which selects annual returns from a distribution based on 15.7% ± 20% would produce a five-year holding return of 14% per annum ± 9.1%.

Dunford knew that the major portion of the investment portfolio, that invested in bonds, could be treated as a guaranteed 6% return. This was because bonds were accounted for at book value, rather than at market value, and the income generated by them was entirely predictable.

Additionally, TCPG's Corporate Planning Group had supplied Dunford with forecasts relating to underwriting performance. Exhibit 6 shows their predictions for TCPG's combined ratio over the next five years. For the next 12 months (June 1980–June 1981) they expected the combined ratio to be about 104, with a worst case scenario of 109. Dunford interpreted their forecast as being equivalent to a probability distribution of 104 ± 2.

With all of this information Dunford was able to determine how sensitive the premium/surplus ratio might be to an increase in the stock/surplus ratio. The current surplus was $1,100 million, the loss reserves were $3,300 million and the premiums to be written during the next year (the size of which was basically a company decision rather than an uncertainty) were reliably estimated at $3.1 billion. If the stock/surplus ratio was increased to 50% then in a "best guess" scenario, in which stocks returned 15.7% and the combined ratio was 104, the cashflow (ignoring taxes) would be as follows:

Return from bonds	$(3{,}300 + 0.5 \times 1{,}100) \times .06$	=	$231 million
Return from stocks	$1{,}100 \times 0.5 \times 0.157$	=	$86.35 million
Loss on underwriting	$3{,}100 \times .04$	=	($124 million).

Hence, the surplus at the end of the year would be 1,100 + 231 + 86.35 − 124 = $1,293 million. This would mean a premium/surplus ratio of 3,100/1,293 = 2.4. Exhibit 7 shows how sensitive the P/S ratio becomes as the stock/surplus ratio is increased.

Weighing the Risks

Bradley and Williams looked over Dunford's analysis. "You've done a great job, David," began Bradley, "but when it comes right down to it, these numbers merely confirm what we already knew, that raising our participation in the stock market is a good strategy if the market cooperates and a disaster if it doesn't. Much as I personally believe that we should be more aggressive, these figures don't especially recommend any one stock/surplus ratio over another. We have to find some way of looking at the problem that gives us more of a solid rationale for our recommendation."

Exhibit 1

THE TRAVELERS CORPORATION AND SUBSIDIARIES—CASUALTY-PROPERTY BUSINESS, COMBINED STATEMENT OF INCOME AND RETAINED EARNINGS (FOR THE YEAR ENDED DECEMBER 31, IN MILLIONS)

	1979	1978	1977	1976	1975	1974	1973	1972
Revenues								
Written premiums	$2,681.6	$2,529.2	$2,524.5	$2,447.8	$2,087.8	$1,811.0	$1,609.5	$1,602.7
Increase (decrease) in unearned premiums	50.1	(12.1)	38.1	22.4	87.3	49.7	1.5	28.4
Earned premiums	2,631.5	2,541.3	2,486.4	2,425.4	2,000.5	1,761.3	1,608.0	1,574.3
Investment income	335.6	315.7	276.8	230.1	183.0	156.3	134.7	119.7
	2,967.1	2,857.0	2,763.2	2,655.5	2,183.5	1,917.6	1,742.7	1,694.0
Losses and Expenses								
Losses	1,674.7	1,633.5	1,676.1	1,758.2	1,463.5	1,240.2	973.3	958.3
Loss adjustment expenses	244.1	202.6	237.8	228.3	166.3	127.7	132.1	135.9
Amortization of deferred acquisition costs	352.5	345.3	329.8	342.7	438.6	403.51	377.6	361.7
Investment expenses	11.6	12.4	13.2	15.3	14.3	16.1	18.4	17.9
General and administrative expenses	402.8	367.9	323.2	280.4	135.2	125.9	128.4	114.4
Dividends to policyholders	48.1	24.5	15.7	23.8	16.1	19.9	14.8	14.6
	2,733.8	2,586.2	2,595.8	2,648.7	2,234.0	1,933.3	1,644.6	1,602.8
Operating Income Before Federal Income Taxes	233.3	270.8	167.4	6.8	(50.5)	(15.7)	98.1	91.2
Federal Income Taxes								
Current	42.6	(1.0)	(5.0)	(1.6)	(.7)	(11.9)	(.6)	4.2
Deferred	(3.0)	83.8	63.2	(30.6)	(51.9)	(36.4)	9.1	11.1
	39.6	82.8	58.2	(32.2)	(52.6)	(48.3)	8.5	15.3
Operating Income	193.7	188.0	109.2	39.0	2.1	32.6	89.6	75.9
Realized investment gains (losses), net of taxes	3.3	(3.6)	3.3	(14.0)	(4.5)	(14.1)	7.7	.3
Net Income	197.0	184.4	112.5	25.0	(2.4)	18.5	97.3	76.2
Retained earnings beginning of year	1,033.6	864.1	677.1	632.2	664.5	639.4	550.6	464.7
Preferred stock conversion	(26.3)	—	—	—	—	—	—	—
Other	—	—	—	—	—	—	.9	(.6)
Transactions with affiliates	84.4	56.4	130.8	69.6	42.4	56.1	35.1	51.2
Dividends to preferred shareholders	(1.8)	(3.4)	(3.4)	(3.4)	(3.4)	(3.4)	(3.4)	(3.4)
Dividends to common shareholders	(89.2)	(67.9)	(52.9)	(46.4)	(46.4)	(46.1)	(41.1)	(37.5)
Retained earnings end of year	$1,197.7	$1,033.6	$864.1	$677.1	$654.7	$664.5	$639.4	$550.6
Change in unrealized investment gains, net of taxes	$5.6	$(1.9)	$(15.1)	$50.4	$53.1	$(131.5)	$(138.2)	$66.1

Exhibit 1 continued

THE TRAVELERS CORPORATION AND SUBSIDIARIES—CASUALTY-PROPERTY BUSINESS,
COMBINED BALANCE SHEET (AT DECEMBER 31, IN MILLIONS)

	1979	1978	1977	1976	1975	1974	1973	1972
Assets								
Bonds	$3,987.3	$3,801.5	$3,228.4	$2,822.3	$2, 243.5	$1,960.7	$1,762.5	$1,706.4
Common stocks	235.1	190.9	146.4	179.1	171.1	245.3	569.7	727.5
Preferred stocks	114.1	93.7	95.8	101.1	88.3	94.8	113.4	91.5
Mortgage loans	170.5	194.8	223.7	125.4	62.4	.9	.9	.9
Investments in real estate	2.2	.6	.6	.4	—	—	—	—
Other investments	.6	.1	.1	.2	.5	.4	.4	.3
Cash and short-term securities	278.1	232.0	414.4	245.6	341.0	226.6	131.4	125.8
Loans to subsidiaries	92.7	77.1	80.8	83.1	81.5	83.8	106.7	163.3
Investment income accrued	92.4	90.1	79.6	66.1	51.9	42.7	35.9	30.2
Premium balances receivable	735.6	611.0	542.6	463.0	401.8	327.4	275.7	260.7
Reinsurance recoverable on paid losses	16.7	13.0	7.1	4.4	2.8	4.2	2.7	3.7
Deferred acquisition costs	153.5	150.8	144.5	132.1				
Other assets	193.5	156.2	158.7	213.4	192.5	124.2	146.9	117.1
Total Assets	$6,072.3	$5,611.8	$5,122.7	$4,436.2	$3,804.8	3,272.4	$3,290.1	$3,357.4
Liabilities								
Losses	$3,051.4	$2,892.3	$2,629.6	$2,274.7	$1,794.4	$1,509.4	$1,329.4	$1,251.2
Loss adjustment expenses	493.0	457.3	423.3	348.0	259.0	218.2	215.7	199.0
Unearned premiums	810.6	760.6	772.6	734.4	712.0	624.7	575.0	573.6
Other policyholder funds	33.4	20.1	20.7	21.4	19.0	19.4	18.3	19.0
Debentures due in 1995	70.8	76.3	86.3	92.0	95.5	97.0	100.0	100.0
Accrued expenses	91.5	74.0	61.0	54.1	53.6	41.8	51.6	48.1
Other liabilities	278.2	230.2	180.3	135.4	169.3	103.4	201.9	285.3
Total Liabilities	$4,828.9	$4,510.8	$4,173.8	$3,660.0	$3,102.8	$2,613.9	$2,491.9	$2,476.2
Equity								
Preferred stock	1.9	4.6	4.8	4.8	4.9	4.9	4.9	4.9
Common stock	113.7	113.6	113.3	113.2	113.1	113.1	113.1	113.1
Additional paid-in capital	5.3	3.4	1.8	1.3	.1	.1	1.9	1.8
Unrealized investment gains (losses)	35.8	30.2	32.1	47.2	(3.2)	(56.3)	75.2	213.4
Retained earnings	1,197.7	1,033.6	864.1	677.1	654.7	664.5	639.4	550.6
Treasury stock, at cost	(111.0)	(84.4)	(67.2)	(67.4)	(67.6)	(67.8)	(36.3)	(2.6)
	$1,243.4	$1,101.0	$ 948.9	$ 776.2	$ 702.0	$ 658.5	$ 798.2	$ 881.2
	$6,072.3	$5,611.8	$5,122.7	$4,436.2	$3,804.8	$3,272.4	$3,290.1	$3,357.4

Exhibit 2_____

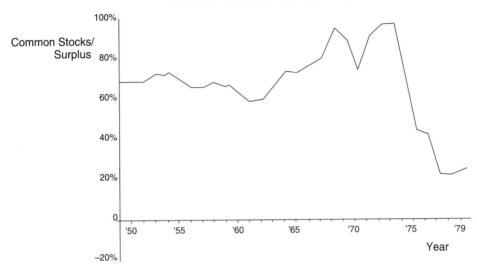

HISTORICAL LEVELS OF COMMON STOCK/SURPLUS RATIO
TRAVELERS CASUALTY-PROPERTY COMPANIES 1950–1979

Exhibit 3_____

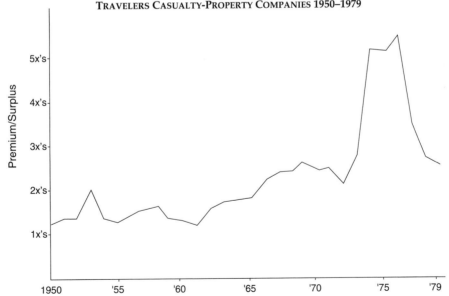

HISTORICAL LEVELS OF PREMIUM/SURPLUS RATIO
TRAVELERS CASUALTY-PROPERTY COMPANIES 1950–1979

Exhibit 4

COMMON STOCKS ÷ SURPLUS/WRITTEN PREMIUMS ÷ SURPLUS   DECEMBER 31, 1979

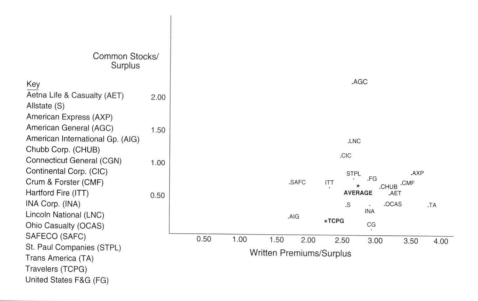

Key
Aetna Life & Casualty (AET)
Allstate (S)
American Express (AXP)
American General (AGC)
American International Gp. (AIG)
Chubb Corp. (CHUB)
Connecticut General (CGN)
Continental Corp. (CIC)
Crum & Forster (CMF)
Hartford Fire (ITT)
INA Corp. (INA)
Lincoln National (LNC)
Ohio Casualty (OCAS)
SAFECO (SAFC)
St. Paul Companies (STPL)
Trans America (TA)
Travelers (TCPG)
United States F&G (FG)

Note: The Connecticut General exposure is probably understated relative to TCBG due to different reporting practices.

Exhibit 5

STOCK RETURNS AND INFLATION RATES, 1948–1978

Year	Stocks[a]	Inflation[b]	Year	Stocks	Inflation
48	5.5	2.7	64	16.5	1.2
49	18.8	−1.8	65	12.5	1.9
50	31.7	5.8	66	−10.1	3.4
51	24.0	5.9	67	24.0	3.0
52	18.4	0.9	68	11.1	4.7
53	−0.1	0.6	69	−8.5	6.1
54	52.6	−0.5	70	4.0	5.5
55	31.6	0.4	71	14.3	3.4
56	6.6	2.9	72	19.0	3.4
57	−10.8	3.0	73	−14.7	8.8
58	43.4	1.8	74	−26.5	12.2
59	12.0	1.5	75	37.2	7.0
60	0.5	1.5	76	23.8	4.8
61	26.9	0.7	77	−7.2	6.8
62	−8.7	1.2	78	6.6	9.0
63	22.8	1.6			

Regression Equation: Stock Return = 20.8 − 2.8 Inflation Rate
(Est. S.D. = 15.9)

[a]Total Return (dividends plus appreciation) of Standard & Poor's 500.

[b]Consumer Price Index.

Exhibit 6 _____

TRAVELERS' COMBINED RATIO ACTUAL VS. TREND 1948–1979 ACTUAL 1980–1984 PROJECTED

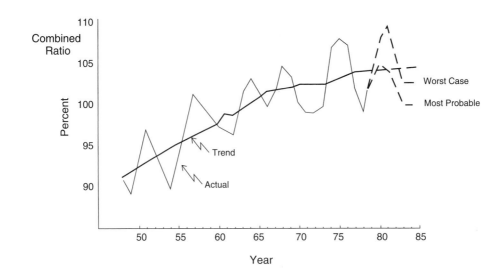

Exhibit 7 _____

SENSITIVITY ANALYSIS OF PREMIUM/SURPLUS RATIO

		Stock/Surplus		
Combined Ratio	**Stock Returns**	**0**	**0.5**	**1**
102	55.7	2.4	1.9	1.4
102	15.7	2.4	2.3	2.2
102	−24.3	2.4	2.7	3.0
104	55.7	2.5	2.0	1.4
104	15.7	2.5	2.4	2.3
104	−24.3	2.5	2.9	3.2
108	55.7	2.8	2.1	1.4
108	15.7	2.8	2.6	2.5
108	24.3	2.8	3.2	3.6

All calculations assume:

Premiums = $3,100 million

Current Surplus = $1,100 million

Loss Reserves = $3,300 million

Fixed Bond Return = 6%

4 PERSONAL RISK

The first three chapters have had a distinctly financial flavor. Yet risks occur in non-financial contexts also. In this chapter, there are cases on health problems, career choice, the bureaucratic perils faced by a public official and, finally, the psychological challenges we all face as consumers. An introductory section shows how to tackle problems such as these, but the real challenge is to be honest with yourself about what is really important to you.

PREFERENCE ANALYSIS

Decision-making can be very hard. Faced with a choice among three alternatives, you may have to evaluate each under ten possible scenarios (uncertainty) and on six different factors of interest (conflicting objectives) for a total of $3 \times 10 \times 6 = 180$ different stimuli. Decision analysis is a methodology based on a set of assumptions that permit us to decouple judgements about the likelihood of scenarios from our relative preference for each scenario. Some probabilities can be assessed fairly objectively (in card games, in repetitive situations such as weather, or demands for inventory). In other cases we may decide it's best to calculate a probability as the product of the probabilities of simpler, more basic events (a method called decomposition and recombination). Occasionally, a scenario is so complex or subjective that we simply trust our holistic judgement. This same range of techniques is applied to the assessment of preferences. In this section we review the basic preference procedure and show how it may be used in more complex circumstances.

Holistic Assessment

Suppose you face a decision that looks like Figure 4.1.

Harvard Business School note 9-184-133. Professor David E. Bell prepared this note. Copyright © 1984 by the President and Fellows of Harvard College.

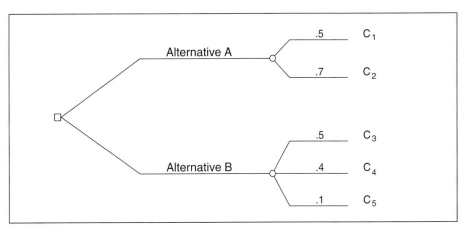

Figure 4.1

In this diagram the C's represent different consequences, which might be simple dollar revenues or complex outcomes that require a several-page description. For example, if the problem centers around the best method for making a new product introduction C_3 might be a completely new competitive structure in the industry.

A simple preference analysis of this problem begins by making a rank order of the consequences. Which outcome is most preferred; which is the least? (We will assume for the moment that the problem is straightforward enough to do this.) Suppose the rank order is $C_1>C_3>C_4>C_2>C_5$. The next step is to assign the best consequence a score of 100 and the worst consequence a score of 0. (The precise scale is arbitrary, but 0 to 100 is usually very practical.) How does C_2 score on this scale? Would you rather have C_2 occur or face a 50–50 gamble between C_1 and C_5 ? If you prefer C_2, then the preference score of C_2 is at least 50. If you prefer the 50–50 gamble, the preference score for C_2 is below 50. Another way to think about the score of C_2 is to consider the two incremental improvements C_5 to C_2 and C_2 to C_1. Which seems bigger?

Let's say that a rough assignment of preference scores is $C_1 = 100$, $C_3 = 60$, $C_4 = 30$, $C_2 = 25$ and $C_5 = 0$. A few consistency checks are usually a good idea. For example, C_4 should be equivalent to a 50–50 gamble between C_5 and C_3. The improvement from C_4 to C_1 should seem greater than that from C_5 to C_3. A 50–50 gamble between C_1 and C_2 should be preferred to C_3.

When the consequences have a natural scale, like dollars, a useful consistency check is to draw the *preference curve* (Figure 4.2).

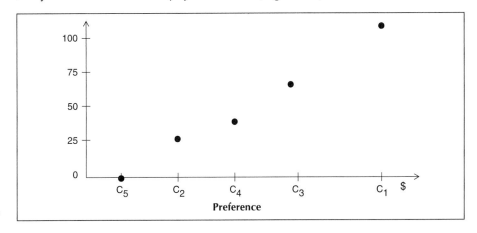

Figure 4.2

It is reasonable to expect a fairly smooth curve to pass through the plotted points. In this graph it looks like the preference value of C_4 may be a little low.

Another helpful consistency check is to add consequences to the list that are not part of the decision problem but that provide useful benchmarks. In this way, the real consequences may be compared with the hypothetical, but plausible, additions in order to calibrate their preference values more accurately.

With preferences assigned, our decision tree looks like Figure 4.3.

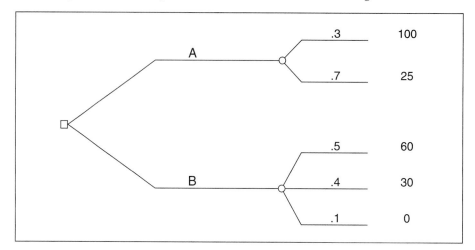

Figure 4.3

The expected preference value of A is 47.5; for B it is 42. Alternative A seems to be better. If your intuition says B is better, try to establish whether it is the analysis or the intuition which is faulty. Both the probabilities and the preference values are candidates for re-examination. Particularly, consider whether there are other factors in your consideration that are not reflected in the preference scores.

Caselet 1: The Somers Mutiny

Alexander Mackenzie, commander of the training vessel *U.S.S. Somers*, was deliberating whether or not to hang three members of his crew for mutiny.[1] It was November 30, 1842, and the *Somers* was in mid-Atlantic; Mackenzie had to make the decision himself. He was not certain that any or all of the men were in fact guilty. The evidence consisted of an informant who alleged that one of the men, Midshipman Philip Spencer, had tried to recruit him for a mutiny, a scrap of paper written in code found on Spencer, and Spencer's history of minor misdemeanors.

Mackenzie already had placed the three men in irons. However, he was concerned that others in the crew, who might also be part of a planned mutiny, could overpower the officers on board and release the three. Nearly all of the crew were apprentices and they would have been unable to sail the ship without the expertise of the three prisoners. In Mackenzie's view, hanging the men would eliminate all possibility of a mutiny.

---

[1] This is a highly condensed version of the case "The Somers Mutiny" by Professors M.C. Voorhees and J.W. Vaupel of Duke University.

Commander Mackenzie had not ordered the hanging yet because of two fairly significant complications. The first was that under naval law, the officers on a single ship could not constitute a court martial and, even if they could, only the Fleet Commander (if a ship were at sea) or the President of the United States (if at shore) could sanction the death penalty. The second complication was that John Canfield Spencer, Philip's father, was the U.S. Secretary of War.

If the men were hanged, Mackenzie himself would be court martialed and quite possibly hanged. However, Mackenzie felt that he might be able to clear his name if he could convince the court that his action was a reasonable necessity.

His dilemma, then, was that whether he hanged the men or not, his own life was in danger. What should he do?

Exhibit 1 shows a decision-tree analysis of Mackenzie's problem. The probabilities have been created for illustration purposes; there is no record of Mackenzie's own views. Note that the first event branch, concerning the likelihood that the men are guilty, does not depend on Mackenzie's action. Mackenzie's odds of "beating the rap" will likely depend on whether the men are guilty or not. The truth might never be discovered, but if they are not guilty, the odds seem greater that the remainder of the crew would be able to present more damning evidence than if they were. If Mackenzie is found guilty, he is more likely to be hanged if the men were innocent than if they were guilty.

To assign preferences: Endpoints *I* and *J* seem to be the best and endpoint *G* the worst. Some people might view *A* and *D* as worse than *G* because Mackenzie has to endure a trial and have his reputation destroyed. On the other hand he does get to live longer. A failed mutiny, *H*, is worse than no mutiny, *I* and *J*, because of the risk to life and limb that occurs even in a failed mutiny, and also because the *Somers* would have to survive the trip to port with an openly rebellious crew.

The preference score of 50 for *E* suggests that Mackenzie would be indifferent between a prison sentence and a 50–50 gamble between a successful mutiny and no mutiny at all. Perhaps the 50 for *E* is too high.

Calculating expected values for each branch of the decision tree leads to a score of 42.68 for "Hang them" and a score of 49.6 for "Wait."

On the morning of December 1, 1842, Mackenzie had the men hanged. The last words of the three men suggested that Spencer and one other man were guilty and that the third was not. On February 1, 1843 Mackenzie's court martial began. On March 28, 1843 Mackenzie was acquitted. After further active service, he died of ill health in September 1848 at the age of 45.

Preferences over Conflicting Objectives

Giving a rank order of consequences can sometimes be the heart of the problem. For example, choosing among job offers can be an extremely difficult task because the uncertainty in your mind is less about the qualities of the various positions available than it is about how well you'll like them. Exhibit 2 shows a hierarchy of considerations that might affect your appraisal of a job offer. The problem is to evaluate each of these dimensions and use them to produce a composite score for each job.

To keep things simple, let's suppose that you only have three concerns about a job: salary, weeks of vacation, and location. The decision tree might look like that shown in Figure 4.4.

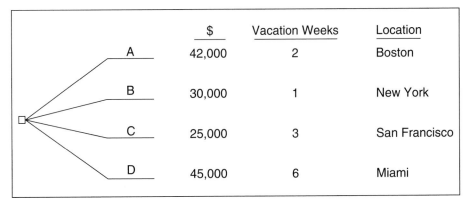

Figure 4.4

One way to solve this problem is to eliminate one dimension at a time. For example, you might convert all these jobs into equivalent jobs in San Francisco (Figure 4.5).

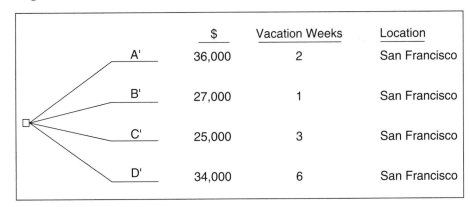

Figure 4.5

Here we're supposing that the salary in job A' has been selected to make the job equally preferred to job A. (We're also assuming San Francisco is your preferred location.) From this revised tree it is clear that A' > B' and that D' > C. It only remains to compare A' and D'. Would you give up $2000 from a $36,000 salary in order to improve your vacation from 2 weeks to 6? I suspect so. So job D is the best. Note that we solved the problem by trading off two objectives at a time. In constructing the revised tree, we traded off location against salary. In picking job D' over job A' we traded off salary against vacation.

This procedure works well when there are only a few alternatives to consider. Otherwise it helps to construct preference scales for each of the attributes. A preference scale is also essential if the precise consequence of an alternative is uncertain. Perhaps your location with job A has not been finalized before the deadline for accepting job D arrives. How do you analyze the situation then?

Additive Preference Decomposition

The following is a systematic procedure for assessing preference values. It is practically common sense if you accept the basic idea of preference.

The first step is to assess separate preference scales for each objective (Figure 4.6).

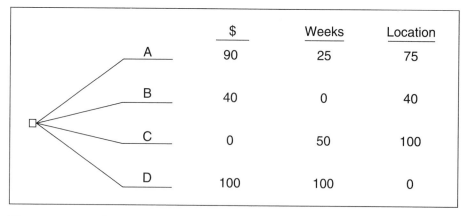

		$	Weeks	Location
A		90	25	75
B		40	0	40
C		0	50	100
D		100	100	0

Figure 4.6

The zero scores do *not* mean that Miami is a worthless location or that a salary of $25,000 should be ignored. A zero only means that that particular alternative scores lowest on that particular objective. (Job B could be eliminated at this stage since it is dominated by job A. We will keep it for the purpose of illustration.)

Now for the hard part. We want to come up with weights for each objective so that we may take a weighted average of the individual scores for each job. Here's one way to assess those weights.

Suppose you were offered a job with a salary of $25,000 in Miami, with one week of vacation. This job would score 0, 0, 0 on our preference scales. Which of the following is the more important improvement?

    A) Raising the salary to $45,000.

    B) Raising the vacation period to six weeks.

    C) Being transferred to San Francisco.

Your rank order of these improvements is the rank order of the attribute weights. Why? Let W_1, W_2, and W_3 be the three weights. With improvement A the resulting job gets a score of $100W_1$; with improvement B a score of $100W_2$; and with improvement C a score of $100W_3$. If you conclude that A is better than B which is better than C, then $W_1 > W_2 > W_3$. The ranking $W_2 > W_3$ does *not* mean that vacation is more important than location to you, only that with these four alternatives the spread of locations is less important an issue to you than the difference in vacation weeks.

Only the *relative* values of the weights matter, so that you could choose W_1 arbitrarily to equal 1. (If the weights turn out to be 1, ½, ¼, it would make no difference if you rescaled them as 8, 4, 2.) To obtain W_3 you must make a *tradeoff* between salary and location. If you have a job paying $25,000 located in San Francisco, what is the smallest salary increase that would induce you to move to Miami? Let's suppose the answer is $3,750. That is, a job with a salary of $28,750 in Miami is just equivalent to a job with a $25,000 salary in San Francisco. To calculate W_3 you need to know what the preference score of $28,750 is. Since $30,000 had a score of 40 let's guess that $28,750 gets a score of about 35. (I'm guessing only for this example. With a decision maker present you would assess the scores.)

Hence you know that:

$$\underbrace{0W_1 + 100W_3}_{\$25,000 \text{ in S.F.}} = \underbrace{35W_1 + 0W_3}_{\$28,750 \text{ in Miami}}$$

Hence $W_3 = 0.35$.

To obtain W_2, let's suppose you say that a job with \$25,000 salary and six weeks of vacation is just equivalent to a \$30,000 job with one week of vacation. Thus:

$$\underbrace{0W_1 + 100W_2}_{\$25,000 + 6 \text{ weeks}} = \underbrace{40W_1 + 0W_2}_{\$30,000 + 1 \text{ week}}$$

Hence $W_2 = 0.4$.

The final step now is to calculate the weighted score for each job.

A: $90 \times 1 + 25 \times 0.4 + 75 \times 0.35 = 126.25$

B: $40 \times 1 + 0 \times 0.4 + 40 \times 0.35 = 54$

C: $0 \times 1 + 50 \times 0.4 + 100 \times 0.35 = 55$

D: $100 \times 1 + 100 \times 0.4 + 0 \times 0.35 = 140$

It appears that job D is the best. Apparently the better salary and vacation were sufficient to overcome the inferior (for this person) location.

Caveats to the Additive Procedure

Certain complications can make the additive approach very suspect. First of all, a salary of \$30,000 may imply a different standard of living in Boston than it does in New York. Six weeks vacation may be ideal on a salary of \$45,000 but of little use on a salary of \$25,000. That is, it may be very hard to evaluate an objective independently of the levels of the other objectives.

Even if preferences are additive, problems can still arise. Suppose the decision tree involves uncertainty and is as shown in Figure 4.7.

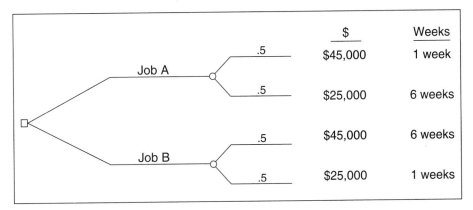

Figure 4.7

Job A may be much more acceptable than Job B because no matter how the uncertainty is resolved something will be good about Job A. Yet both jobs get the same average preference of 70 (Figure 4.8).

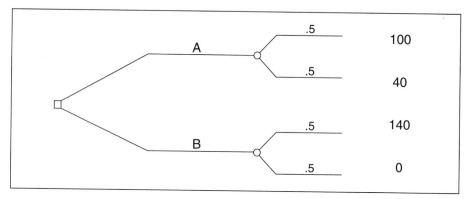

Figure 4.8

(In fact this problem can be resolved by assessing preference curves over preference scores, but this won't be addressed here.)

Despite these caveats, preference analysis is an extraordinarily robust method of analysis. It can be, and has been, used in applications ranging from complex computer models to back-of-the-envelope studies.

In a *Harvard Business Review* article (Sept. – Oct. 82), Brown and Ulvila discuss business applications of this kind of analysis. Examples they use include problems of plant siting, whether to vertically integrate, whether to enter a new business, and allocation of research and development budgets. They also mention the very important application area of bargaining and negotiation, where determining what you want, and the tradeoffs you are prepared to make, are critical.

Caselet 2: William Taylor and Associates

In the late fifties, William Taylor founded an engineering consultants firm.[2] By 1979, the firm had grown and diversified somewhat and Taylor felt it time for a change in the company's legal structure. It was a single proprietorship, but Taylor felt this had a number of disadvantages. It placed the financial and administrative constraints upon him and it created career uncertainty for his senior employees, who felt that the company depended upon the interest and well-being of its sole owner.

On the advice of his son, who had taken a course in multiple objective preference analysis, Taylor spent time at a retreat developing a list of alternatives and objectives. Exhibit 3 shows the result of his efforts. Across the top are seven alternative legal structures (including the status quo), including variations in which Taylor shares ownership with other potential investors. Down the left hand side are 13 objectives, grouped into three clusters according to whether they reflect his concern for his employees, himself, or the business. Note that we could be cynical and say that Taylor is really only concerned about himself and that his other listed concerns are only because of their impact on his own welfare. Whether this is so or not, so long as Taylor does not double count, the objective list is suitable for a preference analysis.

---

[2] This is a highly condensed version of a true, but disguised case "William Taylor and Associates (A)" by Professor S.E. Bodily of the Darden Graduate Business School of the University of Virginia (case UVA-QA-24).

For each objective, Taylor has given each legal structure a preference score from 0 to 100 with at least one alternative getting 0 and at least one getting 100. This system does *not* imply, for example, that the employees have no income and security under the status quo (see Exhibit 3). For example, Taylor feels that Employee Income and Security improves just as much in moving from Alternative 1 to Alternative 4 as it would moving from Alternative 4 to Alternative 7.

Based on this information, what should Mr. Taylor do?

Note that no one alternative is worse than another on all 13 objectives. Alternative 1 comes very close to being dominated by Alternative 6 but is "saved" by Objective 5.

Let us suppose that under each cluster, each objective is valued equally. In this case Exhibit 3 may be collapsed as shown in Figure 4.9.

				Alternatives				
		1	2	3	4	5	6	7
Objectives	A	0	90	200	170	240	100	200
	B	290	70	130	280	220	340	190
	C	330	260	400	350	390	410	320

Figure 4.9

Now notice that Alternative 6 dominates 1, Alternative 3 dominates 2, and Alternative 5 dominates 7. Alternative 5 "virtually" dominates 3.

This leaves us with Alternatives 4, 5, and 6. A more comprehensive analysis showed Alternative 5 to be the overwhelming favorite. After this analysis Mr. Taylor constructed an amalgam of 4 and 5 that he felt was even better than 5. He reported that not only had the analysis helped him to select an organizational form, it also helped him greatly in thinking about strategy for the firm. His son commented that his father would have "gone crazy" without such an analysis. He had put off solving the problem for years and would probably have continued to do so; the company would have suffered as a result. In particular, the analysis convinced Taylor that the Status Quo had to go.

Exhibit 1

DECISION TREE FOR COMMANDER MACKENZIE

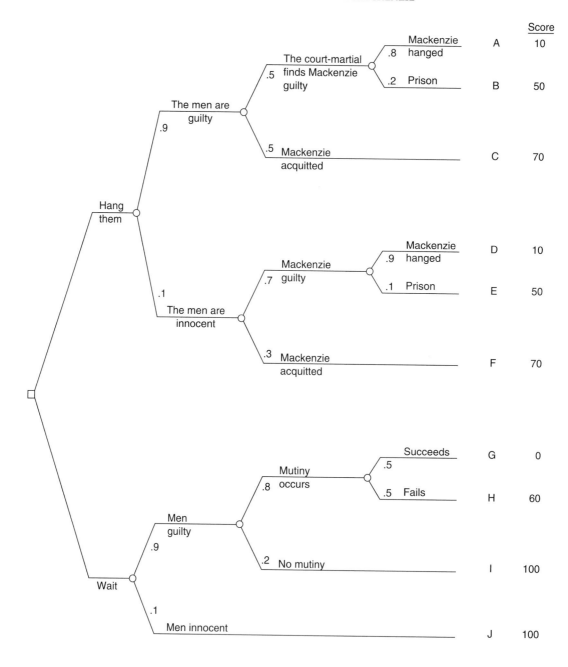

Exhibit 2

HIERARCHY OF OBJECTIVES FOR COMPARING JOBS

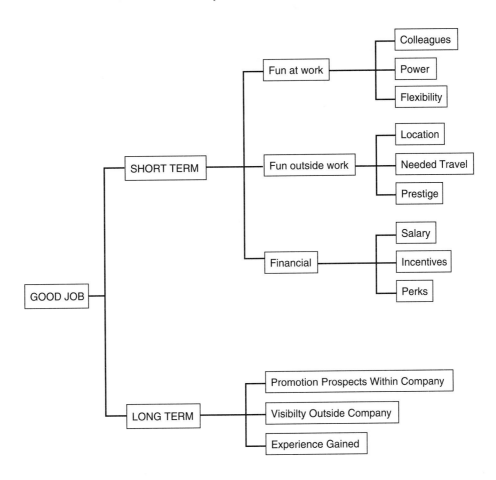

Exhibit 3

	1. Status Quo	2. One Partnership	3. Multiple Partnerships	4. Professional Corporation + Proprietorship	5. Professional Corporation + 1 or more General Corps.	6. Proprietorship w/Responsibility Centers	7. Single Corp w/ESOP
A. Employee Welfare							
1. Employee Income + Security	0	20	40	50	80	20	100
2. Employee Job Satisfaction	0	20	60	80	100	60	50
3. Senior Employee "Entrepreneural Satisfaction"	0	50	100	40	60	20	50
B. Personal Welfare							
4. Personal Income and Security	40	0	20	100	80	50	60
5. Personal Ownership and Control	100	20	40	70	60	90	0
6. Personal Freedom	50	0	20	70	80	60	100
7. Personal Tax Benefits	100	50	50	40	0	100	30
C. Business Welfare							
8. Professional Engineering Entity	50	50	100	100	100	50	0
9. Growth Potential	50	0	100	50	100	80	20
10. Finance	0	40	60	50	90	0	100
11. Unified Marketing	90	90	20	30	0	90	100
12. New Ventures	40	0	100	70	100	90	0
13. Management and Control	100	80	20	50	0	100	100

JOHN BROWN (A)

The following description is the true account of a 42-year-old Englishman, whom we will call John Brown. John was in charge of personnel services and staff development for a major British corporation. His family consisted of his wife (age 41), a son (17), and a daughter (14).

Last Wednesday, I came home from work and decided to saw some wood in the garden. As I was doing it, quite suddenly I felt very odd and decided I ought to go back to the house, a distance of about 10 yards. My balance was failing and about 10 feet from the back door of the house I collapsed. I must have hit the door in my fall because my family heard the noise and came to investigate. I was unconscious for about five minutes. When I came to, they covered me with blankets where I lay and called a doctor. They had not intended moving me until he came but after half an hour I felt considerably better so they moved me into the lounge. We hadn't called an ambulance because there were so many explanations for what had happened. When the doctor did arrive and had performed a series of tests involving my bending and twisting, he announced that he could not explain what had happened. I might say that this gentleman, who, I've since learned, is to retire in a couple of weeks, should never have moved me at all, so far as possible. Fortunately, no harm was done.

I was then taken by ambulance, over rutted roads, to a small local hospital where I was met, about midnight, by a specialist who had travelled 30 miles or so. He gave me a lumbar puncture, which in this case was a test for blood in the brain. He diagnosed a subarachnoid hemorrhage. At this point, my own doctor, a man of the same age, but in whom I have the greatest trust, arrived and consulted with the specialist. He confirmed to me that I had had an aneurism, which having burst caused bleeding within my brain.

An aneurism is a weakness at the joining between two blood vessels. It is something you're born with and more than 3 in 100 people are born with one or more such weaknesses. If the blood pressure causes the wall of the blood vessel to burst, there is a 40% chance of dying before reaching the hospital. In fact, although I lived through that part, a few months ago a colleague of mine died quickly of a cerebral hemorrhage before he could reach a hospital.

The hospital I was in did not have the facilities to help me further. Brain surgery is the only active next step, which must be carried out within a narrow time span, between 5 and 14 days after the original incident in order to minimize the possibility of a recurrence, and at this point I could have gone home and attempted to live a normal life. I'm told, however, that statistics show that after one such incident there is a 50% chance of a subsequent recurrence with fatal consequences. That is to say, half the people who have one attack, subsequently die of a recurrence.

The alternative was to be moved to a larger hospital for tests, in my case here at Westingbrough. The test was not a negligible undertaking. It consisted of injecting radioactive traces through two tubes, inserted into my neck, one for each side of the brain, and then taking an angiogram by X-rays. The test was carried out under anesthesia but recovering from it was extremely painful, a fact that I had not been aware of beforehand. Even now, I am in great discomfort.

A short time after the test, I was informed of the results and now am faced with the principal decision, should I have surgery? The tests show that I had only the one aneurism. Here at Westingbrough they've seen people with five. About 20% of patients like myself prove to have more than one, but I am lucky.

The consultant surgeons have gone to great lengths to explain to myself and my wife the procedures that would have to be followed to correct the problem. Basically they're going to have to saw my skull in a semicircle and then across the middle to get at the particular part of the brain. Then they would clip the blood vessel that has leaked. They know exactly where it is from the X-rays. The danger, apart from that part of the surgery itself, is that cutting off the blood vessel stops the blood flow to a part of the brain. There is a tendency for other blood supplies to compensate eventually for the loss, but it may not be sufficient.

The consequences vary according to which blood vessel is involved. In my case they say there is a probability that I will have impaired speech, perhaps even a total loss. There is a second, larger probability that I will be paralyzed on my right-hand side. There is still a larger possibility that some unknown consequence will occur. There is also the very real possibility that I will die. This morning, the man in the bed next to me died of the same operation. Indeed, in this 26-bed ward that is devoted to this and similar operations, about one person per day has died from various causes while I have been here.

Of course there is a possibility that the operation will be successful. If so, the only possible cloud would be that the clip might not hold or some related problem may arise, but they say that that is a likelihood of about 2 in 500. Other possible consequences of the operation include the chance that the blood vessel cannot be clipped at all, in which case, apart from the surgery, my condition would be unaltered. Another possibility is that the surgeon might be uncertain whether the clip has been inserted properly. If so, this would involve another test, and if relevant, repeat surgery 6 weeks or so from now.

You can be sure I understand the seriousness of my situation. My doctor, I know, has spoken to my children about the consequences to them of my dying. A family friend and experienced pediatrician has also spent time with me and separately with my family. My wife and I have discussed the alternatives at great length; no surgery, with the constant fear of a fatal repetition, and surgery with its attendant risks. If I choose surgery it will be done within 24 hours.

The prospect of dying does not alarm me since, in a sense, that solves the problem. I am well-insured so that there will be no financial headaches for my family. They have had, by now, ample warning of this possibility, so that if I were to die now it would be less of a shock than at some other time.

The prospect of being unable to speak is bad but tolerable. My wife works in social services and deals regularly with a woman who is partially paralyzed as well as being unable to speak, so she has experience in dealing with such people. Nevertheless, this would be a handicap for her as well as for myself.

Paralysis is the worst possibility of all. Again, my wife could care for me, but that would be an unreasonable burden on her and would inevitably restrict her career as well as severely alter our life style. I would have to build a new career, which would be hard.

I haven't thought much about the other possible consequences, since they have not been defined and therefore are difficult to think about concretely. Even if the surgery leaves me no better or worse off, at lease I'll have the satisfaction that I tried. Otherwise, I'll be spending my life wondering if surgery could have put everything right.

The alternative of having no surgery seems like no answer at all. There would always be the uncertainty that death could strike at any moment. This is true for all people one way or another, but in my case the odds would be much greater. What is worse, the effects are nearly instantaneous. What if I were driving my car with my family when it struck? Obviously, I would not feel able to drive with this threat hanging over me. I wouldn't climb a ladder, since, if I'm at the top I stand no chance of avoiding death; at the bottom, at least I have a chance. These are just two examples of the restrictions that would start to encroach on my life. I would always end up taking things easy. My doctor will probably recommend against my travelling; my boss will shy away from charging me with critical assignments.

Above all, I suppose I have tremendous confidence in the eventual outcome. The surgeons, I know, are the best in the country and have been doing this operation for years. This afternoon they told me that only recently a girl, who had had five aneurisms and had had them clipped in five operations, each six weeks apart, had returned to visit them one year later, completely recovered. I have faith, I am optimistic, I'm going to elect to have the surgery.

▼   ▼   ▼

JOHN BROWN (B)

The following is the account of John Brown's wife.

The strange cry made me run for the garden door. John's form lay motionless at the threshold. His ashen pallor told me he was dead.

By midnight it was a hospital scene. Familiar uniforms, for I'd worked in a hospital, but strange roles. John was the patient whom they moved so carefully, I was the relative. They were making preparations for a lumbar puncture, so I realized they were looking for evidence of a brain hemorrhage. This was confirmed by the specialist at 2 a.m. John's condition remained critical.

The next day the children and I went about routine tasks trying mentally to grapple with the enormity of the change. Our own doctor, unavailable the previous evening, was back on duty. Having seen John at the hospital he came to us.

He was very frank in appraising John's chances. Though he didn't put a figure on it my impression was that John had a 50–50 chance of surviving the week. We struggled to comprehend the technical terms of his condition alongside the message that his life was still in danger. The aneurism was a rupture in a blood vessel, temporarily sealed by a clot. Movement might disturb the clot, causing further hemorrhage, so John must remain as still as possible. His drug regime did include strong sedatives which would hopefully provide relief for the pain in his head.

On Friday, John was transferred 40 miles to the neurosurgical unit of Westingbrough Hospital. Every jolt in the ambulance seemed risky and sunlight hurt his eyes. We were just living from minute to minute. Westingbrough is a huge place and I felt like I was losing him in it. But at last he was now in the care of an experienced, specialist, unit.

Finally, on Saturday, there was a sense of respite. John was on a four-hour cycle of drugs, which left him alert only for about one hour out of each four. Even then I was never sure how much he heard or comprehended.

Yesterday, he was taken to the operating theatre for an angiogram. After a full anesthetic, a dye was injected into the carotid artery on either side of the neck and X-rays taken. John was in severe pain afterwards, the disruption and movement had increased his problems, his throat and neck were now swollen and sore. If anything, he now looked worse than after the original incident.

By this morning John was slightly better and the consultant told us the results of the test. He recommended surgery and outlined three options.

1. The aneurism could be wrapped. This was relatively easy to do and didn't take so long, so that there was less chance of complications associated with the operation. The results were not so good, however, and John would have only one in three chance of surviving the first year.

2. A clip could be placed at the "neck" of the aneurism. The clip would usually hold but the complications could be severe. There as a 5–10% chance of death during the operation and there could be a chance of after-effects including paralysis and speech impediments, possibly total.

3. A clip could be placed further back on the offending blood vessel. The consequences were much the same as with option 2, but the clip had a much better chance of success. However, because the clip would cut off more blood the potential after-effects were a little more likely. The chances of operative death were the same, 5–10%.

The surgeon indicated he needs a decision today and he recommended option 3. John asked if the paralysis and speech defects would impair his ability to reason, and the surgeon reassured him on this. John also asked him how many operations of this kind were done at Westingbrough. The surgeon said about 5 or 6 brain operations a week. John said he was eager to go ahead.

This very concept of brain surgery, though we have known since Friday that it was likely, now appears stunning. I said I wanted a little more time to reflect and agreed with the surgeon to see him this afternoon to confirm our decision.

Naturally I have spent a lot of time thinking about the problems that would result from a failed operation. If he had speech then even being in a wheelchair would be tolerable for both of us. It's my understanding that speech difficulties are one of the results of a general paralysis, but not an inevitable by-product. The two consequences that were really threatening were, firstly, paralysis combined with lack of speech which would totally restrict both him and me. I'm not sure that John would be prepared to live like that. The other possibility that scares me is the prospect of having him recover but with diminished faculties. That is a possibility. The operation area is over the frontal lobes of the brain. Mistakes in surgery over such a critical area not only threaten loss of life, but impairment of memory, mental disorientation and possibly change in personality. I've dealt with such people before, in fact a relative of mine recovered from complete incapability to near self-sufficiency in about 6 months. It would be less hard if the retardation were such that John couldn't recognize his own limitation. If he did know about his own condition, both our lives would be intolerable.

These are not idle considerations. John has a private room at the end of a long ward and I have to pass the other patients each time I see him. There are patients with no speech, who are disorientated. One elderly man whom I saw yesterday laughing and joking with his family died today after surgery. Each patient has either shaven heads or are swathed in tremendous bandages. John hasn't really seen these people, but he's heard them.

This afternoon I did go to see the surgeon. I could tell he was reluctant to reexamine the options, probably on the grounds that I was looking for reassurance that he couldn't give. I told him that I wasn't comfortable in my mind with the alternatives we had and wanted to have more information. He asked me if I had any hospital experience and when I said I had, he called me into his office and fetched John's X-rays. He showed me the aneurism which was really quite tiny among all the images of the X-ray. A maze of blood vessels were clearly visible around it and the surgeon confirmed that this was one reason for optimism that a blood deficiency would not occur. You could also see that the neck of the blood vessel was very tiny which explained why the clip needed to be further down. I said, "You really don't know what you're going to do until you open him up, do you?" and he nodded agreement.

He also said that if John had no surgery within 10 days after the first bleeding his chances of surviving dropped greatly, and without surgery most patients are dead within 6 weeks. The subjective part of me was already grieving for what had happened to John, for what suffering might be in store, for what loss lay ahead. The operation was obviously going to be hell and why should he die that way? Maybe it would be better to bring him home to die in familiar surroundings with his family around him. Against that how could I forgive myself if I hadn't given him every chance to live? What would he want?

▼   ▼   ▼

ENVIRONMENTAL PROTECTION AGENCY: EMERGENCY PESTICIDE EXEMPTIONS

The Environmental Protection Agency (EPA) was set up with the goal of preventing significant deterioration of the environment, particularly with reference to man's industrial interference with it. Great attention had been directed by the agency toward pesticides, especially DDT, and the potential harm, often subtle, that they caused to flora and fauna. Not only may the indiscriminate use of pesticides affect the natural environment, but dairy cattle, human drinking water and food are occasionally affected. The EPA is responsible for registering pesticides and only registered pesticides may be used. In some cases a pesticide may be registered for some types of applications but not for others. The EPA may also deregister previously registered pesticides.

Section 18 of the Federal Insecticide, Fungicide and Rodenticide Act, as amended by the Federal Pesticide Control Act of 1972 had given the EPA the authority to permit Federal and State Agencies to use unregistered pesticides in emergency situations subject to case-by-case approval.

Exemptions can only be granted if the following three criteria are all met:

Harvard Business School case 9-180-018. Professor David E. Bell prepared this case. Copyright © 1979 by the President and Fellows of Harvard College.

1. A pest outbreak has or is about to occur and no pesticide registered for the particular use, or alternative control method, is available to eradicate or control the pest.

2. Significant economic or health problems will occur without the use of the pesticide.

3. The time available from discovery or prediction of the pest outbreak is insufficient for a pesticide to be registered for the particular use.

There are three categories of exemption requests. *Specific* exemption requests are those involving pests endemic to the United States. *Quarantine* exemption requests are those for pests foreign to the United States; a decision on these requests could take anywhere from a week to three months. A *crisis* exemption request involves a pest outbreak that was unpredictable and an immediate health or economic hazard, so that there is no time for filing for one of the other two exemptions. A crisis request is usually filed *after* application of the pesticide.

Graham Beilby[3] was in charge of all emergency exemption requests. The EPA rules and regulations largely dictated many mechanical aspects of handling requests. The requestor was required to submit a large amount of data supporting the claim as well as describing the expected detrimental effects of using the requested pesticide. While the EPA did not normally have enough time to collect its own data on a given situation, it was usually evident whether the claims of the requestor were basically true. Inflated claims were sufficient grounds for dismissal of the request. In any case, requestors would not wish to damage their credibility with the EPA for possible future requests.

Requests for crisis exemptions were often discussed on the telephone by Beilby and the head of the requesting agency involved before the official application was filed and before the pesticide was applied. This was because the requestor faced stiff legal penalties if a crisis exemption was not ultimately approved. Therefore, the discussion revolved around reaching an understanding as to what would or would not likely receive approval.

Beilby was concerned that this informal case-by-case evaluation was inadequate in the face of a growing volume of emergency exemption requests. Seven requests had been received in the first two years after the Pesticide Control Act of 1972, but thirty-six had been received in 1974 and even more seemed likely in 1975. (Of the 36 requests in '74, 12 were granted, 14 were denied, 2 were crisis requests, 7 were later withdrawn and 1 was still pending.)

In the spring of 1975 Beilby received an application for a specific exemption request from the U.S. Forest Service to permit the use of DDT on its forests in the Pacific Northwest. The Tussock Moth, endemic to the region, was responsible for periodically defoliating Douglas fir trees. Until 1968, the U.S. Forest Service had used DDT to control the moth but then voluntarily discontinued its use. In 1974 when they again wished to use DDT, by then deregistered, their request was denied by the EPA. The 1974 request, which projected losses of $13 million, was denied based on the belief that the nuclear polyhedrosis virus would cause a natural collapse of the moth. The moth did not collapse, instead became blamed for $77 million in losses.

Beilby was well aware of the difference between a bad decision and a bad outcome, but this event could not have helped EPA's credibility, which was already suffering from the outcome of an earlier exemption decision. In that

---

[3] This name and some dates have been altered. The subjective opinions and probabilities expressed in this case are for illustration only. They do not necessarily reflect the opinion of any EPA staff member.

case, a state had requested an exemption to use DDT, the EPA had granted the request, but the pest had disappeared naturally before doing any serious damage. Fortunately the pesticide had not been applied, but Beilby felt that this incident had undermined not only his own credibility but the image of the EPA in general. Both the U.S. Congress and the general public kept a watchful eye on EPA decisions. Certain exemption requests were politically explosive.

With this background in mind, Beilby looked over the current request. The Forest Service wished to use 490,000 pounds of DDT on 650,000 acres which included part of Washington, Oregon, and Idaho. Two-thirds of the land was federally-owned, one-sixth was state land and one-sixth was the Colville Indian Reservation. Forestry on the Indian land accounted for 40-50% of their employment and 95% of the total income to the tribe. Their forests had been particularly hard hit by the defoliation of 1974. Repeated defoliation leads to tree death, which is not only an economic loss but also substantially increases the chance of forest fires. This would be a severe hazard to the Colville Reservation.

The request was made conditional upon tests of egg mass samples to be taken after the 1975 egg hatch. The tests would show whether the larval population was being controlled naturally by the nuclear polyhedrosis virus. If this natural control was not occurring and if the request for DDT was denied, the Forest Service projected economic losses of $67 million.

Even though the projected losses were high, Beilby was not comfortable with the thought of approving the request. But if he chose to deny the request, he'd have to have his reasoning pretty explicit and defendable. It occurred to him that a study completed only in February for the EPA by a well-known Cambridge consulting firm should be useful for his current decision. After rereading their report he drew the following decision tree (Figure 4-10). Since the request would be withdrawn by the Forest Service if the egg test proved favorable, the probabilities he estimated presupposed that the egg tests were unfavorable.

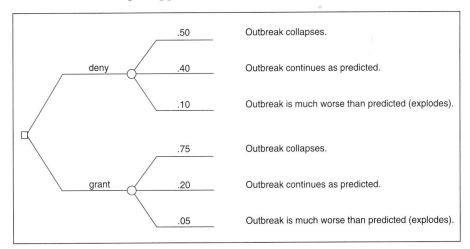

Figure 4.10

Beilby estimated economic losses in the best case (Outbreak collapses) at $3 million and in the worst case (Outbreak explodes) at $90 million. With these figures and the subjective probabilities that he had assessed he calculated expected losses of approximately $20 million for "grant" versus $40 million for "deny." It seemed to Beilby that both of these alternatives were bad and, while to deny resulted in twice the losses as to grant, the use of DDT had to be weighed against the grant decision. Also these numbers did not reflect the desire he had not to appear to make the "wrong" decision again.

He sat and reflected on this further evidence that sophisticated methodologies never seem to work on the problem at hand, before placing a call to the consulting firm.

KENNETH BRADY

Kenneth Brady is a disguised name of the 29 year-old second year MBA student who wrote this case.

I grew up in Dumas, Texas, population 9000, graduating from a small liberal arts college in central Texas. Immediately upon graduation I went to work for Thorne Enterprises in Austin, Texas, as a computer programmer. After six months Mr. Thorne made me president of a subsidiary company that sold conveyor belt scales. The subsidiary had six employees including myself. As a practical matter, I was the chief salesman. Belt scale sales had been flat through the 1973-1974 recession and did not improve much under my management. After eighteen months I quit to go into the life insurance business in Amarillo.

In five years with nothing more than a secretary and a telephone, my income was around $60,000 a year. It was a comfortable living, but the problem was I was a one-man band. When I took a vacation or even the afternoon off, the entire sales process came to a screeching halt. There was no momentum built up in the way I operated.

I applied to the Harvard Business School to see if I could get in. I hadn't considered what I would do if I got accepted. But when I was accepted, I decided that I had to go. I would still be receiving renewal income from my old policyholders, so my wife and I would not have to make too much of a sacrifice in our life style.

But now I'm three months from graduation and I have to figure out what to do next. For the last several months I've been trying to sell a producing oil lease for an exploration company in Kentucky. It's a pretty good deal from my standpoint. They pay my expenses if I don't sell it, and an 8% commission (about $30,000) if I do sell it. If this deal sells, the 30K would make quite a difference in my plans.

At this point, I've got three job prospects. I'll call them Job A, Job B, and Job C. Job A is the one I really want, since it has the most upside potential. But I'd say it has a pretty good chance of not working out at all. Job B had better odds of working out but doesn't have quite the same excitement as Job A. Job C is what I would call a traditional job.

Job A

Mr. Thorne called me last fall about an idea he has for a piggyback rail terminal to be located halfway between Dallas and Houston. I got a group of second year students at the B-school to do a feasibility study of the idea. Thorne's idea is to develop a rail terminal on 9000 acres he owns there and ship truck trailers into and out of Texas via rail. The idea of a truck trailer riding "piggyback" on a rail car is not new. But what is new is the idea of a hub serving two major cities. This terminal would draw business from both Dallas and Houston and would be built on land that is 1/100 the cost of Dallas or Houston industrial property. That's where the economies come in. Thorne also owns a railroad that already serves the proposed terminal site. Hopefully this terminal will transform the surrounding real estate into an attractive industrial site.

Mr. Thorne suggested that the terminal could be segregated from the rest of his business in order to provide a cleaner way for me to participate in the equity. At this stage, we think it will require around $1 million to get started: $300K for equipment and $700K for one year's operating expenses. I'd put in as much money as I could and Mr. Thorne would supply the rest. In addition to profit sharing, I'd be paid $50–70K, salary and bonus, to start-up and run the facility.

I have to give Mr. Thorne an answer by the end of March.

Job B

Robert Irwin owns an oil exploration company in Houston. I met him during the course of trying to sell the Kentucky oil property. Irwin and I have talked about setting up a corporation that would actively seek out producing oil leases that might be for sale. The oil and gas business has been in a severe recession for eighteen months now and a large number of producing properties have been forced on the market at fire sale prices. I would have two petroleum engineers working for me who would evaluate these properties. Irwin's exploration company would receive a standard investment banking fee. I would put up a third of the equity ($100K). In addition, I would receive annual compensation equal to the greater of $60,000 or one-third of the profits.

This is really only a short-term deal. Within two years, the oil and gas glut will be gone and the attractiveness of this business will disappear also.

If the oil and gas glut dries up before we got our business launched, I would probably stay on with Irwin as an agent or broker to sell oil and gas properties. There would be no equity role for me in this but commission at 8% would add up fast if you're good. However, this would give me an opportunity to develop many contacts with prospective buyers and sellers. Hopefully I would develop a strong relationship with a single buyer and then enter into an equity deal with him at some point in the future.

Job C

The third possibility is what I'd call a conventional job. Earlier this spring Mr. Irwin put me in touch with a large pension fund management company in Houston. They have plans to begin an oil and gas investment fund for key executives in the firm. I have interviewed for a position where I'd be working with two or three others to evaluate oil and gas properties for the fund.

This position doesn't open up for another 6-12 months but they'll put me on in the interim as a securities analyst for around $45K until the fund is started. I'm going to Houston in three weeks for another series of interviews and will have to let them know if I'm serious or not.

Analysis

One night after having browsed through all three cases for the next day, I just couldn't bring myself to do any work. I picked up the risk management case for that night again. It was about some quant jock from Wharton who had used preference analysis to assist his father in making a major career change. Since I was facing a major career choice of my own, I tried again to finish the case. About half way through, I decided I should do this stuff for myself and forget about this guy's dad. So I put the unfinished case aside and drew up Exhibit 1.

Exhibit 1 is my rough cut analysis of what makes a job "good." I started by listing all of the attributes that the ideal job would have, such as a high salary, a bonus, equity, etc. Then I made an assessment of how each job I was considering measured up relative to each other. Since I knew that both Job A and Job B had uncertain outcomes depending on the economy and my own ability, I created a Hi and Lo scenario for each of these. Job C was a traditional job and as such had only one scenario to consider. So for each attribute, I now had five scenarios to assess.

For each attribute, I gave the best scenario a raw score of 100 and the worst a raw score of 0. For example, the salary for Job A is poor compared to the salary for Job B or Job C. But the bonus for Job A is better than the bonus for Job B, provided that we are talking about the Hi scenarios for both. However, Job C has a small bonus that is better then the bonus for either Job A-Lo or Job B-Lo.

Travel was easy to assess. Job A has limited travel, just about the right amount, and therefore gets a score of 100. Job C has no travel, which seems confining to me. Job B requires extensive travel. I would prefer extensive travel to no travel, so Job B gets a score of 50 and Job C a score of 0.

The most attractive feature of Job C is the contacts I would make in the Houston business community. Conversely, one of the biggest drawbacks to Job A is that I would be involved in a prosaic industry (railroading) and would make very few contacts outside of the central Texas area. This "contact" issue is one of the most difficult aspects of this whole career decision to assess and as such is one of the motivating factors for doing this analysis.

The next step was to assign weights to each attribute and then to produce "weighted assessments" by multiplying each "raw assessment" by its weight. If I understand this, these weighted assessments mean, for example, that the improvement in quality of contacts between Job A and Job B (either Hi or Lo) is equal to the improvement in work flexibility between Job C and Job B-Hi scenario.

To risk adjust each scenario, I assigned probabilities to each. Job A-Hi has only a 20% chance of working out. I am almost positive that Job C will work out so I've given it a 1.0 chance.

So after all the math is complete, I end up with overall expected preference scores of 366, 356, and 206. This seems to confirm my view that I should forget Job C. I am kind of surprised that Job A and Job B end up so close. In my heart, I want to do the piggyback deal (Job A).

I showed this table to my wife. She was really interested and understood what was going on. She's been after me to take Job C and thinks I'm crazy for "gambling" our money on these other deals. But really all she wants is that I be happy in my work; that's what it comes down to.

One other thing. She'd like to stay in Boston rather than move to some unknown place. We have a house in Belmont and our two kids are in school. It may sound strange but Boston would be a good location from which to pursue the oil and gas deal (Job B). Being from the oil patch (Texas) adds credibility up here. Since most of the action is on the phone or involves flying, it doesn't matter a whole lot where you're based. I think the main thing is she wants to resolve the uncertainty about where we'll live. She wants our next move to be our last move, at least for a while.

Exhibit 1

		Raw Assessments					Weighted Assessments				
		Job A		Job B		Job C	Job A		Job B		Job C
WEIGHT	OBJECTIVE DESCRIPTION	HI	LO	HI	LO		HI	LO	HI	LO	
0.1	Salary	0	0	100	80	80	0	0	10	8	8
0.9	Bonus	100	0	80	0	20	90	0	72	0	18
1.0	Equity	100	0	80	0	0	100	0	80	0	0
0.9	Fun	100	60	50	60	0	90	54	45	54	0
0.6	Travel	100	100	50	50	0	60	60	30	30	0
0.8	Contacts	0	0	60	60	100	0	0	48	48	80
1.0	Ideas	0	0	40	40	100	0	0	40	40	100
0.6	Work Flexibility	100	30	80	30	0	60	18	48	18	0
0.3	Title	100	100	80	80	0	30	30	24	24	0
0.8	Number of Employees	100	100	80	80	0	80	80	64	64	0
0.7	Location	100	100	0	0	0	70	70	0	0	0
	Subtotals (Not Risk Adjusted)						580	312	461	286	206
	Probabilities						× 0.2	× 0.8	× 0.4	× 0.6	× 1
	Intermediate Products						116	+ 250	184	+ 172	206
	Risk Adjusted Preferences						366		356		206

▼   ▼   ▼

CASE

THE TORO COMPANY S'NO RISK PROGRAM

"I really don't see how we can repeat the program at those rates." It was June 1984 and Dick Pollick, director of marketing for Consumer Products, was reacting to an analysis by Susan Erdahl, programs manager. Susan had used available historical data to perform a rough actuarial calculation that confirmed the appropriateness of the three-fold increase in premiums asked by insurance companies to cover a repeat of Toro's "S'no risk" campaign.

Background

Toro had begun in 1914 by making tractor engines and later branched out into lawn mowers. In the early 1960s they added snowthrowers. By 1984 they offered a full range of products for "outdoor care" to both institutional and residential customers. Residential lawn care products constituted about 40–50% of sales, with snowthrowers accounting for a further 10–15%.

Snowthrower sales were channeled through twenty-six regional distributors who supplied snowthrowers to independent retailers, such as hardware stores and lawn and garden centers, across the snow belt. Toro also sold directly to mass merchandisers, like Marshall Field, whose private labels made up about 30–35% of Toro snowthrower sales. Although snowthrowers were sold throughout the year, 60–70% of sales occurred during November, December, and January, dropping off during the ensuing months and becoming minimal during the summer. Sales were especially strong in a year following a severe winter, presumably because people resolved not to be "caught again."

The Toro product line included the newly-introduced lightweight power shovel, as well as the more traditional single-stage and two-stage models. The (smaller) single-stage machines, with suggested retail prices of between $270 and $440, had been selling in excess of 100,000 units per year. The self-propelled two-stage machines, ranging in price from $640 to $1,500, had been selling at somewhat less than 20,000 units per year.

These figures were a far cry from the heady days of the late 1970s when several years of strong growth had culminated in two years, 1978–1979 and 1979–1980, of exceptionally high sales. During this time Toro sold approximately 800,000 single-stage and 125,000 two-stage machines. The severity of the three winters beginning in 1977/1978 created a demand that rewarded dealers for their aggressive inventories.

The following year, 1980/1981 sales plummeted (Exhibit 1). Dealers and distributors were left with unsold inventories that in some cases lasted them three years. Toro not only had to forego the lost income as orders fell to a trickle but they also offered to pay some of the huge holding costs faced by their dealers. The next two winters were equally mild, causing a sharp downturn in Toro's fortunes (Exhibit 3). Dealers had become disenchanted with snow removal equipment. The outlook was bleak.

Harvard Business School case 9-185-017. Professor David E. Bell prepared this case. Copyright © 1984 by the President and Fellows of Harvard College.

The S'no Risk Idea

In November 1982, Susan Erdahl received a phone call from an organization called Goodweather that specialized in arranging insurance to cover weather-related business losses; they had made a reputation insuring rock concerts. They suggested that Toro might wish to insure their snowthrower customers against the possibility of no snow.

Dick Pollick was intrigued. A marketing survey commissioned a few years earlier had emphasized that a major concern of prospective buyers was that their machines might not get enough use. Perhaps Goodweather's proposal would be a way to "guarantee" that a snowthrower purchase would be justified.

By January 1983 the program was set to go: under the plan, each Toro customer (with the exception of those buying power shovels) during the summer and fall of 1983 would receive a full refund of the suggested retail price *and* keep the snowthrower if the total winter snowfall was less than 20% of its historical average. Data from 172 government-run weather stations would be posted at each retail outlet so that a customer could read which weather station would apply and what the relevant historical average had been. If the actual snowfall was less than 50% of average, the customer would be refunded half the retail price. Intermediate percentages would produce a sliding scale of reimbursements (see Exhibit 4). Customers mailing in the registration form (Exhibit 2) would automatically be mailed a check in the event that snowfall in their area was sufficiently low.

Since Toro's potential liabilities ran into many millions of dollars, insurance was felt to be a necessity, and this was where Goodweather came in. They arranged a contract with American Home Assurance Company, who agreed to meet all claims resulting from the campaign in exchange for a premium equal to 2.1% of the retail value of snowthrowers covered.

The Program's Success

At first distributors resisted the new promotion, which was to replace the 10% discount program usually held in the fall. They were apprehensive about the possible administrative complexity and the potential for customer confusion. However, they soon saw the basic simplicity and appeal of the idea. Dealers greeted the promotion enthusiastically and, for the first time in three years, built up inventories to back the campaign.

The accompanying advertising campaign (Exhibit 5) generated a lot of interest, indeed excitement: dealers reported customers demanding nothing but a Toro, and buying larger models to take a greater advantage of the deal. Soaring retail sales were aided in some areas, such as in Toro's home base of Minneapolis, by record-setting fall snows. Dealers sold out of the large models completely and sales of the single-stage machine were also strong. In an attempt to keep pace with demand, Toro made an unprecedented mid-season production run of 2,500 of one of the larger models. They were fortunate to be able to make even this number as they relied on outside suppliers for engines. Production lead times were on the order of months rather than weeks.

Dick Pollick was overjoyed. Not only were sales up and dealers' confidence and interest back, but the campaign had been cheap. Although some modest administrative costs had been incurred due to the set-up required for a new program, the S'no risk promotion had had a basic cost of 2.1% of sales instead of the 10% normally spent on the discount program!

The Present

Despite this success, Dick was not certain that the promotion should be continued. For one thing, the novelty might not carry over to a second year. Also, even though two weather stations had reported snow less than 50% of average (Richmond and Roanoke, both Virginia), customers might be less enthusiastic about the program when they learned that only a few customer had "collected" the previous year. Moreover, since the winter of 1983/1984 had been snowy, sales in the coming fall could be strong even without this kind of promotion. In any case, Pollick regarded the restimulation of the trade as a major benefit of the promotion; this would not likely be reinforced by a repetition.

And now Susan had told him that American Home was asking premiums of around 8% of sales for the coming year. A check of other insurance companies, including Lloyd's of London, produced rate of between 6% and 10%. Susan's own analysis (Exhibit 6) had convinced her that American Home had erred in offering too low a rate for the previous year. Her calculations showed that had S'no Risk been in force for the years 1979/1980 through 1982/1983 the actual payouts would have been 4%, 8%, 1%, and 19% of sales respectively.

Exhibit 1

Snowthrower Sales – Units

Product	78/79	79/80	80/81	81/82	82/83	83/84
Power Shovels	—	107,213	107,896	56,981	89,114	68,141
Single-Stage	426,425	367,253	124,615	111,472	102,718	110,564
Two-Stage	53,700	73,483	17,335	19,683	18,374	31,702

Exhibit 2

TORO S'NO RISK™ PROGRAM REGISTRATION

Press Hard–Print Clearly

MODEL NO._____ DESCRIPTION_____ SERIAL #_____

DATE OF PURCHASE_____ DEALER DESIGNATED WEATHER REPORTING STATION_____
  (Must be between 5/1/83 and 12/10/83)

CUSTOMER NAME _____

ADDRESS _____ ____/____
          Street   City   State   Zip

DEALER NAME _____

ADDRESS _____ ____/____
          Street   City   State   Zip

CUSTOMER SIGNATURE _____ DEALER SIGNATURE _____

IMPORTANT–To participate, the last copy of this Registration Card must be mailed to the address pre-printed on the reverse of card. This registration must be postmarked no later than **December 17, 1983** to qualify. Terms and conditions applicable to this program are those printed on the Toro S'NO RISK™ Program Brochure. Program void where prohibited by law.

Copyright © All Rights Reserved
The Toro Company—1983 Minneapolis, MN 55420
Printed In U.S.A.

White–Customer copy   Gold & Pink–Dealer Copy   Registration Card–Mail to Toro S'NO RISK™ Program

Exhibit 3

SELECTED FINANCIAL DATA 1974-1983 (DOLLARS IN THOUSANDS, EXCEPT PER SHARE DATA)

Operating Data	1983	1982	1981	1980	1979	1978	1977	1976	1975	1974
Net sales	$240,966	$203,761	$247,049	$399,771	$357,766	$223,853	$153,910	$129,978	$131,626	$114,592
Earnings (loss) from continuing operations	$106	$(8,699)	$(12,595)	$5,679	$17,717	$11,733	$5,669	$3,703	$1,809	$4,572
Percent of sales	—	(4.3)%	(5.1)%	1.4%	5.0%	5.2%	3.7%	2.8%	1.4%	4.0%
Per common share and common stock equivalent	$(0.27)	$(1.86)	$(2.57)	$0.97	$3.18	$2.18	$1.08	$0.72	$0.36(a)	$0.92
Net earnings (loss)	$572	$(8,699)	$(13,068)	$5,272	$17,126	$11,085	$5,589	$4,403	$2,480	$5,345
Per common share and common stock equivalent	$(0.19)	$(1.86)	$(2.66)	$0.90	$3.07	$2.06	$1.07	$0.86	$0.50(a)	$1.07
Dividends:										
On common stock outstanding	$0	$0	$1,825	$4,861	$3,670	$2,035	$1,497	$1,286	$1,234	$1,091
Per common share	—	—	$0.33	$0.88	$0.68	$0.39	$0.29	$0.26	$0.25	$0.22
Return on:										
Beginning common shareholders' equity	(2.6)%	(19.3)%	(21.1)%	7.2%	31.5%	24.5%	14.0%	12.1%	7.1%	17.3%
Average common shareholders' equity	(2.4)%	(21.4)%	(23.9)%	7.2%	27.6%	22.6%	13.4%	11.9%	7.0%	16.6%
Summary of Financial Position										
Current assets	$92,662	$89,606	$99,678	$123,180	$139,207	$107,189	$73,234	$65,718	$74,516	$61,063
Current liabilities	$38,925	$43,107	$37,635	$42,676	$68,040	$50,022	$26,640	$22,583	$35,692	$20,172
Net working capital	$53,737	$46,499	$62,043	$80,504	$71,167	$57,167	$46,594	$43,135	$38,824	$40,891
Non-current assets	$58,547	$60,553	$57,353	$60,410	$38,406	$25,817	$21,674	$19,183	$20,061	$11,462
Total assets	$151,209	$150,159	$157,031	$183,590	$177,613	$133,006	$94,908	$84,901	$94,577	$72,525
Non-current liabilities	$2,167	$1,311	$1,488	$816	$591	—	—	—	—	—
Capitalization:										
Long-term debt	$41,858	$47,414	$49,288	$55,315	$39,250	$28,650	$23,100	$22,344	$22,500	$17,210
Redeemable preferred stock	$14,829	$14,829	$14,830	$14,830	—	—	—	—	—	—
Common shareholders' equity	$53,430	$43,498	$53,790	$69,953	$69,732	$54,334	$45,168	$39,974	$36,385	$35,143
Total capitalization	$110,117	$105,741	$117,908	$140,098	$108,982	$82,984	$68,268	$62,318	$58,885	$52,353
Book value per common share	$8.04	$7.77	$9.64	$12.65	$12.63	$10.26	$8.57	$7.97	$7.37	$7.12
Stock Data										
Number of common shares outstanding (in thousands)	6,649	5,597	5,579	5,528	5,521	5,298	5,272	5,016	4,936	4,936
Number of shareholders	4,222	4,528	4,484	4,157	3,345	2,659	2,679	2,188	2,127	1,921
Low bid price	5.375	5.625	9.125	12.625	16.250	6.500	5.875	5.250	4.000	3.500
High bid price	13.875	9.250	19.875	24.375	29.125	16.125	7.250	8.625	6.500	8.250

(a)Earnings per share were lowered by $0.35 in 1975 as a result of the change to last-in, first-out (LIFO) cost method of accounting for substantially all inventories.
All 1975–1978 figures have been restated for the sale of Irrigation & Power Equipment, Inc. and all 1980 figures have been restated for the sale of Barefoot Grass Lawn Service, Inc.
All "per common share" figures have been adjusted to give effect to the 100% stock dividend in December 1978.
The 1979–1981 data has been restated for the implementation of FASB No. 43 accounting for compensated absences.
Earnings per share are computed based on net earnings less preferred stock dividends.

Exhibit 4

CONDITIONS AND TERMS OF TORO'S SN'O RISK PROGRAM

IF IT DOESN'T SNOW WE'LL RETURN YOUR DOUGH! AND YOU KEEP THE SNOWTHROWER.

TORO®

If it snows less than	You keep the Toro and you receive:
20% * AVERAGE SNOWFALL	**100%** REFUND of suggested retail price
30% * AVERAGE SNOWFALL	**70%** REFUND of suggested retail price
40% * AVERAGE SNOWFALL	**60%** REFUND of suggested retail price
50% * AVERAGE SNOWFALL	**50%** REFUND of suggested retail price

CONDITION AND TERMS OF TORO'S S'NO RISK PROGRAM

- Eligible Toro Snowthrower models include only: model S-140, S-200R, S-200E, S-620E, 3521, 421, 521, 524, 724, 824, 826 and 1132.

- Consumer purchases of eligible Toro Snowthrowers must be made between May 1, 1983, and December 10, 1983.

- Eligibility for full or partial reimbursement will be based upon snowfall measurement from 12:10 A.M. July 1, 1983, through 11:59 P.M. May 31, 1984.

- Snowfall statistics and definitions will be based on figures and wording of the United States Department of Commerce/National Oceanic and Atmospheric Administration (NOAA–US Dept of Commerce).

- Determination of full or partial reimbursement will be based upon the NOAA snowfall statistics of a specific, predetermined weather reporting station. The location of the NOAA weather reporting station applicable to your Toro Snowthrower purchase and the terms of reimbursement are displayed in print at the Toro dealer you purchased your Toro Snowthrower from.

- Eligibility for Toro's S'No Risk Program is limited to the original purchaser only and is not transferable. Only new equipment purchased is eligible for the program.

- Toro's product warranty program is a separate program. See operator's manual for product warranty details.

- The territory of this S'No Risk Program includes the 48 contiguous United States and Alaska. Canada is not included.

- Determination of your eligibility will not be made until May 31, 1984, the end of the defined snow period. If eligible for full or partial reimbursement, please allow 8 to 10 weeks for the delivery of your check.

- Your eligibility under Toro's S'No Risk Program shall be void if you, as a Toro Snowthrower purchaser, have concealed or misrepresented any material fact or circumstance concerning your purchase of the Toro Snowthrower. The refund is void where prohibited.

- Inquiries concerning the S'No Risk Program may be directed to your Toro Dealer, or write:

  The Toro Company, ATTN: S'No Risk Program, 8111 Lyndale Avenue South, Minneapolis, MN 55420

*Average annual snowfall for each reporting station will be the "Record Mean" snowfall compiled by the National Oceanic and Atmospheric Administration (NOAA) on file at and/or published by the U.S. Department of Commerce, National Climatic Center, Federal Building, Asheville, North Carolina 28801, as of January 1, 1982, or latest available data.

Purchaser receives Toro's S'No Risk Program at no additional cost. All forms available at participating dealers. Consumer reimbursement is based on Toro's published suggested retail prices exclusive of sales or use tax. Refund void where prohibited.

Exhibit 5

TORO'S ADVERTISING CAMPAIGN

TM 84-3
Prepared by THE TORO CO.
To appear in:
NEWSPAPERS—1983
SAU #19
Copyright © The Toro Company 1983

TM 84-4
Prepared by THE TORO CO.
To appear in:
NEWSPAPERS—1983
SAU #19
Copyright © The Toro Company 1983

Exhibit 6

Reporting Station	Code	Average Snowfall	Actual Snowfall				Actual Sales (at retail value) before 12/10				S'no Risk Refund			
			79/80	80/81	81/82	82/83	79	80	81	82	79/80	80/81	81/82	82/83
Blue Canyon, CA	004	241.6	232.5	146.4	N/A	385.7	86,028	40,257	14,071	51,386				
Colorado Springs, CO	006	40.6	72.6	18.2	34.4	36.3	281,457	110,471	31,900	31,757		55,236		
Denver, CO	007	59.1	85.5	45.1	26.7	81.6	2,428,829	1,302,086	342,171	242,671			171,085	
Grand Junction, CO	009	26.1	21.9	5.9	15.4	14.8	11,157	7,214	3,857	2,100		5,050		
Pueblo, CO	013	30.5	42.6	16.8	N/A	22.3	21,028	23,400	3,371	3,471				
Bridgeport, CT	016	26.1	9.6	11.5	19.7	23.0	571,643	168,700	90,214	288,243	342,986	84,350		
Hartford, CT	017	50.4	16.4	17.7	56.4	46.4	608,886	257,400	117,957	376,900	365,332	154,440		
National Airport, DC	018	17.2	20.1	4.5	22.5	?	145,171	25,900	16,014	42,543		18,130		
Pocatello, ID	021	40.7	35.5	29.7	66.4	58.5	149,228	52,143	31,429	117,914				
Chicago-O'Hare, IL	022	40.4	41.6	35.0	59.3	26.6	39,074,000	3,989,314	1,673,829	3,838,900				
Moline, IL	025	30.8	37.0	18.9	45.3	24.8	2,382,029	386,529	175,128	132,857				
Peoria, IL	026	25.6	27.5	23.8	46.9	19.1	1,307,529	179,214	62,814	86,757				
Rockford, IL	028	35.0	33.9	21.1	41.0	28.0	1,967,143	166,414	59,857	169,829				
Springfield, IL	029	24.7	30.5	17.5	50.4	10.4	836,843	190,271	95,186	404,129				202,064
Evansville, IN	030	13.9	16.3	3.4	15.0	4.1	75,971	8,986	3,886	4,300				3,010
Fort Wayne, IN	031	33.2	28.7	35.7	81.2	14.9	610,571	225,200	83,900	582,086		6,290		291,043
Indianapolis, IN	033	22.9	24.8	17.3	58.2	7.1	1,360,586	312,171	78,000	783,229				469,937
South Bend, IN	036	72.3	66.4	85.0	135.2	35.3	2,654,286	423,557	210,986	499,700				249,850
Des Moines, IA	038	33.8	23.3	20.4	62.9	51.5	2,243,914	399,671	288,057	285,557				
Dubuque, IA	039	43.5	36.0	21.7	N/A	21.4	488,714	70,443	31,400	66,843				33,432
Sioux City, IA	043	30.9	21.7	17.1	56.8	59.5	228,600	52,371	51,800	62,329				
Waterloo, IA	045	31.4	28.2	21.9	39.9	38.9	561,243	146,514	90,228	120,243				
Concord, KS	046	21.6	28.3	6.4	20.6	34.6	165,343	65,157	14,329	9,386		39,094		
Dodge City, KS	047	18.9	35.6	11.8	19.2	33.0	38,443	19,557	2,729	6,100				
Goodland, KS	048	35.9	102.0	41.8	24.4	48.2	2,200	8	2,228	529				
Topeka, KS	049	21.1	18.3	8.9	13.4	27.4	62,814	24,057	15,643	9,743		12,029		
Wichita, KS	050	15.2	12.7	3.1	13.9	25.2	106,600	79,014	16,886	23,057				
Lexington, KY	054	16.4	20.5	3.7	12.6	8.0	10,014	2,371	—	1,057		1,660		528
Louisville, KY	055	17.7	18.3	2.9	11.0	5.2	9,728	3,614	2,100	3,371		3,614		2,360
Caribou, ME	058	113.1	70.6	122.9	158.8	82.9	261,371	68,729	29,571	106,843				
Portland, ME	060	72.9	27.5	38.8	85.3	45.3	1,043,600	270,500	130,500	512,657	626,160			
Baltimore, MD	062	21.7	14.6	4.6	25.5	35.6	41,814	12,200	3,814	18,157		8,540		
Boston, MA	063	42.0	12.7	22.3	61.8	32.7	775,800	258,186	346,457	900,043	465,480			
Worcester, MA	064	70.4	26.6	43.0	73.9	63.4	163,686	89,414	67,000	170,686	98,212			
Alpena, MI	065	84.6	78.2	82.1	89.3	73.7	178,900	46,371	9,343	32,057				

Exhibit 6 continued

Reporting Station	Average Snowfall	Code	Actual Snowfall				Actual Sales (at retail value) before 12/10				S'no Risk Refund			
			79/80	80/81	81/82	82/83	79	80	81	82	79/80	80/81	81/82	82/83
Detroit, MI	40.7	066	26.9	38.4	74.0	20.0	5,353,000	1,256,386	1,016,114	4,111,600				
Flint, MI	45.3	067	39.7	36.4	62.2	33.6	1,128,657	321,429	171,686	224,557				
Grand Rapids, MI	74.1	068	48.5	51.5	74.5	35.9	2,951,729	490,286	257,271	477,529				238,764
Houghton Lake, MI	81.8	069	59.3	74.4	98.7	51.5	914,086	191,629	132,286	297,357				
Lansing, MI	48.8	070	34.7	38.7	62.1	33.5	2,821,128	507,529	276,171	999,529				
Marquette, MI	114.0	071	146.1	176.1	243.8	199.3	230,871	34,214	14,057	14,843				
Muskegon, MI	98.4	072	75.4	107.6	173.9	35.5	2,888,143	471,800	348,071	600,957				360,574
Sault Ste. Marie, MI	113.8	073	108.1	141.7	168.6	87.0	74,957	19,371	6,000	26,486				
Duluth, MN	76.7	076	55.1	36.5	95.7	96.5	351,057	106,471	66,386	190,886		53,236		
International Falls, MN	61.0	077	64.2	45.8	89.9	46.0	51,943	14,614	5,071	22,586				
Minneapolis/ St. Paul, MN	47.4	078	53.3	21.1	95.0	74.4	4,379,943	1,160,014	926,057	982,871		580,007		
Rochester, MN	45.6	080	55.2	25.6	62.7	62.6	401,957	144,143	115,129	114,514				
St. Cloud, MN	43.8	081	44.2	16.5	55.4	53.3	682,971	208,114	120,442	231,329		124,868		
Columbia, MO	23.4	083	31.1	17.6	31.9	4.0	20,686	7,371	857	3,571				3,571
Kansas City, MO	20.1	084	23.5	10.2	29.4	23.4	1,258,214	437,471	163,500	174,014				883
Springfield, MO	16.6	085	24.7	18.2	24.6	5.6	14,071	11,900	2,200	1,471				
St. Louis, MO	20.0	086	25.6	18.1	36.6	7.4	1,211,214	269,143	61,771	777,229				466,337
Billings, MT	57.3	087	59.2	65.9	63.1	49.2	125,200	24,171	14,457	9,100				
Glasgow, MT	27.6	089	17.1	17.1	42.0	30.4	14,629	4,957	1,142	4,086				
Great Falls, MT	58.3	090	34.3	39.2	100.3	45.6	81,600	13,971	15,086	22,443				
Havre, MT	46.0	091	19.8	26.2	N/A	38.1	9,643	1,529	429	1,571	4,822			
Helena, MT	48.3	092	40.3	16.9	56.7	39.0	178,686	109,300	23,157	103,900		76,510		
Kalispell, MT	66.7	093	65.1	50.2	66.2	44.7	98,100	39,043	12,328	16,743				
Miles City, MT	31.1	094	11.6	6.9	21.5	29.6	21,343	1,042	2,729	12,100		729		
Missoula, MT	49.4	095	54.7	14.4	69.3	24.2	65,343	30,271	6,743	19,443		12,806		9,722
Grand Island, NE	30.0	096	36.8	19.2	36.7	40.2	106,071	50,200	20,886	46,429		21,190		
Lincoln, NE	28.0	097	23.3	13.0	32.3	38.0	177,714	74,071	37,757	85,786		37,036		
Norfolk, NE	29.8	098	22.2	10.1	47.1	51.6	113,843	31,929	13,457	38,200		19,157		
North Platte, NE	30.6	099	66.3	3.9	25.1	25.7	65,443	36,043	19,300	15,914		36,043		
Omaha, NE	31.0	100	20.5	9.1	24.3	31.5	1,006,714	506,957	144,814	164,514		354,870		
Scottsbluff, NE	38.8	101	78.5	21.5	15.7	45.2	55,143	24,614	6,757	2,014			3,378	
Valentine, NE	31.2	102	53.3	16.4	47.9	18.9	16,643	11,685	957	2,000				
Reno, NV	25.7	103	22.0	6.1	26.0	23.8	49,517	26,114	12,571	27,671		18,280		
Concord, NH	64.8	104	27.0	54.7	90.0	38.7	491,314	189,985	110,486	436,843	245,657			

Exhibit 6 continued

Reporting Station	Code	Average Snowfall	Actual Snowfall				Actual Sales (at retail value) before 12/10					S'no Risk Refund		
			79/80	80/81	81/82	82/83	79	80	81	82	79/80	80/81	81/82	82/83
Newark, NJ	106	28.1	14.3	19.5	30.8	31.0	62,328	7,971	5,086	8,143				
Albany, NY	107	65.1	27.4	44.9	97.1	75.0	1,016,000	405,129	188,243	436,271	508,000			
Binghamton, NY	108	84.5	56.8	59.3	81.6	81.0	413,443	170,643	54,571	53,186				
Buffalo, NY	109	92.5	68.4	60.9	112.4	52.4	4,803,414	1,208,386	533,229	558,443				
Laguardia, NY	112	26.0	10.3	16.1	25.6	30.2	3,002,686	620,871	573,629	885,729	1,801,612			
Rochester, NY	115	89.7	72.2	94.4	128.4	59.7	1,296,071	232,343	171,500	121,143				
Syracuse, NY	116	110.7	93.4	79.0	137.1	66.0	1,044,314	247,971	118,757	103,686				
Bismarck, ND	119	39.7	26.6	11.7	80.3	32.2	145,900	23,000	17,400	51,329		16,100		
Fargo, ND	121	35.8	39.9	13.1	69.5	23.2	599,786	89,114	59,286	82,371		53,468		
Williston, ND	124	38.1	25.4	19.1	70.4	42.3	101,314	14,829	12,242	31,071				
Akron/Canton, OH	125	48.5	34.2	52.3	61.7	38.8	1,242,429	221,329	193,457	257,300				154,630
Cincinnati, OH	127	24.5	30.1	14.0	24.2	66.0	597,486	312,086	54,100	220,900				
Cleveland, OH	128	53.3	38.7	60.5	100.5	38.0	2,434,443	669,871	521,814	1,032,214				88,443
Columbus, OH	129	28.4	16.6	30.1	35.1	11.5	1,372,500	255,700	120,842	176,886				
Dayton, OH	130	29.0	24.9	19.6	42.9	5.5	2,120,229	588,600	191,371	305,414				305,414
Mansfield, OH	132	42.5	27.6	43.4	66.9	16.6	244,286	75,486	35,786	58,314				34,988
Toledo, OH	134	38.7	17.5	37.7	68.2	12.2	861,571	302,571	213,743	1,376,143	430,786			825,686
Youngstown, OH	135	56.3	32.8	49.1	62.1	39.4	856,971	243,286	213,486	121,157				
Allentown, PA	136	32.2	21.9	25.5	43.9	45.8	451,586	83,357	43,829	134,557				
Avoca-Wilkes Barre, PA	137	49.9	25.5	40.5	59.6	59.1	228,286	159,600	67,671	137,114				
Erie, PA	138	82.4	55.2	89.4	71.3	41.2	793,786	114,329	129,529	49,257				
Harrisburg, PA	139	35.4	14.6	24.9	36.0	35.4	767,800	127,929	68,857	216,943	383,900			
Philadelphia, PA	141	21.7	20.9	15.4	25.4	37.9	818,343	180,886	93,300	129,843				
Pittsburgh, PA	142	45.0	24.1	48.0	45.1	30.1	6,172,600	949,771	434,143	484,043				
Williamsport, PA	143	43.6	20.5	41.6	54.5	17.6	97,471	46,843	18,957	96,957	48,736			48,479
Providence, RI	144	37.2	12.2	21.5	47.4	32.4	115,171	35,529	54,271	223,029	69,103	3,120		
Aberdeen, SD	145	36.1	28.8	8.3	N/A	18.9	21,486	4,457	1,271	7,843		9,010		
Huron, SD	146	38.5	22.2	10.4	59.7	27.3	14,857	12,871	10,743	4,814		3,272		
Rapid City, SD	147	38.0	29.2	16.9	34.8	24.9	11,900	6,543	4,742	5,586		26,830		
Sioux Falls, SD	148	38.8	29.2	10.8	42.4	70.5	98,371	38,329	21,328	28,957				
Salt Lake City, UT	151	58.1	61.6	30.2	57.8	55.8	513,829	389,157	529	434,557				
Burlington, VT	154	77.6	39.6	64.7	81.5	80.5	147,571	44,271	154,086	100,071				
Norfolk, VA	156	8.2	41.9	0.3	6.1	3.4	—	0	32,900	529		3,257		265
Richmond, VA	157	14.6	38.6	1.0	21.2	29.4	528	3,257	528	4,929				

Exhibit 6 continued

Reporting Station	Code	Average Snowfall	Actual Snowfall				Actual Sales (at retail value) before 12/10				S'no Risk Refund			
			79/80	80/81	81/82	82/83	79	80	81	82	79/80	80/81	81/82	82/83
Roanoke, VA	158	24.6	31.8	11.8	30.9	35.0	8,157	3,757	2,000	2,671		1,879		
Spokane, WA	159	51.6	38.3	14.2	47.4	36.6	732,214	363,029	84,000	164,171		254,120		
Walla Walla, WA	160	20.1	27.8	5.4	13.5	3.9	16,443	6,771	—	529		4,739		529
Yakima, WA	161	24.8	47.6	12.0	28.2	21.9	11,714	17,786	1,614	10,000		8,893		
Green Bay, WI	163	44.8	38.1	30.2	54.0	39.7	769,171	199,543	63,529	118,886				
La Crosse, WI	164	42.2	32.0	21.8	36.1	37.1	777,100	220,071	83,786	185,114				
Madison, WI	165	40.4	31.0	26.5	50.0	41.4	2,506,143	406,871	242,414	262,643				
Milwaukee, WI	166	47.0	47.0	41.9	67.2	38.1	9,253,143	1,703,529	786,300	1,035,286				
Casper, WY	168	77.9	101.2	56.9	68.7	151.6	108,086	47,671	11,000	13,829				
Cheyenne, WY	169	52.7	121.5	27.6	26.9	101.0	98,443	68,043	15,000	16,057				
Lander, WY	170	104.0	124.4	67.6	41.8	165.7	78,214	33,914	12,914	14,086			6,457	
Sheridan, WY	172	70.0	75.8	46.7	58.9	66.2	37,100	13,643	7,200	14,700				

	Total Sales	Total Rebate
1979/1980	135,246,551	5,403,592
1980/1981	27,313,192	2,150,357
1981/1982	214,521,866	180,920
1982/1983	30,024,217	5,846,299

MULTI-PERIOD RISKS

The first four chapters were concerned with single-period risks. You make a choice, you face the consequences. That's it. But often a choice merely is the first of many. Risk management requires you to make subsequent decisions in an appropriate manner and to understand at the outset how valuable that flexibility is. In this chapter, we begin with a methodology, *dynamic programming*, for dealing with these kinds of problems. Then we cover options and risk-adjusted discounting. The chapter ends with a description of a multi-period problem that has been analyzed at length using some of the methodologies covered in this chapter and the last.

WORKED EXAMPLES IN DYNAMIC PROGRAMMING

Intuition about decisions under uncertainty is often so faulty that any procedure that assists logical thinking is of benefit. Decision trees were devised to be such a systematic procedure. However, for many problems the decision tree approach becomes unwieldy because of the large number of decision nodes and uncertainties. Options at this point include simplifying the problem, finding a different approach, or getting a large piece of paper. One particular class of problems produces huge decision trees but with an exceedingly simple structure that can be exploited to produce fast answers.

The major signals that a problem involving uncertainty can be solved by dynamic programming are:

- The problem involves repetitive decision making. For example, each period you must decide whether to buy now or later or each period you have to decide how much advertising to buy.

- There aren't many variations in the problem circumstances. For example, in a production scheduling problem it may only be necessary to know how many jobs are waiting to be done. If the optimal production schedule depends on how long each job has been waiting, this introduces too much complexity for dynamic programming.

The best way to describe dynamic programming is by example. As with many techniques, formulating a problem in the required manner is ninety percent of the problem. The case ends with some general advice on how this can be done.

Harvard Business School case 9-183-028. Professor David E. Bell prepared these examples. Copyright © 1982 by the President and Fellows of Harvard College.

Purchasing Exercise: Questions

Imagine that a certain commodity fluctuates in price from day to day; on any given day it is equally likely to be either $2.00, $2.10, $2.20, $2.30, $2.40 or $2.50 per unit weight. Furthermore, the price on any one day is completely unrelated to the price the day before. For example, if today's price is $2.30 and the buyer must purchase exactly one unit of the commodity by tomorrow evening, then since the expected price tomorrow is only $2.25 it would pay, on average, to wait until tomorrow. If the purchaser had reason to be risk averse, or had to pay a daily holding charge, the answer might differ. Without these additional complications it is clear that the most appropriate strategy is to buy now if the price today is $2.20 or less, wait and buy tomorrow if the price is $2.30 or more.

1. What is the best strategy with three days in which to buy the one unit?
2. What is the best strategy with five days to go?
3. Suppose the company requirements are one unit per day. Today there is no inventory. The price today is $2.10. How many units would you buy?
4. How does your answer to question 2 change if there is a 5¢ per day holding charge?
5. Someone comes to you with an offer. He will sell you one unit of the commodity at a fixed price of $2.35 any time during the next three days at your pleasure. That is, if you decide to exercise the option, you pay him $2.35 and receive the commodity. If you decide not to, you pay nothing and do not receive the commodity. What is the maximum that you would be prepared to pay for this option in the circumstances of question 2?
6. Suppose your inventory is currently nil and you can only buy each day's requirements on the day it is needed. Storage for one unit requires a capital investment of $100.00. How would you decide how much storage to take?
7. How does your answer to question 2 change if the buyer is risk averse, e.g., a price today of $2.30 is better than gambling on what tomorrow's price might be?

Answers

1. With three days to go, a decision tree would look like Figure 5.1. If you can follow it you can see that with three days to go you may either buy now or wait. If you wait, tomorrow you will see one of six prices—at which time you will either buy or wait. If you wait again, you are forced to buy at whatever price occurs on the last day. Clearly, with two days to go you should buy only if that day's price is less than $2.25, the average price expected on the last day. This means that, depending on the actual price seen on day two, your *expected* (in a probability sense) cost will be either $2.00, $2.10, $2.20, $2.25, $2.25 or $2.25. Thus the decision to wait on day three implies an expected cost of $2.175. Hence with three days to go you should buy now only if the price is $2.10 or $2.00. Even if the price is $2.20, you should wait because there's a good chance of paying less in the two days that remain.

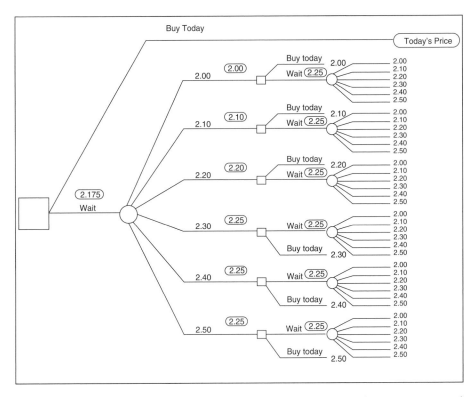

Figure 5.1

Got that? If you haven't, I strongly urge you to review the argument and Figure 5.1 until you fully understand the problem and its solution. Note that it makes sense that the more time you have to buy the commodity, the less you are likely to pay. Try it with six pieces of paper in a bag if you don't believe it.

Now for the dynamic programming approach. The logic is exactly the same but the effort is considerably easier. The procedure starts by recognizing that you have 18 decisions to make. What do I do if the price is X on day Y? Since there are six prices and three days, this makes 18 decisions. (Actually you would know the price on day 3, but dynamic programming produces the strategy for all possible prices so we'll pretend we're doing our calculations just before dawn when the day 3 prices are not yet known.) I will make the notation easier by dropping the $2.00 for all the prices and doing the calculations in cents.

What we are going to do is calculate the expected cost of being in each of those 18 situations assuming that you have not yet bought the commodity. We will fill out table 5.1.

Table 5.1

Today's price is	0¢	10¢	20¢	30¢	40¢	50¢
Today is						
Last Day						
Day 2						
Day 3						

What does it cost us if we haven't bought the commodity by the last day and the price then is 0¢ (i.e. $2.00)? Clearly 0. Fill in the appropriate box in Table 5.2. Repeat for all other boxes on the last day.

Table 5.2

Today's price is	0¢	10¢	20¢	30¢	40¢	50¢
Today is						
Last Day	0	10	20	30	40	50
Day 2						
Day 3						

Now let's fill out the row for day 2 in Table 5.3. The decision is to take either the price available on that day or the average of the cost in the row above ($2.25 → 25¢). It's clear what we do on day 2 and thus what we expect to pay.

Table 5.3

Today's price is	0¢	10¢	20¢	30¢	40¢	50¢
Today is						
Last Day	0	10	20	30	40	50
Day 2	0	10	20	25	25	25
Day 3						

On day 3 it is clear that we can either take today's price or pay the average of the day 2 expected costs [which is $(0 + 10 + 20 + 25 + 25 + 25)]/6 = 17.5$.

In Table 5.4 we get:

Table 5.4

Today's price is	0¢	10¢	20¢	30¢	40¢	50¢
Today is						
Last Day	0	10	20	30	40	50
Day 2	0	10	20	25	25	25
Day 3	0	10	17.5	17.5	17.5	17.5

This table gives us both the purchasing strategy to be followed and the expected cost of following it. On day 3 if the price is $2.30 then you can expect to pay $2.175 (this is achieved by waiting). On day 3 if the price is $2.10 then you can expect to pay $2.10 (achieved by buying now). At dawn on day 3 how much are you expecting to pay?

Answer: $(0 + 10 + 17.5 + 17.5 + 17.5 + 17.5)/6 = 80/6 = 13.333$.

That is, $2.1333.

So the procedure is simple. For each row compare today's price with the average cost of waiting for tomorrow.

2.   Without reading on, complete Table 5.5 out to five days.

Table 5.5

Today's price is	0¢	10¢	20¢	30¢	40¢	50¢	Average
Today is							
Last Day	0	10	20	30	40	50	25
Day 2	0	10	20	25	25	25	17.5
Day 3	0	10	17.5	17.5	17.5	17.5	13.33
Day 4							
Day 5							

Your table should look like Table 5.6.

Table 5.6

Today's price is	0¢	10¢	20¢	30¢	40¢	50¢	Average
Today is							
Last Day	0	10	20	30	40	50	25
Day 2	0	10	20	25	25	25	17.5
Day 3	0	10	17.5	17.5	17.5	17.5	13.33
Day 4	0	10	13.33	13.33	13.33	13.33	10.55
Day 5	0	10	10.55	10.55	10.55	10.55	8.70
Day 6	0	8.70	8.70	8.70	8.70	8.70	—

I included day 6 as well just to show that, when you get back far enough, even buying at $2.10 is not worth it. In my calculations I've kept track to two decimal places of cents, but of course there is no need to be so meticulous—17.5, 13.3 etc. is quite accurate enough.

One attractive aspect of this procedure is that it allows a simple method of communicating the optimal strategy to an assistant, who, after all, does not have to worry about average cost.

Table 5.7

Today's price is	0¢	10¢	20¢	30¢	40¢	50¢
Today is						
Last Day	BUY	BUY	BUY	BUY	BUY	BUY
Day 2	BUY	BUY	BUY	WAIT	WAIT	WAIT
Day 3	BUY	BUY	WAIT	WAIT	WAIT	WAIT
Day 4	BUY	BUY	WAIT	WAIT	WAIT	WAIT
Day 5	BUY	BUY	WAIT	WAIT	WAIT	WAIT
Day 6	BUY	WAIT	WAIT	WAIT	WAIT	WAIT

3. We can regard each day's requirements as a separate problem. Imagine that different people are responsible for different days. Each person has the same strategy table (Table 5.7). The person who is in charge of today must buy. The table also tells the person in charge of buying for tomorrow to buy today (which is day 2 for him). Ditto for the person who is responsible for two days from now. Only when we get to the person who regards today as day 6 (she's buying for five days from now) will $2.10 be too high. Thus five people will buy today.
The answer to the question is 5.

4. Now try your hand at solving question 2 when there is a five cent per day holding charge. I've filled in rows 1 and 2 of Table 5.8 to get you started. Don't forget that if you buy early you have to pay the holding charge. The box with the asterisk happens to be 25¢ for either of two reasons. You could buy now and pay $2.20 plus a 5¢ holding charge for a total of $2.25 or wait and pay an average of $2.25 tomorrow.

Table 5.8

Today's price is	0¢	10¢	20¢	30¢	40¢	50¢	Average
Today is							
Last Day	0	10	20	30	40	50	25
Day 2	5	15	25*	25	25	25	20
Day 3							
Day 4							
Day 5							

The table in full should look like Table 5.9.

Table 5.9

Today's price is	0¢	10¢	20¢	30¢	40¢	50¢	Average
Today is							
Last Day	0	10	20	30	40	50	25
Day 2	5	15	25	25	25	25	20
Day 3	10	20*	20	20	20	20	18.33
Day 4	15	18.33	18.33	18.33	18.33	18.33	17.78
Day 5	17.78	17.78	17.78	17.78	17.78	17.78	17.78

The strategy box now looks like Table 5.10 (breaking ties as buy now):

Table 5.10

Today's price is	0¢	10¢	20¢	30¢	40¢	50¢
Today is						
Last Day	BUY	BUY	BUY	BUY	BUY	BUY
Day 2	BUY	BUY	BUY	WAIT	WAIT	WAIT
Day 3	BUY	BUY	WAIT	WAIT	WAIT	WAIT
Day 4	BUY	WAIT	WAIT	WAIT	WAIT	WAIT
Day 5	WAIT	WAIT	WAIT	WAIT	WAIT	WAIT

Comparing the strategy box with the earlier one we see an emphasis on waiting. Of course this is what we'd expect, given there is a penalty on buying early.

5. We can answer this one by figuring out the best strategy taking advantage of the option and then comparing how much lower our costs are than when we do not have the option (Table 5.6). I will assume we cannot sell the option to someone else. The mechanics are exactly as before, except that row 1 looks different. Clearly you will exercise the option only if you are faced with paying more than $2.35. (Note that this can only happen on the last day because before then you can expect to pay at most $2.25).

Try the calculations yourself. I've filled in row 1 of Table 5.11 for you.

Table 5.11

Today's price is	0¢	10¢	20¢	30¢	40¢	50¢	Average
Today is							
Last Day	0	10	20	30	35	35	21.67
Day 2							
Day 3							
Day 4							
Day 5							

Table 5.12 shows how you should have ended up:

Table 5.12

Today's price is	0¢	10¢	20¢	30¢	40¢	50¢	Average
Today is							
Last Day	0	10	20	30	35	35	21.67
Day 2	0	10	20	21.67	21.67	21.67	15.84
Day 3	0	10	15.84	15.84	15.84	15.84	12.23
Day 4	0	10	12.23	12.23	12.23	12.23	9.82
Day 5	0	9.82*	9.82	9.82	9.82	9.82	8.18

By comparing Table 5.12 with Table 5.6 we can see how much we would pay for the option depending on our circumstances (Table 5.13).

Table 5.13

Today's price is	0¢	10¢	20¢	30¢	40¢	50¢	Average
Today is							
Last Day	0	0	0	0	5	15	3.33
Day 2	0	0	0	3.33	3.33	3.33	1.66
Day 3	0	0	1.66	1.66	1.66	1.66	1.10
Day 4	0	0	1.10	1.10	1.10	1.10	0.73
Day 5	0	0.18*	0.73	0.73	0.73	0.73	0.52

The Before Dawn column tells you how much you'd pay for the option just before seeing the new day's prices. Note that there is no shortcut that gets straight to Table 5.13. The reason is that the optimal strategy alters with the option. The only instance in Table 5.13 where this occurs is marked by an asterisk.

6. With no storage we will pay an average of $2.25 per day. With one day's storage we can cut this average to $2.17 1/2 (Table 5.6). This saves 7 1/2¢ per day. If there are $50 \times 5 = 250$ business days, this saves a total of $18.75 per year. Does this exceed the capital cost of $100? Two units of storage gets the average cost down to $2.13 1/3, a further average saving of 4 1/6¢ per day, for an annual total of $10.42. Does this exceed the capital costs of $100?

7. We may use a preference curve to reflect the risk aversion (Table 5.14):

Table 5.14

Price	2.00	2.10	2.20	2.30	2.40	2.50
Preference Value	0	10	20	30	60	100

This says that when the price gets up to $2.40 the financial situation is fairly serious and at $2.50 it is really terrible. (Imagine the prices are in millions). The solution by dynamic programming is no harder than before (Table 5.15).

Table 5.15

Today's price is Today is	0¢	10¢	20¢	30¢	40¢	50¢	Average
Last Day	0	10	20	30	60	100	38.33
Day 2	0	10	20	30	38.33	38.33	22.78
Day 3	0	10	20	22.78	22.78	22.78	16.39
Day 4	0	10	16.39	16.39	16.39	16.39	12.59
Day 5	0	10	12.59	12.59	12.59	12.59	—

Note that the strategy now differs from Table 5.7 in that on day 2 we buy at 30¢ instead of waiting (as question 7 requires) but also on day 3 we buy at 20¢ instead of waiting. This is because the penalties for getting stuck with a high price are now much greater, increasing the desire to settle for a reasonable price.

Option Pricing Exercise: Questions

Suppose that General Foods stock is selling today at $32 per share. Suppose that each week it will go up by $1, down by $1 or stay the same—all with equal probability (1 in 3). Someone offers to sell you one share of General Foods at any time during the next five weeks for $35.

1. How much would you pay for this option?[1]
2. How much would you pay if today's price was $36?
3. How much would you pay if the price movements were in increments of $2 instead of $1?

Answers

1. In five weeks the price could end up anywhere from $27 to $37. At that time the option will be worth either $1 or $2 so long as the stock price is worth at least $36. What is the option worth in the last week but one if the stock price is then $35? Well, in the last week it will be worth either 0, 0, or $1 depending on whether the stock price is $34, $35, or $36. Thus the option has value $1/3 in the last but one week. To avoid getting fractions all over the place, I'm going to solve the problem for 243 shares (243 = 3 × 3 × 3 × 3 × 3). Entries in Table 5.16 are thus 243 times bigger than for one share.

---

[1] Ignore the opportunity cost of money. This assumption is not serious in this example but would be if GF were expected to have a net gain over the period, for then buying the stock itself would be a competing investment. Also, for the purposes of this example, assume that GF has no systematic risk component so that expected value is an appropriate criterion.

Table 5.16

Question 1	26	27	28	29	30	31	32	33	34	35	36	37	38	39	40
Last Week	0	0	0	0	0	0	0	0	0	0	243	486	729	972	1215
Week 2	0	0	0	0	0	0	0	0	0	81	243	486	729	972	1215
Week 3	0	0	0	0	0	0	0	0	27	108	270	486	729	972	1215
Week 4	0	0	0	0	0	0	0	9	45	135	288	495	729	972	1215
Week 5	0	0	0	0	0	0	3	18	63	156	306	504	732	972	1215
Week 6	0	0	0	0	0	1	7	28	79	175	322	514	736	973	1215

Each entry in this table is derived by averaging the three nearest entries in the row above. The 18 figure in week 5 is the average of 0, 9, and 45—the three values the option could have by week 4.

The conclusion is that, at a current price of $32 with five weeks to go the option is worth 7/243 dollars or about 2.9¢. The answer to question 2 can also be obtained from Table 5.17. At $36 the option is worth 322/243 dollars or $1.32 1/2. Clearly the answer had to be bigger than $1 since the option is worth $1 immediately.

Table 5.17

Question 2	26	27	28	29	30	31	32	33	34	35	36	37	38	39	40	41	42	43	44
Last Week	0	0	0	0	0	0	0	0	0	0	243	486	729	972	1215	1458	1701	1944	2187
Week 2	0	0	0	0	0	0	0	0	81	162	324	486	729	972	1215	1458	1701	1944	2187
Week 3	0	0	0	0	0	0	27	54	135	216	378	540	756	972	1215	1458	1701	1944	2187
Week 4	0	0	0	0	9	18	54	90	180	270	423	576	783	990	1224	1458	1701	1944	2187
Week 5	0	0	3	6	21	36	81	126	219	312	462	612	810	1008	1236	1464	1704	1944	2187
Week 6	1	2	8	14	28	56	107	158	254	350	497	644	836	1028	1250	1472	1709	1946	2188

The option value at a stock price of $32 is now worth 107/243 dollars or 44¢. At $36 the option value is $2.12.

Discussion

The two examples analyzed above were, of course, simplifications of reality. The discrete values of prices is unrealistic as well as the rather specific way in which they move. However, with a computer to do the work, these restrictions are not important. Indeed the great virtue of the dynamic programming solution technique is that it is easy to tell a computer what to do and the computation involved is much less than with a conventional decision tree approach. (This is because certain calculations are repeated over and over in the decision tree approach. See Figure 5.1 where the average "2.25" is calculated six times instead of once.)

This simplicity arises because of the simple structure of the problems we have solved:

1. The problem can be separated into a number of *stages*, usually time periods.
2. There are a (usually small) number of *states* which, together with the stage number, completely define the circumstances of the decision maker.

Two more conditions help to simplify the analysis a great deal:

3. The alternatives available at each stage and in each state are identical.

4. The probability curve that determines which stage the decision maker moves into at the next stage as a function of the current state and decision is the same for all stages.

These last two conditions are not necessary, but were present in the example given above.

The key concept is that the decision you make in a given state at a given stage *should not depend* on how you got to that state at that stage.

In the purchasing example, as long as I tell you there are three days to go, the current price is $2.20 and you haven't yet bought the commodity, then it's irrelevant what the price was yesterday. Similarly, it doesn't matter what General Foods was selling at yesterday if you have possession of the option today.

EXERCISES ON DYNAMIC PROGRAMMING

The Job Search

You are looking for a job and have arranged a series of interviews with prospective employers. The interviews are sufficiently far apart that you will receive any job offer from one interview before going to the next. You will not be required to respond to a job offer until all of your interviews are over.

You are considering two interview strategies. The first, your "sensible approach," involves demonstrating to the interviewer that you have a well-rounded education and are a perfect match for them. This strategy, you estimate, will give you a 30% chance of receiving a job offer from any given interview. The second approach is your super-aggressive, "brash" strategy. You project the image of one who is destined for the very top. You flick through a copy of the company's annual report, making suggestions here and there about how they can restructure their business. This approach is rarely successful (10% of the time) but if it works the company will mark you as a high flyer and offer you a great position and superior starting salary.

To summarize, the "sensible" strategy will yield an average job offer or nothing. The "brash" strategy yields a great job offer or nothing. On a scale in which no job scores 0 and a great job scores 100, an average job scores 60. This means that if you are going for your last interview and have not yet received a job offer you should adopt the sensible approach, since 0.3 × 60 is bigger than 0.1 x 100. Obviously if you have already had one average job offer there is nothing to be lost from adopting a brash attitude thereafter.

1. If you have lined up 15 interviews, reason intuitively as to whether you should be brash or sensible in your first interview.

2. Use dynamic programming to develop a contingency strategy when you have arranged only four interviews. In particular how should you approach your first interview?

Harvard Business School exercise 9-184-132. Professor David E. Bell prepared this exercise. Copyright © 1984 by the President and Fellows of Harvard College.

Hint: The *stages* are the number of interviews remaining. The *states* are:

- You have had no job offer yet
- Your best job offer so far is only an average one
- You already have a great job offer

Chutes and Ladders

This exercise in dynamic programming is based on the children's game Chutes and Ladders, shown simplified as in Figure 5.2.

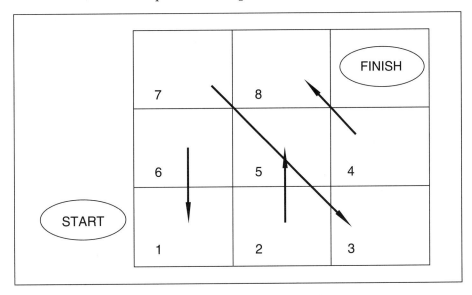

Figure 5.2

Placing your marker at "Start," you toss a coin to determine which square you go to next. A Head moves you two places forward, a Tail only one place forward. This procedure is repeated until you land on or past "Finish." Should you land on the tail of an arrow you move at once to the square it points to. From "Start" a Tail takes you to square 1, a Head to square 5. From square 8 you are bound to reach "Finish" on the next toss. Each toss of the coin costs you $1. You may quit at any time. You receive $10 if you reach "Finish."

1. If you have $5 in your pocket, do you wish to play?
2. How much profit would you expect to make on average from playing the game?

Hint: The *stages* are the number of dollars you have in your pocket. The *states* are which square of the board you are on.

CASE   **AT&T—8.70 BONDS**

In 1970, AT&T issued $350 million of 32-year bonds at a coupon of 8.70%. The terms of the issue allowed AT&T to call the bonds at any time after five years. In 1975 when the bonds did became callable, AT&T considered replacing the

Harvard Business School case 9-183-083. Professor David E. Bell prepared this case; it was adapted from a paper by W. M. Boyce and A. J. Kololay in *Interfaces*, November 1979. Copyright © 1982 by the President and Fellows of Harvard College.

issue with noncallable bonds which they felt would require a coupon of about 8.00%. Even allowing for the cost of recall and reissue, the lower interest rate would provide AT&T with net savings of about $6 million. However, by calling the bonds now they might forego the opportunity to do so sometime in the future when interest rates were even lower and the savings still higher.

Another advantage of delaying the recall was that the call premium would be reduced. The terms of the issue required AT&T, if they called the bonds after five years, to pay the bondholders a premium equal to 22/27 of one year's interest. This would amount to $22/27 \times \$350,000,000 \times .087 = \$24,811,111$. However this amount was reduced by 1/27th for each additional year before recall, so that if the bonds were called less than five years before maturity, no such premium would be paid. Commissions on the reissue were estimated at 0.875% of the face amount, or $3,062,500.

Analysis

To trade off current gains with foregone opportunities required an estimation of the potential gains as a function of interest rate and date of reissue, as well as a forecast of where interest rates might be over the next several years.

We have seen that if AT&T were to call the bonds now they would have an immediate cash outflow of $27,873,611 (the call premium plus the reissue cost). This "investment" would return interest savings of (8.70%–8.00%) × $350 million or $2,450,000 each year for 27 years. Since the corporation was taxed at around 50%, the real cash flow would only be half these amounts.

A net present value calculation requires a discount rate which represents the return on competitive investments. One competitive investment is for AT&T to *buy* bonds for which their return would be 4% per annum (8% before taxes). The net present value of the above cash flow at 4% is $6,066,937.

Table 5.18 repeats the calculation for a variety of interest rates assuming recall now, in 1980 or in 1985. For example if the bonds are not recalled until 1985 at which time the prevailing interest rate is 7%, the call premium would be $12/27 \times 8.70\% \times 350,000,000 = \$13,533,333$, for a savings of $(8.70\% - 7.00\%) \times 350,000,000 = \$5,950,000$ for 17 years. At a discount rate of 3 1/2% (7% before tax) this cash flow gives a net present value, in 1985, of $29.34 million.

Table 5.18

| | Call Date | | |
	1975	1980	1985
9.0	−22.1	−18.4	−14.4
8.5	−8.4	−6.2	−4.1
8.0	6.1	6.6	6.6
7.5	21.3	20.0	17.8
7.0	37.5	34.0	29.3
6.5	54.6	48.7	41.4
6.0	72.7	64.2	53.9
5.5	91.8	80.4	66.9
Breakeven Rate	8.21%	8.26%	8.31%

On the matter of forecasting interest rates, it was decided to model interest rate movements as a *random walk*. The premise was that interest rate trends were unpredictable but that the rate of variation was. The random walk model assumed that *change* in interest rates over a month was describable by a probability distribution having mean 0% and standard deviation 0.12%. Monthly changes were assumed independent of one another, from which one may deduce that annual changes have mean 0% and standard deviation 0.40%. The probability distribution for five yearly changes has a mean of 0% and a standard deviation of 0.90%. Table 5.19 shows a discrete approximation to this distribution that can be used for the analysis.

Table 5.19

EXPECTED CHANGE IN INTEREST RATES OVER FIVE YEARS

Probability	Change
.2	−1%
.2	−0.5%
.2	0%
.2	0.5%
.2	1%

Entries represent the net present value of calling the bonds at a given year and interest rate. Note that to compare the value of calling in different years requires discounting of the more distant savings. For example, calling at 6 1/2% in 1985 is better than calling at 7% in 1980 if the effective annual discount rate between 1980 and 1985 is less than 4%.

The information in Tables 5.18 and 5.19 should be enough to determine whether the bonds should be recalled now. If they should not be recalled, it would be useful to have a criterion for determining at what "trigger level" of interest rates the bonds should be recalled in the future.

▼   ▼   ▼

OPTIONS CONTRACTS

Trading in options began at the Chicago Board Options Exchange in 1973. There are contracts available on commodities such as sugar but most trading activity is in stock options, stock index options, and most recently on futures options.

An option contract is characterized by its maturity date, its strike price (exercise price), the underlying property, and whether it is a call or a put.

Buying a *call* option gives you the right, at any time up until the maturity date, to buy the underlying property at the strike price. (In Europe options only give you the right to buy *at* the maturity date, but for tradeable options this feature rarely makes a difference in practice.) Selling a call option requires you to deliver the property at the strike price on demand at any time up to the maturity date.

Buying a *put* option gives you the right to *sell* the underlying property at the strike price at any time up until maturity. Selling a put option requires you to buy the underlying property at the strike price on demand at any time up to the maturity date.

Harvard Business School note 9-184-141. Professor David E. Bell prepared this note. Copyright © 1984 by the President and Fellows of Harvard College.

Exhibit 1 shows some stock option contracts and their prices for Boeing Company on two days in 1983. On October 28, 1983 it was possible to trade in any of 30 options contracts on Boeing. There were five different strike prices, three different maturities, and two types (calls and puts). In addition, since one could buy or sell each of these, 60 different actions were possible. As we can see from Exhibit 1, only 15 out of the 30 were traded on this day (but 19 on November 2, 1983).

The Options Exchange opens up trading in a new strike price category whenever the current stock price falls outside the range of strike prices currently being traded. For example, if on November 3, 1983 Boeing stock had jumped to $51, an option would have been opened for trading at a strike price of $55. The more volatile the stock price, the more options available for trading. Most of the trading volume tends to be concentrated on the options with strike prices closest, above and below, the current stock price.

On October 28, 1983 (near the close of trading) one could have bought a call option at a strike price of $45, valid until February, for 87 1/2¢ per share. One option is for 100 shares, so the price would be $87.50 (plus commissions of about $25 for an outside investor). At the maturity date, which will be the Saturday after the third Friday in February (February 18, 1984) if Boeing is above $50, it will make sense to *exercise* the option. If Boeing is below $50, the option will expire worthless. Note that in order to make a profit on the deal, the Boeing stock price has to be sufficiently above $50 to cover not only the option premium and the various commissions, but also the time value of money on these up-front payments and the taxes on any gain.

Note from Exhibit 2 that an option is always worth at least the difference between the current price and the strike price, since this is the profit that could be made by exercising the option at once. Also, the value of an option increases with the maturity date, since a longer term option could always be exercised earlier. The option price also falls as the strike price increases. The few anomalies in the November 2, 1983 prices are probably caused by the thin volume in these contracts. The stock price may have moved up after the last option trade in these contracts. (Example 1: The November call at 30 is *exactly* the amount that could be gained by exercising at once; one would expect it to be slightly higher. Example 2: The November calls at 45 and 50 have equal prices.)

Relationship between Calls and Puts

Exhibit 2 shows the payoff from various combinations of stock and option ownership. Note that the graphs only represent the value of portfolios at maturity; they do not reflect any of the costs required to purchase the positions or the value of any dividends paid or received. It is apparent that options can be used as a form of investment insurance (protecting the downside) or as a cheap form of speculation. Considerable effort has been put into understanding how options should be priced to reflect their fair value. Though this section discusses option pricing, it is worth emphasizing that for risk management purposes, it is sufficient to recognize that in high volume trading we can assume that the options are fairly priced; our only concern will be with the usefulness of options in *manipulating* risk profiles.

Note that a portfolio consisting of a stock and a put is identical to one in which one owns a call and at maturity an amount of cash equal to the strike price plus the accumulated dividends. Graph (v) of Exhibit 2 shows the payoff under either portfolio. Since they have identical payoffs, we can expect them to have equal prices.

Let C be the price of the call at a given time before maturity. Let P be the cost of a put. Let E be the strike price, S the current value of the stock, and r_F the risk-free interest rate.

The cost of the first portfolio is thus $S + P$. The cost of the second is $C + E/(1 + r_F)^T + D$ where T is the number of years to maturity and D is the discounted value of any dividends. The formula:

$$C - P = S - \frac{E}{(1 + r_F)^T} - D$$

should hold (in practice, approximately) for all options. Let's test this out on Exhibit 1. Using the November 2, 1983 data, the May call at 35 is $7.50, the May put at 36 is $1.75. We should have

$$7.50 - 1.75 = 40 - \frac{35}{\sqrt{1 + r_F}} - D$$

where we take a square root because of the six-month maturity. If $D = 0$ the breakeven value of r_F is 4.4%. If we take r_F as 8% the breakeven dividend value would be 57¢. Let's try another example. The May 40s have $C = 4.375$ and $P = 3.25$. We should have

$$4.375 - 3.25 = 40 - \frac{40}{\sqrt{1 + r_F}} - D$$

for a breakeven r_F of 5.9% if $D = 0$. If r_F were 8%, the breakeven divided value would be 38¢.

Portfolio Management

Consider an investment manager who actively trades in the stock market but who nevertheless tries to keep his portfolio approximately equivalent to the S&P 100. He is disturbed at the wide range of returns possible from this portfolio and is thinking about different ways to reduce this risk. How would the following risk management strategies affect the probability distribution of returns?

a. Liquidate part of the portfolio in favor of cash invested at the risk-free rate.
b. Sell futures contracts on the S&P 100 to lock-in return.
c. Liquidate the portfolio and, instead, buy calls on a set of stocks representing the S&P 100.
d. Buy puts on a set of stocks representing the S&P 100 in a way that guarantees a minimum return (say 0%).
e. Buy puts as in (d). Also sell calls on a set of stocks representing the S&P 100 in a way that eliminates any returns above, say 30%.

You may want to sketch your answers on Figure 5.3, a probability *density* distribution of the existing portfolio, which has mean return 15% and a standard deviation of 20%.

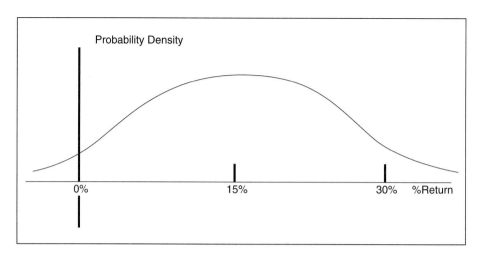

Figure 5.3

Converting half the portfolio into cash at a risk-free rate of 8% would produce a portfolio with a mean of 11 1/2% and a standard deviation of 10% (see Exhibit 3a). Selling futures would completely remove all risk (apart from any basis risk) and thus produce a portfolio with mean return 8% and standard deviation 0%. Why only 8%?

Suppose that he replaces every 100 shares he owns by a call option at the strike price nearest to the current stock price. The money he does not spend on options premiums (most of it, say 90%, for illustrative purposes) is left in cash, earning 8%. If the market drops, his only income will be from the cash. For every $100 of total investment he will have 90×1.08 or $97.20 at the end of the year. The options will be worthless. He will have had a net loss of 2.8% on the year. Since the market is equally likely to go up as down (roughly), this will be his net position half of the time.

If the market goes up, say by 20%, he will make an amount of money on the options equal to the amount he would have earned from his original portfolio because he "controls" an equivalent number of shares, at least on the upside. In *addition* he still has the interest income on the cash. Hence he has $97.20 plus $20 made on the options, for a total return of 17.20%. Hence he has sacrificed a little of the action on the upside in return for removing all of the downside below –2.8% (see Exhibit 3(c)). Note that to guarantee a total return of at least 0%, he would have to have at least $100/1.08 = 92.59\%$ of his portfolio in cash. The rest can be used to buy calls. Question (d) is essentially the same analysis, and results in a graph similar to Exhibit 3(c).

Just as we may buy puts to ensure a minimum return we may also sell calls to guarantee a maximum return. Why would anyone ever want to guarantee a maximum return? For one thing, while downside risk is usually feared, upside potential may not be all that great. Making 50% on your portfolio is better than making 45%, but for those investors having decreasing marginal value for money, the additional income becomes less and less useful. At a more cynical level, a portfolio manager may well be afraid of doing *too* well in one year lest he be expected to repeat the performance. However, there is a very practical reason for selling calls. The premiums earned from selling calls can be used to pay for the purchase of the puts that protect the downside risk. The manager can trade off the high upside against the low downside without the need for any current cash flow. Exhibit 3(e) shows the resulting distribution of returns.

Option Pricing

The mathematical details of option pricing go beyond this chapter, so the following discussion is intended only to show some of the ideas involved. Recall that pricing options is complicated because:

a. Option returns are correlated with the market so that their price should reflect the systematic risk they contain.

b. The distribution of returns is not even approximately symmetrical, so standard deviation may not be an adequate measure of risk in a portfolio containing options.

c. An option transaction has an up-front cash flow as well as the one at the maturity date.

d. A call option that is attractive only because the underlying stock is expected to appreciate is an illusion, since the money used to buy the option could have been used to take a leveraged position in the stock itself.

We begin with a simple example. You hold General Machines stock, currently worth $66 a share and paying no dividends. You expect that GM stock will be worth either $72 or $64 by the end of the year, with equal probability. Someone asks you to sell a call option on that share with a strike price of $70. What would be a "fair" price to charge for such an option? Suppose you charge $V. Let's look at your net cash flow under various scenarios (Figure 5.4).

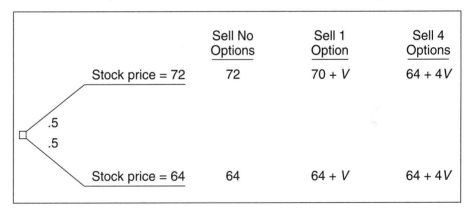

		Sell No Options	Sell 1 Option	Sell 4 Options
Stock price = 72		72	70 + V	64 + 4V
Stock price = 64		64	64 + V	64 + 4V

Figure 5.4

If the stock price drops to $64, you will owe nothing on the option but still own the stock worth $64 and the $V you received as a premium. If the stock price goes up to $72 the option will be exercised for which you will receive $70 plus the $V premium.

If you sell four call options you will have 64 + 4V if the stock price falls. If the stock goes up to $72, you will lose $2 on each of the options, leaving you with 72 + 4V − 8 = 64 + 4V. Therefore if you were to sell four call options you'd have a guaranteed income of 64 + 4V no matter what the ultimate price of GM stock. The net present value of this income is:

$$4V + \frac{64}{(1 + r_F)} \quad .$$

The option premium is not discounted since it is received up front.

Figure 5.5 shows one way to think of your decision problem:

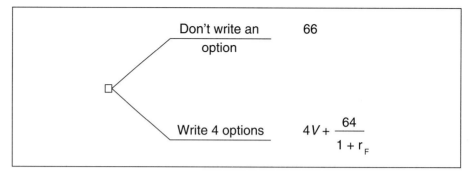

Figure 5.5

Remember, $66 is the fair value of the GM stock—we don't have to fold back the decision tree in this case.

So, a fair value for four options is given by:

$$4V + \frac{64}{(1 + r_\text{F})} = 66$$

or

$$V = 16.50 - \frac{16}{(1 + r_\text{F})} \quad .$$

Since options will trade at a common price, this calculation must also give the fair price for one option.

Note that if we were to ignore opportunity costs, or equivalently if we assumed $r_\text{F} = 0$, then the value of the option would be 50¢. Now that seems strange, because there is a 50–50 chance that the option will be worth $2 (if the stock goes to $72) or $0 (if the stock drops to $64). So why isn't the option worth $1?

The answer is that we have neglected to consider the opportunity value of the stock itself. Note that the EMV value of GM stock is (72 + 64)/2 or $68, yet it is priced at only $66. This is because of the systematic risk in the stock as well as the time value of money. If β is the beta of GM stock we should find that:

$$66 = \frac{68}{(1 + r_\text{F} + \beta (r_\text{M} - r_\text{F}))}$$

where r_M is the return on the market.

Just to make sure this story hangs together, let's assume for a moment that $r_\text{F} = 0$ and that β = 0 so that the current price of GM under this scenario would be $68. In this case, selling four options would give a guaranteed return of 64 + 4V so that a fair price would be found by setting 64 + 4V = 68 or V = 1, which is what we had hoped. With these assumptions the obvious solution is correct.

Now that we know how to do the pricing, here is a trick way to get straight to the answer. For the moment, let's continue to assume $r_\text{F} = 0$. *Suppose* the probability that GM stock will be $72 were 1/4 and that the probability that it will be $64 were 3/4. The EMV would be $66, which is consistent with the facts. Suppose we now use the naive approach for pricing the option (Figure 5.6).

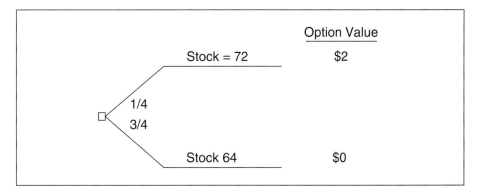

Figure 5.6

The EMV of the option is $1/4(2) + 3/4(0)$ or 50¢! This is no coincidence. If you pick a probability that makes the current stock price fair (ignoring risk), the same probability can be used to price the option, also ignoring systematic risk.

Let's try one more example to make sure this really works. IBM stock will be worth $100 or $200 in one year's time. It is currently worth $130. What is the value of a call option issued with a strike price of $120?

Trick Method

Set:

$$130 = 200p + 100(1 - p)$$

so that $p = 0.3$.

The value of the option is thus:

$$0.3 \times 80 + 0.7 \times 0 = \$24 \quad .$$

Old Method

Let's use the examples given in Figure 5.7 to review the old method.

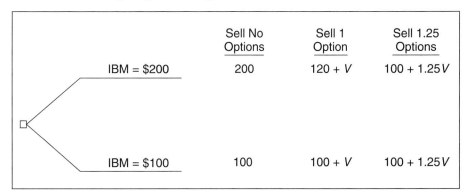

Figure 5.7

The fair option value is found by solving the equation

$$\frac{100}{(1 + r_F)} + 1.25V = 130 \quad .$$

Since we are, for the moment, assuming $r_F = 0$, this solves with $V = 24$!

It is a bit more complicated if we do *not* assume $r_F = 0$, but the principle is the same. Let's go back to our original GM example. The steps to follow are:

Step 1 Find p such that:

$$\frac{72p + 64(1 - p)}{(1 + r_F)} = 66$$ (the discounted value of the stock, ignoring systematic risk)

We find $p = 0.25 + 8.25r_F$.

Step 2 Calculate the discounted value of the option (ignoring systematic risk):

$$\frac{2p + 0(1 - p)}{1 + r_F}$$

$$= \frac{(0.5 + 16.5r_F)}{(1 + r_F)} \frac{(16.5(1 + r_F) - 16)}{(1 + r_F)}$$

$$= 16.5 - \frac{16}{(1 + r_F)}$$

The following observation may help. It is *irrelevant* that I chose 50–50 as the probability that GM was \$72 or \$64. If you go through this section again (carefully) you will find that the option price does not depend on that probability. This is because the *current* share price (\$66) already embodies information about the distribution of prices in one year's time. The current price also embodies information about the degree of systematic risk in the stock. That is why the trick works. You just interpret the current price as being due *entirely* to the probability distribution of returns as if there were no systematic risk in the stock.

The two-outcome simplification above turns out to give the right intuition. The way to price an option is to revise the probability distribution of stock price at maturity in a way that removes the excess price appreciation due solely to the stock's systematic risk. Then the option may be valued using this revised distribution by taking the EMV of the option's value at maturity discounted back at the risk-free rate. This is a fairly complicated procedure, however, and is beyond the scope of this note. A discussion of the Black-Scholes formula for the pricing of stock options may be found in many textbooks, for example Sharpe's *Investments* (pp. 438-444).

Exhibit 1 _____

| | | | | CHICAGO BOARD | | | | |
| | | | | Calls | | | Puts | |
Option	NY Close	Strike Price	Nov	Feb	May	Nov	Feb	May
Boeing	38	30	–	–	–	–	–	–
		35	$3\frac{1}{2}$	5	$5\frac{7}{8}$	$\frac{3}{8}$	$1\frac{5}{8}$	$2\frac{1}{4}$
		40	$\frac{1}{2}$	$2\frac{1}{4}$	$3\frac{1}{2}$	2	4	–
		45	$\frac{1}{16}$	$\frac{7}{8}$	$1\frac{13}{16}$	–	–	–
10/28/83		50	–	$\frac{3}{8}$	–	–	–	–
Boeing	40	30	10	–	–	–	–	–
		35	5	$6\frac{1}{4}$	$7\frac{1}{2}$	$\frac{1}{8}$	$1\frac{1}{16}$	$1\frac{3}{4}$
		40	$1\frac{1}{16}$	$3\frac{1}{8}$	$4\frac{3}{8}$	$1\frac{3}{8}$	$2\frac{3}{4}$	$3\frac{1}{4}$
11/2/83		45	$\frac{1}{16}$	$1\frac{3}{16}$	$2\frac{1}{8}$	$5\frac{1}{2}$	–	–
		50	$\frac{1}{16}$	$\frac{1}{2}$	–	–	–	–

– No Trade

Exhibit 2

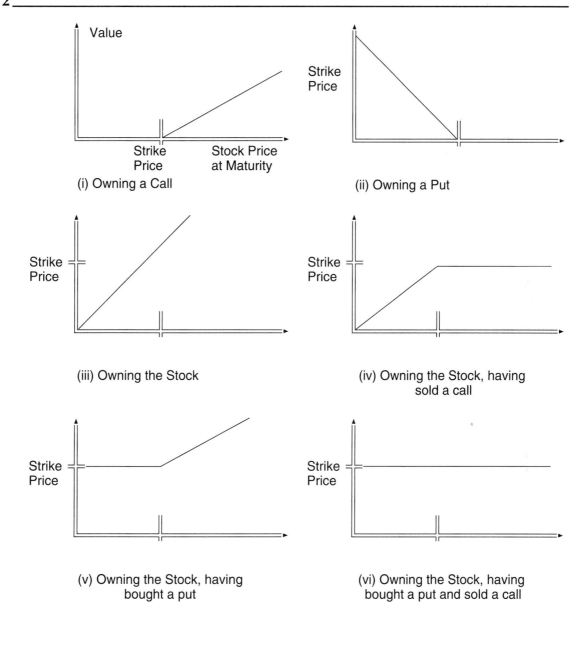

Exhibit 3

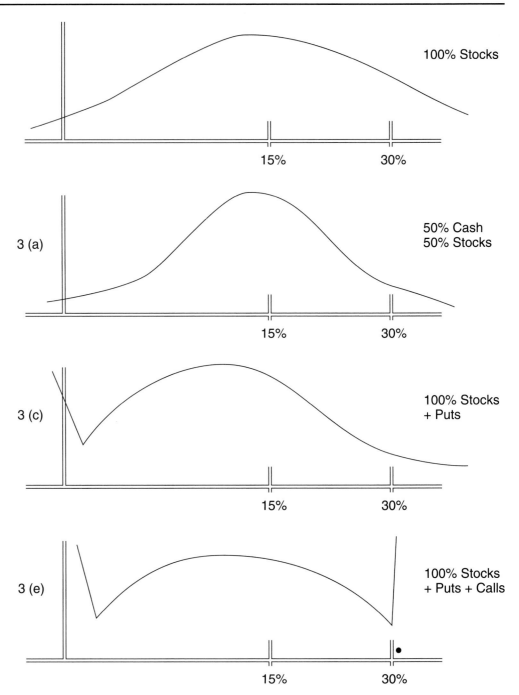

Note: These graphs are only sketches. The near vertical lines represent the discrete probability at these points.

EXERCISES ON OPTIONS

Since options are difficult enough as it is to analyze, these exercises, while reflecting realistic scenarios, have been simplified greatly to permit analysis in a reasonable time. Ignore taxes and the time value of money throughout, except where noted.

1. **The Wilmington Wire Company** Wilmington Wire Company makes gold-plated wire for the jewelry and electronic industries. Industry practice is to offer both date-of-shipment and date-of-order pricing at the customer's preference. Moreover, the customer may select the pricing method at the time of shipment. Since the raw metal is expensive, comprising anywhere from 80–98% of all costs of producing a product, a drop in the price of gold between order and delivery could be disastrous.

   Company practice is to purchase gold to cover an order immediately after the order is received. If gold options are traded in the obvious way, describe a hedging procedure that would eliminate Wilmington's risk.

2. **The Arkwright Medal Company** Arkwright Medal Company has been granted a license by the International Olympic Committee to produce silver medallions in commemoration of the upcoming games. As part of the licensing agreement the price and production level are fixed, indeed, the medals have already been manufactured by Arkwright. Also part of the licensing agreement is a requirement that the medals only be sold during the games. Arkwright recognizes that two factors lead people to buy the medals:

   ▶ enthusiasm built during the games, inspiring the desire fora keepsake,
      and

   ▶ speculative instincts

   Since there was no way to hedge against the general success of the games, Sally Zimmerman decided to concentrate on the relationship between expected sales and the price of silver during the games. Table 5.20 shows her estimate of expected revenue as a function of the silver price prevailing during the games.

Table 5.20

Silver Price ($1/oz.)	$2\frac{1}{2}$	3	$3\frac{1}{2}$	4	$4\frac{1}{2}$	5	$5\frac{1}{2}$	6	$6\frac{1}{2}$	7
Expected Revenue (Millions)	.5	1.0	1.5	2.5	3.5	6.5	9.5	9.5	9.5	9.5

At low silver prices the revenue reflects modest sales combined with the salvage value of unsold medals. At high silver prices the inventory will be sold out and since the price has been fixed, revenue will be constant.

If silver options trade in the usual way in units of 5,000 ounces, at strike prices at intervals of 50¢, what hedging action eliminates Arkwright's exposure on the medals?

Harvard Business School exercises 9-184-137. Professor David E. Bell prepared these exercises. Copyright © 1984 by the President and Fellows of Harvard College.

3. **American Business Machines** British Electronics, PLC, was offering for sale, by sealed bid auction, its U.S. subsidiary, Supertronics Inc. ABM thought that Supertronics was worth $25 million and on October 31, the deadline for submission of bids, they had submitted a bid of $20.2 million. The bids would not be opened until the end of December. ABM felt confident that they would be the highest bidder, but by November 2, they were not so sure. They heard that a number of British companies were making bids denominated in *pounds*. It was clear that if the pound rose against the dollar before the end of December, British Electronics might find it more valuable to accept one of the pound-denominated bids.

ABM felt that the current exchange rate of $1.50/£ was equally likely to be either $1/£, $1.50/£ or $2/£ by the end of December. Table 5.21 gives prices for options, based on a unit of £1200, at various strike prices:

Table 5.21

Options on £1200 Expiring December 31

Strike Price	Calls	Puts
$1.00/£	$600	$0
1.25	400	100
1.50	200	200
1.75	100	400
2.00	0	600

Current Exchange Rate = $1.50
Dec. 31 Futures Price = $1.50

- Determine the net cashflow from (a) buying a call at a strike price of $1.50; (b) selling a put at a strike price of $1.25; (c) buying a put at a strike price of $1.75 as a function of the exchange rate on December 31.
- If ABM is sure to win the bid if the exchange rate is at $1.00/£ or $1.50/£ and is sure not to if the exchange rate is $2.00/£, what action in the options market (see Table 5.21) would most hedge ABM's risk?

4. **Ivy Investment Inc.** Ivy Investment Inc. has its entire capital in a commodity that will have one of five equally likely values in one year's time. III feels that its position is somewhat risky and is considering ways to reduce it. Fortunately the commodity is traded on the futures and options market. III is also prepared to consider replacing some of the commodity with a risk-free investment. Ian Ibbotson III, CEO and only employee of III, is preparing a synopsis of investment possibilities. Assuming efficient pricing, all the missing numbers in Table 5.22 are uniquely determinable from those given. Complete the table. (Both futures and options are based on an underlying unit at a current price of 100.)

Table 5.22

	Current Investment	Risk-Free	Buy One Futures Contract	Buy One Call Option at 105 Strike Price	Buy One Put Option at 105 Strike Price
Cost Now	100	100		5	
Investment Value After One Year					
Outcome #					
1	95	105			
2	105				
3	115				
4	125				
5	135				

RISK-ADJUSTED DISCOUNT RATES

Net Present Value (NPV) calculations are used as a way to determine whether a stream of cash flows generated by an investment offsets the opportunity cost of the capital used to purchase it. When those cash flows are uncertain, a popular adaptation of the NPV technique is to raise the discount rate by an amount which reflects the degree of uncertainty in the returns. This idea is fairly reasonable at first glance, for it reduces the value of the returns and emphasizes short-term payback. Selecting an appropriate discount rate is a challenge even when the cash flows are certain, but choosing a risk-adjusted discount rate is even harder. Moreover, just as the opportunity cost of funds can vary over time in a way that may be known in advance, so too the degree of uncertainty can vary over time in a way that may be known in advance.

To see some of the problems involved, consider two investments having exactly the same average returns in each year, with the same degree of uncertainty about them. In the first cash flow, the uncertainty about one period's return is completely independent of the uncertainty in all other periods. Just because the first year turns out well tells you nothing about how well you will do in the other periods. A farm, at the mercy of the weather, might be an example. In the second investment all the uncertainty stems from a single event which will be resolved in period 1. Thus, by the end of period 1, all future cash-flows will be known with certainty. If the first year's income is high, all the rest of the cash flows will be high. An R&D venture might be an example.

Which investment would you rather have? The first has a diversification advantage in that good years and bad years will tend to balance out over time, whereas the second investment is all or nothing. On the other hand with the second investment you'll know where you stand after 12 months and be able to plan your future activities with greater precision.

Any methodology that ignores the distinction between these two cases is missing something important. The manner in which the uncertainty about future returns gets resolved as time passes is crucial to our evaluation of them.

Harvard Business College note 9-184-151. Professor David E. Bell prepared this note. Copyright © 1984 by the President and Fellows of Harvard College.

The analysis that follows takes as a premise that the investor wishes to evaluate investments in a manner compatible with the Capital Asset Pricing Model (see "Diversification and Investment Risk" section in Chapter 1.) In this model a one-year investment should be priced in such a way that its expected return r and standard deviation of return s satisfy the formula

$$r = r_F + \frac{cs}{s_M}(r_M - r_F)$$

where r_F is the risk-free rate, r_M is the average return of a fully diversified portfolio ("the market portfolio"), s_M is the standard deviation of return from that portfolio, and c is the correlation between this portfolio and the one-year investment under consideration. To simplify the algebra in what follows we will always assume $r_F = 6\%$, $r_M = 13\%$ and $s_M = 20\%$.

A Danger Signal

Someone offers you an investment that is expected to pay off $100 in one year's time. What is the most you will pay for it? If the risk-free rate were 6% and the $100 were certain, you would pay up to $94.34 for it. But suppose the $100 is uncertain and suppose you feel that the uncertain $100 is worth an equivalent *for sure* of only $80. (This might be because the risk is correlated with the market or, if you're not diversified, it may reflect straightforward risk aversion.) Hence you are now only prepared to pay 80/1.06 or $75.47 for this investment.

What risk-adjusted discount rate would have got us to $75.47 directly? All we have to do is find the value r such that:

$$-\$75.47 + \frac{100}{1 + r} = 0$$

and the answer is 0.325 or 32.5%.

Now let's change the example. Someone would like to pay you money up front in exchange for you becoming responsible for a debt of $100 to be paid in one year. If the debt is a sure $100, you'd take on this liability for $94.34.

But suppose the $100 is not certain and suppose you feel that the uncertain $100 is just as bad as a liability of $120 *for sure*. (This might be because the uncertainty is positively correlated with the market or, if you're not diversified, simply because of risk aversion.) Hence, to meet this obligation you'd require a payment of at least 120/1.06 or $113.21 up front.

What risk-adjusted discount rate would have got us to this answer immediately? That is, for what value r does:

$$+ 113.21 - \frac{100}{1 + r} = 0 \ ?$$

The answer is –0.117 or –11.7%.

A negative discount rate? Not only didn't the rate get adjusted up, it actually fell below zero! When future cashflows are expected to be negative they require a *lower* discount rate, not a higher one. This makes sense; you are adjusting the discount rate in order to penalize the returns for the riskiness of them but raising the discount rate *improves* a negative return.

Many investments have some years in which a net outflow can be expected (in the first few years or at the end) and, presumably, some years in which there is expected a net inflow. Suppose you are offered a cash flow that will require you to pay $100 at the end of year 1 but receive $100 at the end of year 2. Both amounts are uncertain and positively correlated with the market (from your perspective). The equivalent verifiable cashflow is −120 in year 1 and +80 in year 2. Hence it has an NPV of −$42.01:

$$-42.01 = \frac{-120}{1.06} + \frac{80}{(1.06)^2} \ .$$

You should be paid at least $42.01 to take this cashflow. What discount rate gets us the answer immediately? It is r where:

$$-42.01 = \frac{-100}{1 + r} + \frac{100}{(1 + r)^2} \ .$$

Surprisingly this equation never holds no matter what r we pick. (Try it with your calculator.) Putting it another way, there is no risk-adjusted discount rate that correctly values this cash flow.

One-Period Discounting

Consider a one-year investment whose return is estimated at $X with a standard deviation of $S. The uncertainty in the investment has a correlation c with the market. What is its fair value today? If we pay a price $P for it then our expected return is:

$$\frac{X - P}{P} \times 100\% \ .$$

The standard deviation of that percentage return is $\frac{100S}{P}$. (This is because $X \pm S$ becomes $\frac{X-P}{P} \pm \frac{S}{P}$ or $\frac{100(X-P)}{P} \pm \frac{100S}{P}$ in percentage terms.) The correlation is still c. Plugging these values into the first equation in this section gives the equation:

$$\frac{100(X - P)}{P} = 6 + \frac{c\dfrac{100S}{P}}{20}(13 - 6) \ .$$

Multiplying by P and simplifying we get:

$$100X - 100P = 6P + 35cS$$

or

$$100X - 35cS = 106P$$

so

$$P = \frac{100X - 35cS}{106} = \frac{X - 0.35cS}{1.06}$$

This formula is very revealing: to eliminate the risk in the cashflow we would be prepared to pay up to an amount $0.35cS$, the *risk premium*. The net amount $X - 0.35cS$ is the *certainty equivalent*. The net present value is equal to the certainty equivalent discounted back at the *risk-free rate*. Note that this procedure does not depend on whether X is positive or negative!

An investment is expected to return 6000 ± 3000 in one year's time. What is its fair value today if its correlation with the market is 0.75?

$$Answer: \frac{6{,}000 - 0.35 \times 0.75 \times 3{,}000}{1.06} = \$4{,}917 \ .$$

So, as it turns out, the equivalent risk-adjusted discount rate is 22% found by solving the equation

$$4{,}917 = \frac{6{,}000}{1 + r} \ .$$

What would the fair value of the above investment be if $c = -1$?

$$Answer: \frac{6{,}000 + 0.35 \times 3{,}000}{1.06} = \$6{,}651 \ .$$

The equivalent risk-adjusted discount rate is now –10%.

Two-Period Discounting

Multiple periods are easy to handle once you know how to handle one period. All you need to do is "fold back" the cash flow from the horizon just as you would a decision tree.

An investment will return a single payment in two years' time, currently estimated at $6,000 \pm 3,000$. The uncertainty is not dependent at all on events in year 1, but has a correlation of 0.75 with the market in year 2. How much is it worth today?

Answer: At the end of year 1 we will be in exactly the same position as we were in Question 2. Hence we are indifferent between the current cash flow and one in which we receive $4,917 for sure at the end of one year. And that has an NPV of

$$\frac{4{,}917}{1.06} = \$4{,}639 \ .$$

Note that

$$4{,}639 = \frac{6{,}000}{1.06 \times 1.22}$$

so we could think of the $6,000 as having been discounted back at a rate of 22% during the second year (when it's risky) and at 6% in the first (when it's not). Alternatively we could say that the appropriate risk-adjusted discount rate was 13.7% (found by solving $\frac{6{,}000}{(1 + r)^2} = 4{,}639$).

An investment will pay off $2,000 \pm 1,000$ in year 1 ($c = 0.75$) and $4,000 \pm 2,000$ in year 2 ($c = 0.75$). How much is it worth?

Answer: The value of the cash flow in year 2 is

$$\frac{4{,}000 - 0.35 \times 0.75 \times 1{,}000}{(1.06)^2} = \$3.092.7$$

The value of the cash flow received in year 1 is:

$$\frac{2,000 - 0.35 \times 0.75 \times 1,000}{(1.06)} = \$1,639.15 \quad.$$

The total value is \$4,731.85. The internal rate of return (IRR) is given by solving

$$-4,731.85 + \frac{2,000}{1 + r} + \frac{4,000}{(1 + r)^2} = 0 \quad.$$

The IRR is 15.5% which is the "appropriate" single risk-adjusted discount rate.

As we have seen, the discount rate should be adjusted for the risk characteristics of the investment on a period by period basis. Yet there is a certain appeal to using *one* discount rate for all periods. The question we take up in the next section is, when is single rate discounting correct?

When Is One Rate Enough?

The One-Period Case

Suppose we express the standard deviation of a cash flow as a *fraction* of the average cash flow. For example with $6,000 \pm 3,000$ and $10,000 \pm 5,000$ the standard deviation is half the average. Suppose all the cash flows we are going to look at have standard deviations equal to half their mean. Then the formula for the fair current value becomes:

$$\frac{X - 0.35c(0.5X)}{1.06}$$

or

$$X\left(\frac{1 - 0.175c}{1.06}\right) \quad.$$

Now it makes some sense to think of this as X discounted at some rate. We solve for the rate with the relation:

$$\frac{1}{1 + r} = \frac{1 - 0.175c}{1.06} \quad.$$

In general, if the standard deviation is sX (a constant multiple, s, of X) when the average cashflow is X then the formula:

$$1 + r = \frac{1.06}{1 - 0.35cs}$$

gives an appropriate risk-adjusted discount rate r. Table 5.23 gives you an idea of how quickly the risk-adjusted rate increases with cs. Note that cs is a quantity proportional to the systematic risk in a project. When $cs = 0$ the risk-adjusted rate is 6%, the risk-free rate.

Table 5.23

cs	0	0.1	0.2	0.375	0.5	1
r (in percent)	6	9.8	14.0	22.0	28.5	63.1

The interpretation of this table is that if you have a risk that is entirely systematic whose standard deviation is about half the average cashflow, then you should use a discount rate of 28.5%. This is also the rate you should use for a risk that has a standard deviation equal to the average mean but which only has a 0.5 correlation with the market.

An investment is expected to return \$6,000 ± 2,400 in one year's time. Its correlation with the market is 0.5. What is its current fair value?

Answer: We have $s = \frac{2,400}{6,000} = 0.4$ and $cs = 0.4 \times 0.5 = 0.2$. Hence the appropriate discount rate is 14% (from the table). Therefore the fair value is $\frac{6,000}{1.14} = \$5,263$.

Note that the idea of a constant ratio $\frac{S}{X} = s$ isn't so far-fetched. If you had to guess how much money a construction job would take, it seems reasonable to imagine that you could be off by 10% or so no matter what the size of the job. In estimating costs and revenues, people are apt to make percentage errors, not absolute errors.

The Two-Period Case

You have an investment that will give a single payoff in two years' time. As time goes by you will get more and more information about the size of that cashflow. At the moment you feel that in one year's time, your estimate of the actual payoff will be about \$6000 but this is by no means certain. Your forecast now of what your *estimate* will be *then* is \$6,000 ± 3,000. (Think of a random number being drawn from the distribution \$6,000 ± 3,000. This will be your *estimate* of the actual payoff.) Now this estimate is, itself, not an accurate predictor of the actual payoff. You feel that if your estimate in one year is \$E, then your forecast distribution for the actual payoff is $E \pm E/2$.

Your uncertainty about the estimate has correlation c with the market. Also the correlation of your uncertainty about the actual payoff *given* the estimate is also c.

Now let's value this cash flow.

At the end of year 1, if the estimate is E the discounted value of the payoff will be:

$$\frac{E - 0.35c\frac{E}{2}}{1.06} = \frac{E}{1 + r}$$

$$\text{where} \quad 1 + r = \frac{1.06}{1 - 0.175c}.$$

At the time your distribution for E is $6,000 \pm 3,000$, so that the investment is equal in value to one with a payoff of $\frac{6,000}{1+r} \pm \frac{3,000}{1+r}$ at the end of year 1. The value of this right now is:

$$\frac{\frac{6,000}{1+r} - 0.35c\frac{3,000}{1+r}}{1.06} = \frac{6,000}{1+r}\left(\frac{1 - 0.175c}{1.06}\right) = \frac{6,000}{(1+r)^2}.$$

This $6,000 has been discounted back two years (legitimately) at the same rate.

The Bottom Line: A cash flow may be discounted with a single risk-adjusted discount rate for all periods if you expect your estimates of the cash flows in future periods will be updated each year in the following way:

$$\text{New Estimate for a period} = \text{Old Estimate for that period} \pm \left(\begin{array}{l} \text{Constant} \\ \text{Fraction} \end{array} \times \begin{array}{l} \text{Old Estimate} \\ \text{for that period} \end{array} \right)$$

and if the correlation of all the errors with the market is c. In this case the risk-adjusted discount rate is given by the formula:

$$1 + r = \frac{1.06}{1 - 0.35c \,(\text{Constant Fraction})}$$

Example

An investment costing $9,000 will produce revenues at the end of years 1, 2, and 3. Your current estimates of those revenues are $3,000, $4,000 and $5,000 respectively. The standard deviation of the uncertainty associated with the first year's return is $1,000. How the cash flow turns out in year 1 will tell you something about the value of future cash flows. If the $3,000 turns out to be $3,300 you will revise your estimates of future cash flows up by 10% also, that is, to $4,400 and $5,500 respectively. You feel that your estimate of the next year's cash flow will always have a standard deviation equal to about a third of your estimate, so that in this case your standard deviation for the second year cash flow will be 4,400/3 at the end of year 1 and so on. The uncertainty resolved in any given year has correlation 0.6 with the market. Is the investment attractive?

Naturally, I have set things up carefully so that the whole flow can be discounted back at a single rate. And what is that rate? The estimates go up or down by a factor with standard deviation 1/3. The correlation is 0.6 so cs is $\frac{1}{3} \times 0.6 = 0.2$. From Table 5.2 the appropriate discount rate is 14%:

$$\text{NPV} = -9,000 + \frac{3,000}{1.14} + \frac{4,000}{(1.14)^2} + \frac{5,000}{(1.14)^3} = \$84.31$$

The project is just acceptable.

Technically, all that is required to have one discount rate is that the correlation times the "constant fraction" must always be the same, but this is a more complicated condition than we would expect to find in examples.

The "constant fraction" property may well work on revenues alone and on costs alone but is unlikely to work on net cash flows since these may be small or even negative. Since it is also likely that revenues and costs will have different risk characteristics (e.g., debt payments are virtually riskless) it is important to disaggregate the cash flows into component parts that are inherently positive.

How Rates Get Set

For long-term investments, the NPV is very sensitive to the discount rate used. Getting it wrong can have a huge impact on your valuation. Risk- adjusted discount rates, like chain saws, are very efficient if you know how to use them, very dangerous if you do not. The above analysis may be very well in principle, but it does not help us to establish a discount rate in practice. (Rather it provides us with warning signals for when adjusting the discount rate for risk may be very wrong.) To use the above analysis you would need to estimate means, standard deviations, correlations, and risk-free rates way into the future.

Most companies set discount rates as follows. They find a project *whose fair value is known* that is similar in risk characteristics to the one they are valuing. The discount rate depends on such things as the real rate of return, inflation, liquidity, taxes, nature of the systematic risk, and how that risk is resolved over time. All very complicated. But if you know of a project that has the same properties as yours and if you know the fair value of it, you can solve for the discount rate (by finding the IRR). However, given the chain saw analogy above, how can you rely on the two projects being "close enough?" Also, if we assume that most people use rates that are too high, will the use of other people's rates lead you to systematic undervaluation of projects? (You don't want to pay more than the market value, but that's a bidding problem, not a valuation problem.)

EXERCISES ON CAPITAL BUDGETING UNDER UNCERTAINTY

1. A production manager has negotiated a deal in which he will pay only 20% of the cost of some new machinery up front; he will pay the rest after two years. After accounting for inflation and all tax effects, the net cash flow of savings minus costs from the purchase of the machinery is shown in Table 5.24.

Table 5.24

Year 0	Year 1	Year 2	Year 3
$ – 40,000	$136,400	$ – 154,640	$58,300

His company's usual hurdle rate for investments is 10%. Since the savings are speculative, he is wondering if he should use a risk-adjusted discount rate of 25%. On the other hand, the uncertainty in the savings is clearly a matter of chance, unrelated to any other factors, so perhaps the risk-free rate of 6% would be more appropriate.

a. Calculate the net present value of the cash flow for each of the three hurdle rates.

b. Provide an intuitive explanation for these answers.

c. From what you know about the situation, should the investment be made?

2. In this question, assume that the risk-free rate is 6% and that the expected market return is 13% with a standard deviation of 20%.

Investment I_1 is expected to pay off $10,000 in year 1 with a standard deviation of $7,000 and a correlation of 0.75 with the market. In year 2 it is expected to pay off $10,000 with a standard deviation of $3,000 and a correlation of 0.75 with the market.

Investment I_2 is expected to pay off $10,000 in year 1 with a standard deviation of $3,000 and a correlation of 0.75 with the market. In year 2 it is expected to pay off $10,000 with a standard deviation of $7,000 and a correlation of 0.75 with the market.

a. Reason intuitively as to whether you prefer I_1 or I_2.

b. What is the most you should pay for I_1? I_2?

3. Today is January 2, 1994 and you are about to learn whether you will collect an annual bonus of $10,000 or not from your employer. Your employer pays you this bonus, apparently at random, 50% of the time. The bonus is significant to you since your only source of income is your base salary, also $10,000. However, your employer does offer one service. He will borrow or lend money at 0% interest. There is no inflation. No one else will lend or borrow money from you at any rates. Starting January 1, 1996, you will begin a new extremely well-paid job. Your future employer will not loan you any money.

In short, your disposable income (you do not pay tax) will be $10,000 or $20,000 for each of the next two years. If you knew that you'd be getting $20,000 in one year and $10,000 in the other you would borrow or lend $5,000 to equalize the disposable income in the two years.

Your preference curve for a standard of living consistent with various levels of consumption in a year is given by Table 5.25.

Table 5.25

Amount Spent 1 Year (Thousands)	Standard of Living (Thousands)
0	0
1	1.0
2	1.9
3	2.8
4	3.6
5	4.4
6	5.1
7	5.8
8	6.4
9	7.0
10	7.5
11	8.0
12	8.4
13	8.8
14	9.1
15	9.4
16	9.6
17	9.8
18	9.9
19	10.0
20	10.0

For example, consuming $8,000 for each of two years would give the same satisfaction as spending $5,000 in one year and $12,000 in the other. It is always the case that an even distribution of a fixed income over two years would maximize total preference.

a. How much should you borrow if your first-year bonus is $0?

b. How much should you lend if your first-year bonus is $10,000?

c. If your bonus is $0 this year, how much would you pay to know now what your bonus next year will be?

d. Would you, before hearing this year's bonus, agree to have next year's bonus exactly the same as this year's?

THE SPRUCE BUDWORM

In early June 1976, Richard Hatfield, Premier of New Brunswick, sat with his cabinet in the provincial capital of Fredericton. Twenty miles away, planes loaded with chemical insecticide sat on a runway awaiting Hatfield's permission to begin spraying the forest. The spruce budworm was responsible for decimating the timber forests of Eastern Canada, and New Brunswick's economy would be crippled without the annual spray program. Environmental groups had long objected to the extensive, indiscriminate use of pesticides but with the province's economy at stake, these objectives had been overridden. In 1975, however, a health scare had begun when two children died of a disease called Reye's Syndrome, shortly after local forests were sprayed.

To be maximally effective, spraying must take place in a 3-4 day "window" at a crucial stage of the budworm's larval development. Each year the cabinet met at the very last minute to decide whether to call off the spraying for that year. Each year, despite the escalating cost of spraying and the unfavorable publicity that the morning newspapers would bring, the spectre of economic disaster forced them to spray, and 1976 proved to be no different.

Background

The spruce budworm is a moth which during its larval stage feeds on the buds and needles of balsam fir and spruce trees. Historically, spruce budworms generally remain at population densities so low that it could be called a rare species; but periodically, when forest conditions and weather are favorable, it is "released" from this endemic level and erupts to cause severe defoliation and tree mortality over large areas, for five to ten years.

Budworm epidemics have occurred in the spruce-fir forests of Northern America in 1770, 1806, 1878, 1910, and intermittently since 1950. Exhibit 1 shows the map of Eastern North America, indicating the area of spruce budworm infestations since 1909.

Another outbreak would probably kill 40% or more of the forest's spruce-fir volume. Because larger trees suffer a higher mortality rate, this would probably mean an end to spruce-fir saw milling in the area within a decade if the epidemics were not controlled or prevented. The pulp and paper industry could continue longer by conducting intense salvage operations and utilizing surviving timber and small trees, but the level of activity would be greatly decreased. After an outbreak it would take 40 years to establish and grow another crop of merchantable timber; recovery could take even longer if an intense outbreak also destroyed the spruce-fir regeneration.

Harvard Business School case 9-183-134. Professor David E. Bell prepared this case. Copyright © 1982 by the President and Fellows of Harvard College.

In 1952 when it became clear that an outbreak had begun, New Brunswick began spraying large acreage of the forest with DDT. This controlled the budworm population, but only for one year. The 10% or so of the budworm that survived were sufficient to maintain the threat the next year. So the province sprayed again. While regular spraying has undoubtedly saved the lumber industry in the short term, it has had a number of undesirable side effects. The most direct effect has been the increasing cost of the spraying operation. It is estimated that one-time aerial spraying costs $3.00 per acre, and millions of acres are sprayed. A second consequence of the spraying program has been that the outbreak has never subsided. Thirty years after it began, the threat remains. Earlier outbreaks collapsed after five to seven years because the budworm multiplied to such an extent that they consumed all the available foliage and then starved. Only a few would survive and the population would remain low during the 40-50 years it would take for the forest to regenerate, providing the food supply to fuel another outbreak.

A third consequence is the environmental harm caused by such large-scale doses of DDT. But leaving the forest to face destruction by the budworm would have environmental implications too. The change in wildlife habitat would alter the composition of wildlife populations. Elimination of the mature forest cover would reduce the numbers in some songbird species, while increasing the number of birds in species suited for a regrowing bushy forest. The exposure of streams to direct sunlight would raise water temperatures, decreasing dissolved oxygen levels causing lower fish growth and vigor; cool water is needed for good trout habitat. Large areas of dead and dying timber creates a major fire hazard; dead balsam fir makes fire line construction difficult and provides a bed for ignition and spread of spot fires. Moreover, the decreased aesthetic beauty of the forest and the increased hazard from falling trees and fire would affect campers and hiking enthusiasts.

Substitutes for DDT were tested in an effort to find a chemical that had similar effectiveness on the budworm but less damage on flora and fauna. Control measures other than aerial spraying of chemical insecticides had been tried and were under development. Releases of budworm parasites and predators had not been effective because the introduced species had not become established. Aerial spraying of budworm pathogen had not achieved foliage protection or adequate suppression of budworm population densities. Silviculture control had some potential and was being implemented. For example, a budworm-resistant species of fir, black spruce, was being planted (from airplanes) by an independent forester. Silviculture by itself was not a complete solution because of the time required for its implementation and its inability to eliminate infestations; it could only reduce the forest's susceptibility.

The 1976 Task Force

The pressures on the New Brunswick government increased every year. The lumber industry grew more mechanized and capital-intensive, and faced stiffer competition in world markets from regions such as Georgia where tree growth was faster and pest problems fewer. Environmental groups became increasingly vocal. The Reye's Syndrome incident, thought by health officials to be unrelated to the spray program, was nevertheless a public relations nightmare. In the summer of 1976 the cabinet set up a special task force to evaluate budworm control alternatives for the future, and to evaluate the effectiveness of those used in the past.

This was not the first time such a study had been performed. Every few years a report had been written and duly assigned to collect dust on ministerial shelves. Gordon Baskerville, who was to lead this task force, felt he might have an advantage over his predecessors in that a group of researchers at the University of British Columbia had built a simulation model of the New Brunswick forest that was sophisticated enough to give reliable forecasts of the effects of differing forest management strategies. All that had to be done was to try various combinations of spraying and logging strategies and see which came out best.

Baskerville appreciated, though, that previous reports had been ignored because what was "best" for one person was not necessarily "best" in the eyes of another. This was especially true of politicians, in his view. It was always difficult to predict what they really wanted.

He thought back to February when he had been interviewed by one of the simulation model research team, who had been interested in establishing by what criterion the outcomes of the simulation trials should be judged. It was only then that Baskerville had realized how difficult it was to express exactly what one's objectives are in a complex problem such as this. (A brief summary of the morning's discussion is shown in Exhibit 2.)

It occurred to him that if this same person could interview a spectrum of policy-making individuals within New Brunswick, he, Baskerville, would have a much better idea of what management alternatives he could propose in his report that would give it some chance of being implemented.

The Simulation Model

A computer program which simulated one year of a 6 × 9 mile region of forest was constructed based on 50 years of data assembled by provincial biologists and foresters. Initial data are the number of trees, by species and by age, the foliage density on the trees (which will vary according to budworm activity) and the density of budworm eggs. The program would then estimate survival rates of the budworm according to randomly generated weather patterns, the foliage supply and any spraying activity. It would produce an end-of-year inventory of trees recognizing mortality due to budworn, logging, and natural death (old age).

This program would be replicated 265 times to reflect a 265 × 6 × 9 = 14,310 square mile area of forest that approximated the province of New Brunswick.

One last calculation was the end-of-year egg count. The moths tended to lay their eggs near to their own tree if foliage conditions were good, but if overcrowding was a problem they would fly above the trees and be carried by the wind for distances of up to 100 miles, and an average of 50. (A strong westerly wind that would carry the moths out into the Atlantic, or at least into Nova Scotia, was very desirable but for the fact that Ontario, to the west, had outbreaks too.) A wind pattern was generated according to the historical distribution of prevailing winds and the eggs assigned to new sites according to a historical distribution of distances travelled (Exhibit 3).

This completed the simulation of one year (Exhibit 4). To test the reliability of the program, it was necessary to run it for 200-year periods. This was to make sure the model correctly reproduced the 40-70 year cycle of outbreaks that was known to occur without man's intervention. At first, the model only produced seven-year cycles. Finally, it was realized that this was because the predatory action of birds had been omitted. When the budworm is at very low densities, birds feeding on them are sufficient to keep populations low. Since the budworms thrive only on new foliage from old trees, it takes 40 years or so after an outbreak for there to *be* any old trees. The next outbreak occurs when a sequence of warm, dry summers allows the budworm to reproduce faster than the food requirements of the local birds. When the bird consumption was ignored, the budworms were able to "break out" whenever the foliage was plentiful. Because there was less time between outbreaks, there was less foliage, the outbreaks were not so intense, the majority of trees survived and quickly produced more foliage, precipitating another outbreak.

This accidental discovery led to the idea of killing the birds rather than the budworm, since more frequent outbreaks, while slowing the growth of trees, did not kill them. This proved to be an impracticality.

Extensive testing of the model demonstrated that it was consistent with qualitative insights about the way the forest would develop under a variety of starting conditions. In particular, when the model was given the 1952 forest inventory, and the historical weather, wind and spraying conditions were used, it reproduced the 1976 forest conditions quite accurately. Exhibit 5 provides an illustration of the graphic capabilities of the model and shows how the forest would develop under three different spraying strategies. Each rectangle is a three-dimensional graph of egg densities. The exhibit demonstrates the tendency of spraying to extend rather than eliminate outbreaks. Exhibit 6 continues the no-spray trial to demonstrate the recurrence of an outbreak after a period of dormancy.

Use of the Simulation Model

The model was used to investigate various management strategies for the forest. Since future weather is uncertain, it was necessary to test each strategy over many trials to get a sense of the stability of the forest's response. The most important strategy the cabinet wanted to test was to see what would have happened had they not sprayed at all since 1952; that is, they wanted to know if spraying had been worth it.

The simulation was run with three strategies:

1. Historical logging and no spray.
2. Historical logging and historical spray.
3. Historical logging with budworm assumed extinct.

Exhibit 7 shows the status of the forest and industry in 1952 and under the two realistic scenarios. The lower half of the exhibit shows projections of the damage done by pursuing these two strategies in the future, in comparison with a no-budworm scenario. For these calculations the starting point is the actual 1976 conditions.

A problem with the simulation model was that it was very expensive to test strategies. One fifty-year trial cost $50. While this was acceptable for testing obvious strategies, it did not permit experimentation with complex new strategies. Also the output from one trial was substantial, since reporting was for 265 sites times 50 years. Two developments were needed. The first was some simplification of the simulation model that would permit reliable screening of alternative strategies. The second was the development of a quantitative preference function which would permit the screening to take place without direct human involvement.

The Dynamic Program

A simplified model was constructed of a 6 × 9 site in which the *state* of the forest was represented by four variables: the percentage of young trees (≤ 9 years), the percentage of old trees (≥ 30 years), the egg density, and the foliage density. A preference function was formulated which discounted back at 5% the profits from the logging industry less the spraying costs.

Exhibits 8 and 9 show samples from the optimal strategies produced by the optimization program. Each graph shows what to do with a tree of a given age, foliage density, and egg density. Young trees should not be sprayed or logged because they are not worth anything and are easily replaced. Old trees should be logged whatever their budworm condition. Middle-aged trees should be treated according to their age, foliage and egg densities, The odd-square gap in many of the graphs is perplexing and no satisfactory explanation was ever found. The possibility that it was caused by a programming error was investigated at length.

After detailed examination of these results, it was concluded that the dynamic program was suggesting a strategy that was subtly different from historical management. Historically, spray was applied to trees that were about to die in order to save them. This was a very myopic strategy that was rejected by the forward-looking dynamic program. It calculated (implicitly) that trees that were saved from immediate death would only have to be resprayed the following year if they had not been logged. It was recommending to spray only those trees that were just beginning to be infected in the hope of extinguishing the budworm from that area for more than just a year.

This idea of prevention rather than cure suggested two other strategies to the scientists. Both were designed with a view to reducing dependency on insecticides. The first was to be more flexible in where to cut. Mills, quite naturally were apt to cut those trees of reasonable size that were nearest to its mills because this reduced haulage costs. If money could be diverted from insecticides to subsidizing haulage costs, trees that were heavily infested could be cut down rather than sprayed. The second strategy relied on the introduction of a budworm disease to an area to keep the population in check once it had been controlled by natural collapse or by logging.

These four strategies (historical, dynamic program, active logging, and controlling by disease) were run on the simulation model. Exhibits 10, 11, 12 and 13 show plots of five key criteria against time for one fairly typical trial in each case. Forest volume is the amount of growing wood. Harvest cost varies with distance travelled and the size of trees being cut (bigger ones are cheaper per cunit). Relative unemployment is the proportion of people unemployed relative to the maximum that could be employed if mills were running at achievable capacity. The recreational index was constructed to illustrate how desirable the forest was for camping, hiking and so on. Insecticide applications are shown as a fraction of the forest sprayed, though no adjustment was made for dosage.

The Preference Study

In August 1976 Baskerville wanted the preference analyst from the simulation team to interview a variety of influential individuals in New Brunswick including the Premier and Cabinet officers to ascertain a criterion for selecting among the different strategies. The following are summaries of what he heard, categorized by profession.

Silviculturists

Their main concern was to improve the predictability of the forest. The age structure of the forest was one key to this since an elderly forest (which was currently the case) was extremely susceptible to budworm outbreaks. Their thought was that if the budworm outbreaks could be controlled so that outbreaks occurred sequentially in different parts of the province, rather than simultaneously, as had been the case historically, a more stable age structure would result. Then there would always be areas in which to lumber. One expert pointed out that total eradication of the budworm was in fact undesirable, partly because of the way in which it preserved the balance between balsam, spruce, and birch tree populations, and partly for the rationale that "better the devil you know."

Civil Servants

The prevailing view was that the forest economy was so vital to the welfare of New Brunswick that no expense or strategy could be ignored if it led to the continued health of that economy. Issues such as the negative effects of spraying were felt to be wholly secondary. One person pointed out that tourism would not be affected by any policy changes because most tourists came to New Brunswick only for the purpose of passing through to Nova Scotia. In any case, most of the money they spent was ultimately destined for the United States since many tourist stops were owned by Americans. At the very worst, $40 million in sales could be lost.

It was the day-to-day lives of the population that was the greatest concern. The forest was a way of life so that any interruption to it meant more than sheer dollar loss. People had to have good quality, satisfying jobs in forest-related industries. Nor could a temporary suspension of activities be allowed because a continued presence of New Brunswick wood in world markets was required.

Subject to these concerns their goals tended to be to preserve the forest for the indefinite future and secondly to alleviate acquired disparities within the province. It would be unfortunate if forest conditions improved in the south relative to those in the north, for example.

Politicians

The message here is quite clear. If you intend making policies that involve a reduction in jobs you'd better have a cast-iron provable reason for doing so. A forest policy once chosen has to be self-justifying to the people. The general view was that even if the forest would be gone within 25 years if present policies were continued, it would not be feasible to reduce employment by more than 10%–15% over a period of several years. If there was a substantial public awareness that something drastic had to be done, unemployment might be a possibility, but even then it would be undesirable.

In reference to the problem that a forest policy is necessarily a long-term proposition, the feeling was that a clearly defined policy could be expected to have continuity between changing administrations.

Federal Government

Substantial funds for forest preservation had been paid regularly in recent years to the province without any sign that the situation was improving or that the funds were being used for long-term improvements. They felt it was not their role to provide day-to-day support for a province's economy but rather to provide one-time capital to get the region permanently on the right track. Future funding would likely require them to be convinced that long-term improvement was likely.

Forest Industry

A major concern was that if policies were introduced that cut back on production opportunities, investors would go elsewhere. There had been substantial investment in large, modern, expensive equipment over the last 10 years, building for the future, and that future was now. It would be difficult to have investor confidence at a future time if those past investments were to fail now.

Their goals were the continued profitability of their company and preservation of the forest. They were somewhat surprised at the thought that these two goals might be contradictory.

They saw their jobs as being complicated by three sets of uncertainties: the world market, government policy, and the budworm—in decreasing order of importance. They felt that the latter two could be controlled and should be.

The analyst summarized his report to Baskerville in these words:

"We know now which policies would *not* be accepted if presented. We can exclude, in order of importance:

a. those that cause more than a 10% reduction in employment in the near future,

b. those that fail to give any long-term improvement in the forest,

c. those where continued extensive spraying is the expectation indefinitely."

Baskerville grinned as he laid down the report.

The problem is that they all believe that if we only think hard enough we can come up with a solution that allows us to continue cutting down the forest and protect the long-term growth of the forest. Until they realize those aren't both attainable we'll never settle down with a fixed long-term policy. And as for not lowering employment by more than 10% over the next few years, normal year-by-year fluctuation can be of the order of 30%. I'm going to have to find some way of presenting the alternatives in such a way that it will be clear there is no magic solution.

Exhibit 1

MAP OF EASTERN NORTH AMERICA SHOWING THE AREA OF SPRUCE BUDWORM INFESTATIONS SINCE 1909

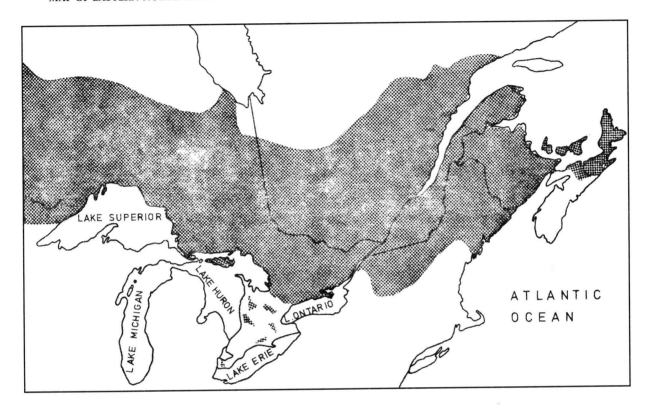

Exhibit 2 _____

PREFERENCES OF BASKERVILLE FOR FOREST ALTERNATIVES

GENERAL CONCERNS

1. That the forest economy be stable over time.
2. Providing an opportunity for the small holder to sell his wood.
3. Some mills had been forced to swap their timber lands for crown lands so that a new government-owned mill could have a large enough service area. It was especially important that all these mills did not lose their harvest potential (at least 10 cunits/acre).
4. Must not clear out more than 300 acres in one place because this would impact deer and moose survival, as well as causing erosion. No clearcutting around rivers because this might harm the salmon population.
5. Potential effects on tourism should be minimized or enhanced.

ATTRIBUTES

	Title	Units	Range
X_1	Amount of saw woods (hardwood) harvested	% of mill capacity	0–100
X_{2i}	Amount of pulpwood in region i i = 1, 2, 3, 5	% of mill capacity	20–100
X_3	Salmon population	Avg. cunits/acre harvested	5–15
X_4	Tourism	Proportion of "Good" areas	0–1
X_5	Delivery Cost to the Mill of a Harvest Cunit	Dollars	30–60
X_6	Acres Sprayed by Insectide	Acres	0–5.5 million

Exhibit 3 _____

MOTH DISPERSAL IN HYPOTHETICAL FOREST

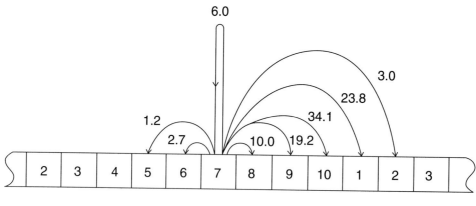

West   East

(Examples of dispersal probabilities for moths dispersing from site 7 are given as percentages, not necessarily resulted in an average distance of 50 miles.)

Exhibit 4

THE BASIC MODEL STRUCTURE FOR THE BUDWORM/FOREST SIMULATION MODEL

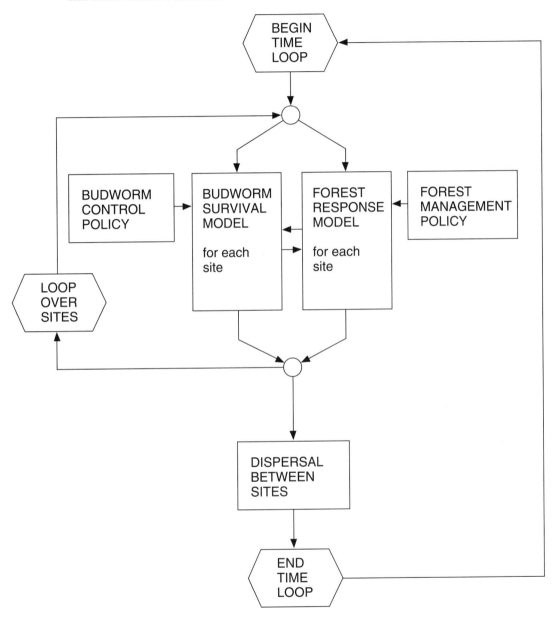

Budworm survival, forest response and control policies are independent for each of the 265 sites. Once each year dispersal occurs between the sites and then the process is repeated for the next simulated year.

Exhibit 5A

COMPUTER SIMULATION MAPS OF BUDWORM EGG DENSITY FOR THREE SCENARIOS: (1) NO SPRAYING; (2) SPRAYING AT INTENSITY 2; (3) SPRAYING AT INTENSITY 6.

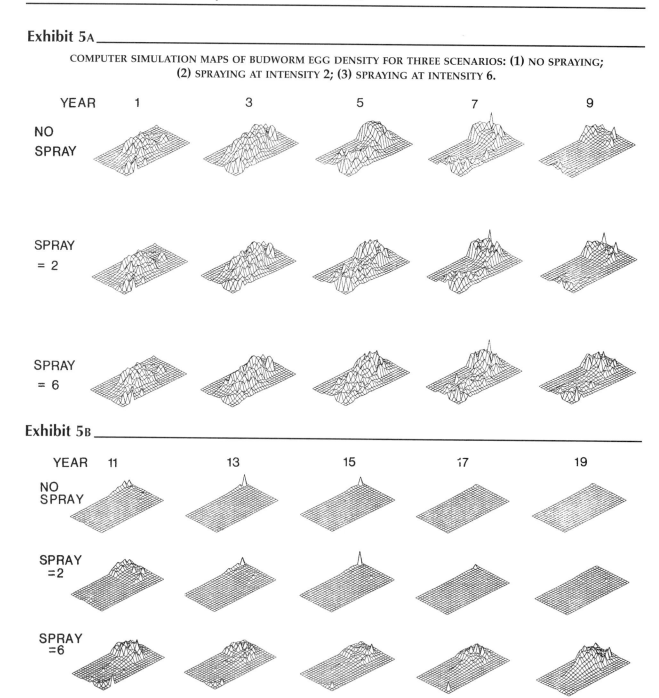

Exhibit 5B

Exhibit 6 _____

THIS IS A CONTINUATION OF THE NO SPRAY SIMULATION IN EXHIBIT 5.
IT SHOWS HOW A SECOND OUTBREAK BEGINS IN THE FOURTH DECADE.

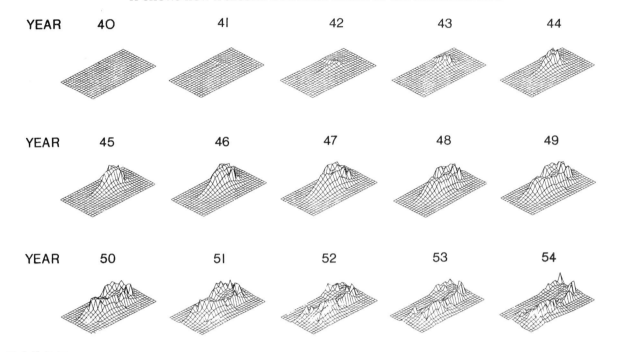

Exhibit 7 _____

	1952 level	1976 level with no protection 1952-1976	1976 level with historical protection 1952-1976
	PROJECTIONS FROM SIMULATION MODEL		
Annual harvest (cunits)	1,404,000	1,268,000	2,500,000
Annual value added ($)	143,000,000	128,000,000	416,000,000
Annual wages ($)	63,000,000	43,000,000	128,000,000
Annual man-years employed	11,150	4,313	11,055
Total forest inventory (cunits)	104,000,000	32,120,000	100,000,000

Deterministic run using historical weather.

	If we protect and maintain present passive management	If we don't protect
Total loss of harvest (cunits) 1977-2027	3,000,000	50,000,000
Total loss of value added ($) 1977-2027	87,200,000	2,079,000,000
Total loss of wages ($) 1977-2027	27,600,000	709,000,000
Total loss of man-years employment 1977-2027	8,900	186,000
Total forest inventory (cunits) in 2027	34,000,000	6,000,000

Typical results from simulation for next 50 years starting from 1976 conditions.

Exhibit 8

POLICY TABLES FOR REPRESENTATIVE AGES
(PRICE = $55/CUNIT; ρ =.05; F_T = FOLIAGE LEVEL; LGE_D = LOG (EGG DENSITY))

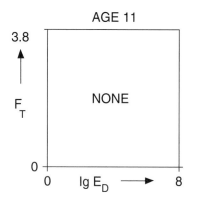

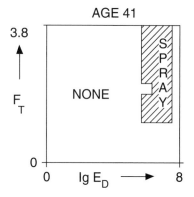

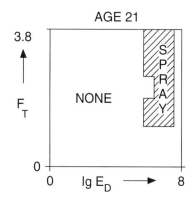

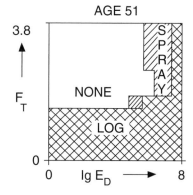

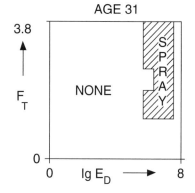

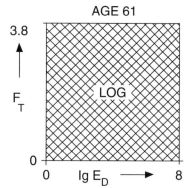

From IIASA Project Status Report.

Exhibit 9

POLICY TABLES FOR AGES **42-47**
(PRICE = **$55**/CUNIT; ρ =.05; F_T = FOLIAGE LEVEL; LGE_D = LOG (EGG DENSITY))

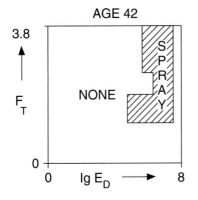

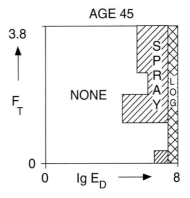

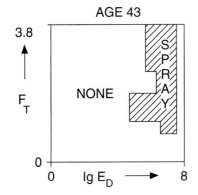

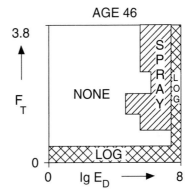

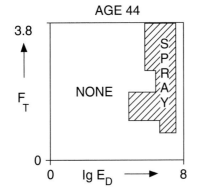

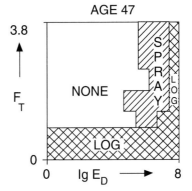

From IIASA Project Status Report.

Exhibit 10

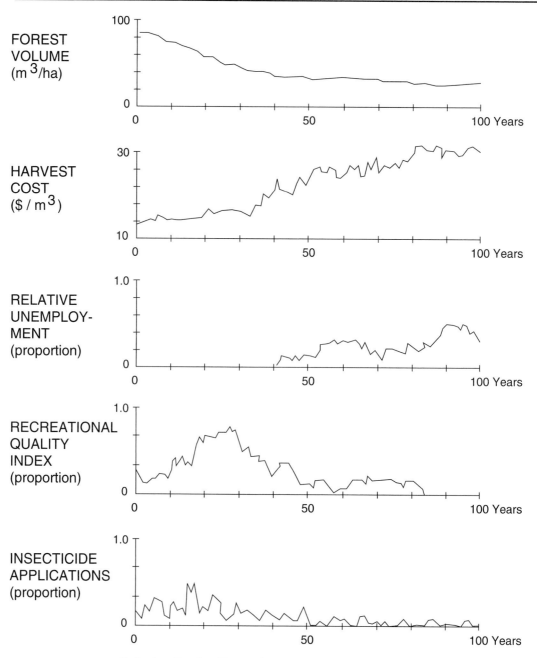

FOREST
VOLUME
(m³/ha)

HARVEST
COST
($ / m³)

RELATIVE
UNEMPLOY-
MENT
(proportion)

RECREATIONAL
QUALITY
INDEX
(proportion)

INSECTICIDE
APPLICATIONS
(proportion)

Projections Based on Historical Management

Exhibit 11

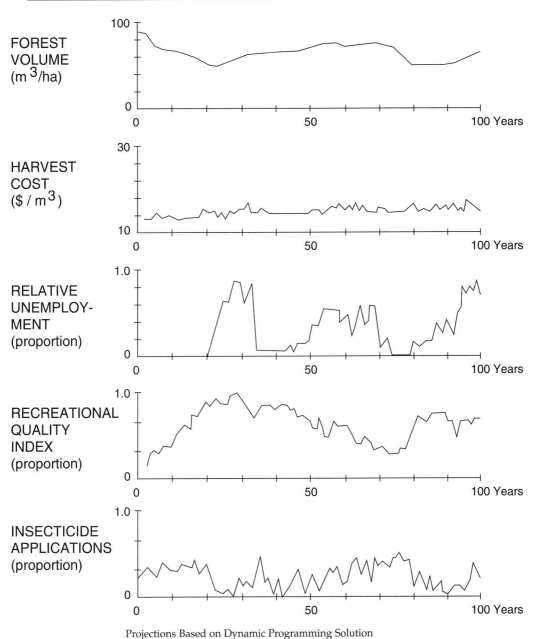

Projections Based on Dynamic Programming Solution

Exhibit 12

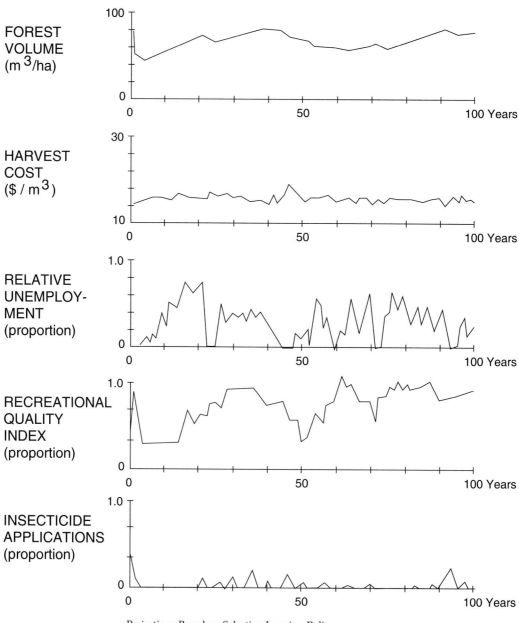

Projections Based on Selective Logging Policy

Exhibit 13

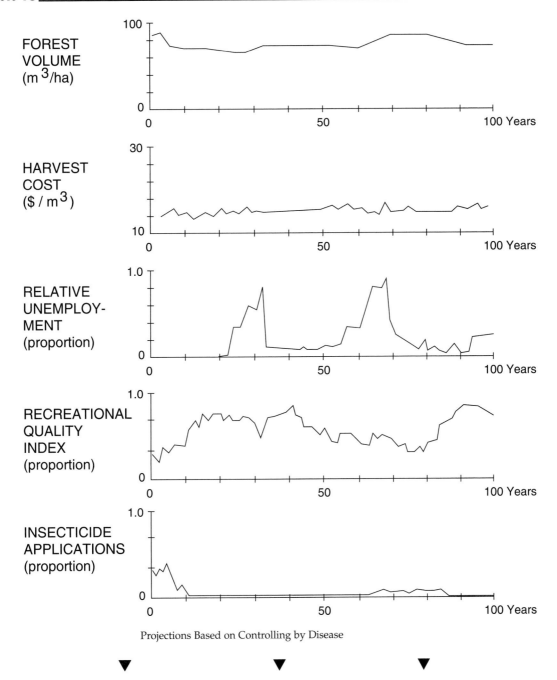

FOREST VOLUME (m^3/ha)

HARVEST COST ($ / m^3)

RELATIVE UNEMPLOY-MENT (proportion)

RECREATIONAL QUALITY INDEX (proportion)

INSECTICIDE APPLICATIONS (proportion)

Projections Based on Controlling by Disease

MULTI-PERSON RISKS

In this last chapter we look at situations where much of the risk derives from the actions of others. What can we do to lower the risk to ourselves in these situations? The chapter begins with a traditional risk management situation in which a self-insurance strategy leads to a proactive emphasis on loss prevention. Written contracts are a way to encourage others to be attentive to risks that concern you: in three cases we explore some of the essentials in designing such contracts. Our final case brings us back to the cast of characters at Breakfast Foods. This short case strikes at the heart of all we have covered.

THE RISK MANAGEMENT FOUNDATION OF THE HARVARD MEDICAL INSTITUTIONS

Late one evening in August 1981, Daniel Creasey, Harvard MBA '67, was reviewing the medical malpractice self-insurance program of the Harvard Medical Institutions. Twelve institutions with a total of 4,100 beds and 4,300 physicians were involved in the program (Exhibit 1). The following morning he was to make a presentation of the annual financial statistics to the overseeing committee and make proposals for the future development of the program.

When the premiums dam burst in the medical malpractice insurance business, Creasey had been hired by the Harvard affiliated medical institutions to examine the possibility of setting up a self-insurance program. After a decision had been taken to go ahead with the program, he had been placed in charge of it.

The program had been a success from the outset in terms of yielding a reduction in premium costs. However, the problem of reducing the frequency of medical mishaps had been less tractable. Institutionally, the Risk Management Foundation had been successful in penetrating the organizations of the participating hospitals, but its impact could not yet be seen in a statistical reduction of mishaps.

Harvard Business School case 9-182-170. Professor David E. Bell prepared this case. Copyright © 1982 by the President and Fellows of Harvard College.

Medical Malpractice Background

Of all malpractice incidents resulting in an indemnity payment 78% occur in hospitals. This was one of several significant findings reported in a special medical malpractice closed-claims study conducted by the National Association of Insurance Commissioners of 71,782 claims closed between July 1975 and December 1978 by 128 insurers throughout the country.

During that period $876 million was paid out in total indemnity, with 40% of the amount paid in 1978 alone. In 1977 and 1978 the average indemnity payment rose 30%, leading some experts to project annual national payouts of $1 billion in the next few years.

This increase appeared to be due in part to a growing number of large settlements, rising defense costs, and general inflation. Single indemnity payments of $50,000 or more increased by 20% in 1978. Awards of over $1 million were also on the upswing with 23 such awards reported in 1978 compared with only five in 1975. This inflation in claim sizes was most noticeable in cases of grave permanent injury such as cardiac arrest and severe brain damage. These injuries occurred often from anaesthetic mishaps, patient monitoring difficulties, and birth injuries. The average indemnity for a single grave injury jumped 63% during the study period to almost $350,000.

Reason for High Malpractice Premiums

When Dan Creasey had first looked at medical malpractice in the early seventies, the increasing volume of claims was already very noticeable. However, little effort had been made within hospitals to launch programs to minimize the likelihood of medical mishaps with an *ex ante*, preventative focus or, to limit liabilities *ex post* after a mishap had occurred.

Part of the reason for this neglect lay in the organizational structure of hospitals. The hierarchies of the medical and administrative professionals are completely independent. Few mechanisms exist to integrate their efforts to come up with joint solutions to problems that have both medical and administrative aspects. Thus, instead of setting up collaborative measures to deal with medical malpractice, the standard procedure had been to transfer the problem out to the insurance companies.

The insurance companies, for their part, regarded the medical malpractice business as a stepchild among their various lines of insurance. They did not examine the particular risk problems of the medical business and simply used procedures developed in the more traditional lines of the property and casualty business. Mr. Creasey noticed for instance, that insurance companies did not adequately discriminate between geographical areas with differing malpractice histories. Twenty-five percent of the premium was based on local loss experience but the other 75% was based on national figures. States like Massachusetts with low claims histories were penalized by being pooled with states like California that had high claims histories. Nor were institutions with higher levels of practice and peer review recognized by lower premiums. Also, premium rates were determined in part by projections of *future* claims resulting from malpractice occurrences that took place during the policy year. There was an in-built conservatism in these protections which resulted in inflated premium charges.

These drawbacks suggested some clear-cut possibilities for insurance cost reductions. They were still shaping in Creasey's mind when a severe turmoil in the insurance industry in 1974 severely curtailed their underwriting programs and led to the withdrawal of insurance companies from the less attractive lines of business including medical malpractice. In the seller's market that resulted, medical care institutions began to lose their institutional policies and ran into increased administrative difficulties and costs simultaneously with a severe acceleration in rates. Renewals were at premium rates of 10 to 20 times those of the prior year and bore no relation to the level of claims being paid. This crisis resulted in urgent discussions between the Harvard affiliated medical institutions to investigate means to control their insurance costs.

CRICO

A committee proposed collective self-insurance for the institutions via a "captive" insurance company. The program was to provide an aggregate coverage of $50,000,000 of which $5,000,000 would be collective self-insurance provided through the captive and $45,000,000 would be in the form of excess insurance purchased jointly from conventional excess insurance carriers.

The captive was named the Controlled Risk Insurance Company Limited (CRICO), and for tax reasons it was located in the Cayman Islands. The paid-in capitalization of CRICO at the outset was $253,000 divided equally among the participating institutions through the ownership of 253,000 shares @ $1 per share. Since the company would collect $3,200,000 as premiums in the first year, and its maximum possible liability was $5,000,000, the share holders were obligated to meet additional assessments of no more than $1,800,000 (divided up according to share-holding) in the event of the program running into financial adversity through unanticipated claims volume in the first year.

The initial premium rates were established at 73% of the Joint Underwriting Association (JUA) rates with the expectation that this figure would decline to 60% of the JUA rate over time. The JUA was a residual underwriting pool created under the auspices of the state of Massachusetts in 1975, when all of the conventional underwriters withdrew from the state.

The premium charged to cover the malpractice and general liability of an institution as a corporate entity and its nonphysician employees as individuals was calculated as the sum of a specified charge per bed and a specified charge per outpatient visit. The premium charged for the personal coverage provided to physicians was a function of their specialty.

The primary policy provided a coverage on claims-made basis. That is, only claims actually made during the period of coverage were to be covered, in contrast with the conventional occurrence-based policy which covered all claims resulting from events during the coverage period no matter at what subsequent date they materialized. The advantage of the claims-made arrangement was that it did not need to anticipate future financial flows, and thus could relate current premiums to current claims. As the program progressed over time, the coverage would expand backwards, covering all events since the date of its inception.

The Risk Management Foundation

Setting up the captive proved to be fairly straightforward. As far as the individual hospitals and physicians were concerned, all that had changed was the name of their insurer. But Creasey's next step was to set up The Risk Management Foundation (RMF) to handle all loss control and claims management services for CRICO. The outside insurance company (AIG), which had been replaced by CRICO, had continued to provide these services. Creasey was able to minimize the visibility of this most recent change by hiring Jack Coughlan as RMF's claims manager. Jack was already running the claims management process for CRICO but as an employee of AIG.

An entirely new face, however, was that of Jim Holzer, a lawyer with a background in medical administration, hired by Creasey to run the loss control function. While Coughlan typically only met with physicians *after* an incident, Holzer would be considerably more visible as the one responsible for finding ways to reduce the chance of such incidents occurring at all. Since loss control measures had been minimal up to this time, there was a possibility that medical staffs might resist attempts at "bureaucratic intervention" in their activities.

Loss Control

The risks that need to be controlled in a hospital are of three kinds:

) Physical plant and equipment inadequacies or malfunctions
) Deficiencies in standards and practice
) Human error

Holzer's first efforts were to set up information gathering and monitoring operations within each hospital. Various sources of information—from clinical reports to financial data—were put under the charge of a single coordinating administrator who was in turn under the direction of a top level quality assurance committee. This coordinator was Holzer's contact in each hospital and thus a link in the chain forged between the risk management areas in the various hospitals.

One of the basic information flows through this system was the *incident report*. This was a record of all abnormal happenings in the hospital from trips and falls to apparatus malfunctions. Included in these reports would be events resulting from human errors, e.g., drug and nursing errors. This provided a vital database from which to assess the nature of incidents and was a vital component in the claims management process. Incident reports originated at the source of a mishap and would be made out by the medical personnel involved or by a witness. They would then be handed over to the risk control coordinator within the hospital who would make a record of them and forward copies to Mr. Holzer's central office. The subset of these reports that might possibly result in liability claims would be passed on to the claims office.

Holzer also tried to raise the consciousness of medical personnel to the need for minimizing risk. He gave lectures and presentations and published a bi-monthly newsletter—the *Forum*—providing a miscellany of materials bearing on risk management through sections like "Legal Forum," "Safety Forum," and case studies of individual incidents.

Holzer felt that the number of incidents related to equipment could be reduced. However, deficiencies in practice and, more importantly, attitudes towards loss control appeared a good deal less tractable.

The problem of physicians with declining capacity illustrates the difficulties in this area. Current procedures require a doctor to establish his or her credentials to practice only once in his career—at the outset, when he collected his qualifications. It is true that a physician's association with a hospital is reviewed each year by that hospital's Chief of Service, but these reviews are apt to be formalities after the initial accreditation.

This was a key concern, yet little could be done due to the unique structure of the medical profession and its status with respect to the lay public. Medical education, medical research, standards of practice and the supply of qualified professionals were entirely in medical hands. Furthermore, the profession was jealous in preserving its prerogatives. Fraternal links within the profession were strong, which frequently acted in favor of a practitioner with diminished capabilities but against the public at large. With the growth of consumerism generally, medical practice was coming under larger public scrutiny but in a very gradualist fashion. The large claims awarded by courts could be regarded as symptomatic of this trend.

Claims Adjustment

The handling of claims may be viewed as a tripartite task: investigation, evaluation, and negotiation. In order to establish medical malpractice, it is not sufficient merely to identify damage. Damage as the outcome of negligence is essential to sustain malpractice charges.

The case history of Mr. Rajiv illustrates some of the problems of claims adjustment. The patient had been the victim of an arthritic condition since birth that severely limited his ability to move his joints. By means of new techniques it became feasible to replace the defective bone structure of the joints with a synthetic bone-like cement and other artificial materials. The Brigham Hospital specialized in this procedure and Mr. Rajiv was brought over from his home town, Delhi, to the hospital for the operation. The operation was demanding both in terms of technical skills and due to its length and complexity. The surgical team had to work in shifts. Nevertheless, the operation itself was successful. However, in removing the patient from the anaesthesia, the anaesthetist inadvertently switched off the wrong button on the anaesthesia machine. The patient was deprived of oxygen and died. Pinning down the responsibility for the damage was complicated by the fact that (a) the anaesthetist had been on duty throughout the operation so that fatigue became a factor in his actions. The responsibility for the consequences of these actions might thus have been transferred to the hospital for establishing unsatisfactory standards of practice. (b) The machine was an outmoded English make, which, though functioning satisfactorily, had nonstandard controls. The oxygen and nitrous oxide (the anaesthetic) controls were in fact in the opposite configuration to the new machines. Thus machine deficiencies were also implicated.

A problem in the investigation of potential suits arises from the tendency of medical personnel to suppress relevant information, including occasional attempts by doctors to rewrite records. This arises from the basic instinct of self-defense complicated by the medical/nonmedical professional gulf discussed above and from a lack of knowledge of legal procedure. There is little realization that tainted evidence can be more damaging before a jury than a straightforward record of negligence. In hospitals where the reporting mechanisms are thin, the difficulties of gathering good evidence can be awesome.

The claims management function could in theory be performed by external agencies—as an adjunct function of the insurers or by assigning it to a law firm. However, there are factors that make in-house operation of damage control desirable especially in the hospital context. The most important of these is the ability to conduct comprehensive investigations efficiently and quickly and conserve evidence which is crucial in settling claims. Outside agencies are unlikely to have the same access to and confidence of the doctors involved. Additionally, the data-gathering activities may be coordinated with the loss control function, thus contributing further to efficiency. Under the pre-CRICO system, it was common to see several claims adjusters investigating one incident because each doctor or hospital involved had separate insurance arrangements.

In the case of Mr. Rajiv a suit by the bereaved family was imminent. Litigation was avoided by last minute negotiation with the family before their return home by employing the services of an attorney of Indian origin able to converse with the bereaved family in their native language. In fact, the settlement (of $83,000) with the family was made in the airport lounge as they awaited their return flight. It is improbable that an insurance company casualty claims department could have moved with as much flexibility and speed. The passage of time and litigation would probably have escalated the costs of settling the claim.

Though Coughlan was emphatic about the virtues of a flexible and case-by-case approach in dispatching claims, there was a formal procedure for dealing with each actual or putative claim. On the basis of the evidence assembled in the file, an effort was made to evaluate the potential size of a damages award. The evaluation was based on two kinds of factors: one set of factors was concrete and objectively measurable, e.g., actual financial loss such as income and medical expenses ("special damages"). The other set of factors attempted to capture intangible considerations. In this category would fall considerations like the shock value of the mishap (e.g., a facial disfigurement in a young woman would have a different impact in court than a similar disfigurement in an older man) and the composition of the jury ("general damages"). Exhibit 2 is the evaluation sheet used.

On the basis of this, negotiations are entered into with the opposing party. The objective is always to prevent a particular incident from "developing," there being a presumption that the longer a claim pends, the longer the mishap will fester. The growing commitment of financial and emotional capital will make mutually amicable settlements progressively difficult. Massachusetts law allows suits for malpractice to be brought within three years of the date of discovery. Thus, if it is obvious that a mishap has occurred which has a high probability of ultimately leading to a suit, Coughlan's staff will volunteer to make a settlement even before the patient has begun considering a suit or sought external legal assistance.

Only a third of all active claims are actually converted into suits. Even at the trial stage, negotiated settlement is not excluded. At each step in this process Coughlan will have a mental figure of the sum for which he is prepared to settle. The initial evaluation is only a benchmark and is constantly modified as the case unravels. A representative of the claims department will be present at all stages in the court to evaluate the nature of the evidence and the impact on the jury.

The estimate of an eventual settlement price is used not only for negotiation purposes but also to set up loss reserves. The precise amount put into the reserve is a function of the estimate and the probability of losing the particular suit. Loss reserves are funded by premiums so Coughlan is quite sensitive about accuracy in establishing the reserves.

Planning for the Future

Creasey could see from his financial data, (Exhibit 3), that claims losses had begun to escalate rapidly. Although this was of concern, CRICO's rates were less than 60% of those charged by the JUA, the goal originally aimed for.

As he looked ahead, Creasey wondered if, with five years of experience behind him, the premium-setting system could (or should) be revised to reflect the different loss experience of member institutions. Should he expand the domain of RMF beyond malpractice insurance to include other lines of property and casualty business? He had received many inquiries from outside the Harvard medical group by medical institutions wishing to join the program. Should he pursue them? Finally, as always, he wondered if there were any further ways to improve the loss control and claims adjustment process.

Exhibit 1 _____

SHAREHOLDER INSTITUTIONS—CONTROLLED RISK INSURANCE COMPANY, LTD.

The Beth Israel Hospital Association
Brigham and Women's Hospital
The Children's Hospital Medical Center
Sydney Farber Cancer Institute, Inc.
Harvard Community Health Plan, Inc.[a]
President and Fellows of Harvard College[b]
Joslin Diabetes Center, Inc.
Judge Baker Guidance Center
Massachusetts Eye and Ear Infirmary
Massachusetts General Hospital[c]
Mount Auburn Hospital
New England Deaconess Hospital

a. Includes: The Hospital at Parker Hill.

b. Includes: Harvard Medical School, Harvard School of Dental Medicine, Harvard School of Public Heath, Harvard University Health Services.

c. Includes: The McLean Hospital Corporation, The General Hospital Corporation.

Exhibit 2

BODILY INJURY EVALUATION WORKSHEET

FILE NO: _____ NAMED INSURED _____   CLAIMANT: _____

DAMAGES TO DATE (Verified?)_____ FUTURE DAMAGES (Approximate and Explain)

(A) MEDICAL	
Doctors _____	_____
Hospitals _____	_____
Nurses _____	_____
Rx _____	_____
Other _____	_____
(A) TOTAL	
(B) EARNING CAPACITY	
_____Wks> @ _____ Per Wk. _____	
(B) TOTAL	
(C) PAIN & SUFFERING	
_____Wks. Tot. @ _____ Per Wk._____	
_____Wks. Part. @ _____ Per Wk._____	
(C) TOTAL	
(D) MISCELLANEOUS	**TOTALS** (Including future damages)
Cosmetic Defect _____	**(A)** _____
Shock Value of Injury _____	**(B)** _____
Jurisdiction _____	**(C)** _____
Other _____	**(D)** _____
(D) TOTAL	**TOTALS**
COMMENTS	
_____	High-Low Jury Verdicts _____
_____	Liability Exposure Factor _____
_____	Approximate Settlement Value

_____
_____
_____

DEFINITIONS:

Total Disability – Prevented because of the accidental injury from performing every function of the usual work, duties or activity.

Partial Disability – Ability to perform only part of the usual work, duties or activity.

Jury Verdicts – Your estimate if no suit. – Defense attorney's estimate if suit.

Liability Factor – On all clear liability claims where there is no contribution possible, factor 100%.

Miscellaneous Damages – if pertinent, show an amount and explain in comments.

Wrongful Death – Addendum required.

Exhibit 3 _____

CONTROLLED RISK INSURANCE COMPANY, LTD. UNDERWRITING RESULTS

	Year Ending 3/31/77	Year Ending 3/31/78	Year Ending 3/31/79	Year Ending 3/31/80	Year Ending 3/31/81
Retention level	$5,000,000	$10,000,000	$12,000,000	$15,000,000	$15,000,000
Net premium	3,239,110	3,281,298	3,385,658	3,108,625	3,257,265
Claims losses	729,523	897,648	1,526,790	3,026,487	4,919,479
Underwriting profit (loss)	2,509,587	2,383,650	1,858,868	82,138	(1,662,214)
Investment income	85,050	284,993	676,590	914,753	2,013,403
Net profit (loss)[a]	$2,594,637	$ 2,668,643	$ 2,535,458	$ 996,891	$ 351,189
Cumulative surplus	$2,594,637	$ 5,263,280	$ 7,798,738	$ 8,795,629	$ 9,146,818
Total assets	$3,826,614	$ 7,144,420	$11,016,209	$14,515,038	$19,137,648

▼   ▼   ▼

DON'T PUT YOUR COMPETITIVE ADVANTAGE AT RISK

On September 17, 1991, an incident at an AT&T switching center temporarily cut phone service to and from Manhattan and halted air traffic along the East Coast for several hours. Angry phone users and disgruntled air travelers soon learned the cause of their difficulties. "AT&T Outage Caused by Negligence, Faulty Alarms, Sloppy Record-keeping" was a headline in *The Wall Street Journal.* AT&T spent many millions of dollars over the previous two years positioning itself as "The Right Choice," touting the reliability of its service over its upstart rivals. MCI and Sprint were not slow to capitalize on the situation. The day after AT&T's problems, both published ads suggesting that subscribers having difficulties should in future connect themselves to their alternative networks. The incident occurred because no one at the switching center noticed that power had reverted to back-up emergency batteries, which soon failed.

Perrier also learned the consequences of negligence the hard way. In January 1990, laboratory workers at the Mecklenburg County Environmental Protection Department who were accustomed to using bottles of Perrier as their source of purified water, noticed the presence of minute traces of benzene, a carcinogen. "It's perfect. It's Perrier," Perrier's U.S. advertising slogan had a hollow ring as it withdrew 160 million bottles worldwide at a total cost of $200 million and lost its entrenched position at the forefront of the mineral water trend. The incident began when company employees failed to replace charcoal filters used to screen out impurities present in the waters of the Perrier spring. Perrier's problems were exacerbated by its failure to provide prompt reassurance to the public that the benzene problem had been located and solved. Since this incident occurred, the chairman of Perrier was pressured to resign and the company was taken over by Nestle.

Text prepared by David E. Bell and Pascal A. Onillon. This article first appeared in the May–June 1992 edition of *Risk Management Reports,* a Tillinghast Publication. Used with permission.

Accidents will, of course, happen. But there's something to be said for making doubly sure to avoid accidents that strike at the heart of a company's competitive advantage are avoided. How much would Perrier now pay to improve its filter replacement process? What advice would you give AT&T about the need to guarantee uninterrupted service, at least in high- visibility areas like New York City and air traffic control centers?

Four Corporate Assets at Risk

The source of a company's competitive advantage is a major asset, to be guarded and protected with at least the same vigilance that might be accorded the company's infrastructure. Indeed for many companies, a key patent, a fanatically loyal workforce, or a quality image may be worth far more than all the buildings put together.

Take a moment to consider the value you have at stake in the following four categories:

1. **Physical Assets**

    Bricks and mortar, machinery, and equipment have been traditional targets for insurance protection. When the Piper-Alpha oil rig collapsed into the North Sea three years ago, taking 167 lives and a substantial part of the UK's oil revenues with it, the owners were reimbursed more than $1.2 billion for their loss, the largest man-made (versus natural) disaster ever.

2. **Cash Flow**

    A company will cease operations in fairly short order if it is denied access to funds, whether its bank withdraws its credit line or its retained earnings turn negative. In March 1989, an explosion ripped apart a BASF ethylene oxide production plant in Antwerp, Belgium; the explosion caused nearly $90 million worth of property damage, but worse than that, it eliminated production at the plant for two years. BASF now estimates the lost net income over this period at around $200 million, more than twice the property loss. Happily for the company, this business interruption loss was well within the $300 million of coverage they maintained with Gerling-Konzern Insurance AG of Cologne, Germany. BASF has since doubled its business interruption coverage to $650 million.

3. **Goodwill**

    While debates rage over methods of measuring the value of corporate goodwill—the favorable disposition of company partners such as suppliers, distributors, customers, and the government—and over whether to include an allowance for such value on a company's balance sheets, the consequences of a loss of goodwill can be dramatic.

    Drexel-Burnham-Lambert collapsed into bankruptcy after Michael Milken and other employees were indicted for insider trading. In the fall of 1991, Salomon Brothers, one of the most prestigious of Wall Street firms, drastically cut back its trading activities after losing customers following an announcement that key employees admitted to violating the auction rules for Treasury bills. An intangible asset such as goodwill is rarely insurable, nor are many losses from the criminal activity of employees. Other companies may learn from the active steps Salomon took to avoid similar mishaps in the future.

4. **Competitive Advantage**

Michael E. Porter[1] has taught us that a company will go nowhere without a competitive advantage. In the late 1980s, TRW viewed air bags as the potential rising star for its automotive business. TRW's position as a market leader in the supply of this emerging product began when the Ford Motor Company announced that TRW would be its sole supplier of air bags. But two incidents quickly soured this prospect. In early 1990, a chemical fire destroyed a Canadian plant where TRW jointly produces air bag propellant with ICI. This prevented TRW from supplying Ford with passenger side air bags for its 1990 Lincoln Town Car and Continental models. Then, on October 26, 1990, Ford had to announce the recall of 55,000 1990 and 1991 model year cars because of possible problems in air bags supplied by TRW. On December 17, 1991, an explosion in a TRW plant in Michigan halted production for all of Ford's passenger-side air bags. These incidents have postponed the targeted break-even date for TRW's strategy and a key competitor, Norton International, is quickly gaining new market position. These events come at a bad time for TRW as General Motors and Chrysler are each greatly expanding their use of air bags, planning to introduce them in all of their light vans and trucks by 1995.

Is Insurance the Answer?

Of the four asset categories we have described, only physical assets are readily insurable. Insurance to cover the loss of income during business interruption is available, but it rarely does more than cover the near-term shortfall in cash flow due to a temporary loss of revenue. It will never make up for the lost opportunity caused by your absence from the market for that period. Goodwill and competitive advantage, though potentially more valuable than short-term operations, are impossible to insure. These assets lie, like the bottom of an iceberg, large and unseen (Figure 6.1). But unlike an iceberg they are forever exposed.

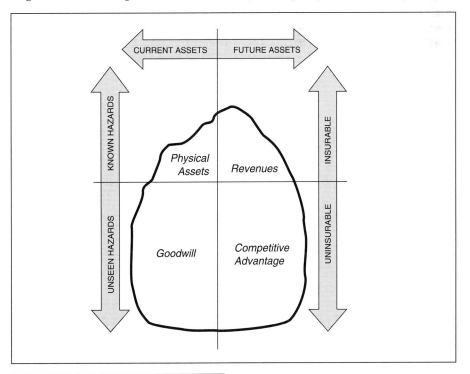

Figure 6.1

[1] M. E. Porter, "How Competitive Forces Shape Strategy," *Harvard Business Review,* March–April 1979.

Even where insurance *is* a possible solution, it may soon not be cost-effective. The insurance industry is being rocked by large losses and poor investments while at the same time management and societal trends are placing companies in positions of greater risk.

Fairgrounds, ice rinks, and physicians are being forced out of business through an inability to obtain adequate liability insurance at reasonable cost. Where insurance rates are regulated, for example in the automobile markets of New Jersey and Massachusetts, insurance companies are threatening to withdraw. Medical costs, currently 11% of GNP, continue to rise at triple the inflation rate. More and more corporations require worker contributions to family health coverage. If the trend continues, insurance will not be the vehicle for health financing. Also, because of a change in U.S. accounting regulations, companies were required, as of January 1, 1993, to capitalize their future obligation for the medical costs of retirees. In 1991 large firms like GE and IBM recognized one-time accounting losses as high as $2 billion for this purpose. The corresponding figure for GM is expected to be about $24 billion, a sum which could endanger their credit rating, according to an authority at Standard & Poor's.

The insurance industry is concerned that recent industrial disasters are not simply statistical freaks, but symptoms of greatly increased business interruption exposures. A single loss, the 1989 explosion at Phillips Petroleum's Pasadena, Texas, cost $1.4 billion, representing 80% of worldwide premium payments for property damage and business interruption for hydrocarbon and chemical processing industries. The largest single fire loss in 1990—in July at the ARCO petrochemical plant at Channelview, Texas, had a property loss amounting to $20 million while the business interruption loss was 10 times that amount. Business interruption losses can be up to 50 times or more the property loss amount as companies have larger plants with increasing concentration of equipment and inventory and longer, more complex, production stages.

Insurance is increasingly hard to find in areas like director's liability (one of the consequences of a rising tide of litigation) and environmental pollution. Recall that Exxon's bill for the Alaskan oil spill is estimated in the billions of dollars. The current $150 billion surplus held by property-casualty insurance companies would be exhausted even if they only had to pay 15% of costs associated with known Superfund clean-up sites.

Even without an insurance crisis, the fact remains that most of the value in our four categories (Figure 6.1) is simply *not insurable*. Some other mechanism must be found. And matters are getting worse.

Trends to Greater Risk

Two major trends are raising the general level of risk faced by corporations.

1. **Business Consolidation**

    The latest management ideas lead companies in the direction of greater interdependence and concentration of resources. For example:

    a. **Global Strategies** While global corporations benefit from many strategic advantages, they also trade these advantages against organizational costs, in the form of interdependencies across countries within the same product groups and across product groups, worldwide or within specific countries. A U.S. television assembly plant discovered recently that its $700 million annual sales were at the mercy of a small Brazilian subsidiary that was producing parts vital to its operation.

Do you now have a global positioning strategy? The same product in all countries with a single message? For most of its history, Gillette allowed its individual brands to stand alone in the marketplace. With the introduction of its new Sensor product, Gillette adopted the use of its own name as a "Superbrand" with all of its products. This gamble paid off. Not only was Sensor a big success, the corporate identification generated carry-over effects. But with all your eggs in one basket you must be especially careful that the basket isn't dropped. Perrier and Tylenol suffered worldwide exposure from global media coverage when their products underwent recalls after calamitous events. It's not that we advocate a return to regional marketing—simply that greater concentration implies greater risk.

b. **Single, Just-In-Time Supplier** Now that we all manufacture to zero-defect standards with no down time, surely there's no harm in designing our operations in a way that assumes all our supplies will arrive just when we need them and in perfect shape. But is the supplier as risk-management-conscious as the manufacturer? It only takes one member of a narrow value chain to have difficulties that send shock waves throughout the system. In 1988, a leading U.S. computer manufacturer was forced to spend $12 million expediting shipments to meet a product introduction deadline after a fire at its Taiwanese supplier halted production.

c. **Mergers and Acquisitions** An inevitable consequence of any merger or acquisition is that plants are consolidated leading to greater concentration of resources and centralization of activities. And since risk management personnel are typically at a fairly low level in most organizations, they are rarely to be found ironing out details in takeover deals. With huge environmental bills awaiting the unwary, caution is in order. Following its $1.5 billion acquisition of Koppers in 1988, Beazer was obliged to make a $500 million provision for cleaning up pollution from the U.S. company's chemical business.

d. **Technology** Factories of the future, with their robotics and sophisticated software, represent enormous concentrations of value in specialized production units. With fewer humans in control, the consequences of a single error become magnified. Technology brings its own unforeseen risks. The electronic transfer of funds heightens the potential for embezzlement and fraud, computer viruses can bring a computer center (even a nation) to its knees. Technology transfer is often a not-so-hidden goal of your joint venture partner. Guarding your proprietary technology requires vigilance[2]. Technology has also made a moving target of quality standards. What used to be measured in parts per million is now measured in parts per trillion.

2. **Changing Societal Goals**

Goodwill is a state of mind brought about by years of harmonious relations. These days, partners expect more from you than just value for money. More challenging still, the global corporation must track societal changes in multiple countries as global reach also means global responsibility.

a. **Ethics** Not so long ago it seemed that corporate ethics was delegated to the legal staff. So long as it was legal, it was ethical. But that is no longer sufficient, at least for companies who expect to retain goodwill. When

2 D. M. Spero, "Patent Protection or Piracy—A CEO Views Japan," *Harvard Business Review,* September–October 1990.

the basketball star, Magic Johnson, announced he was HIV positive, attention quickly turned to the companies for whom he was retained as an advertising symbol: would they continue to retain his services?

The tuna industry refused for quite some time to respond to the demands of activists who complained that dolphins were being trapped by the tuna nets. The canners paid attention only when activists led a boycott of their products. In retrospect, one might argue that the canners should have seen the writing on the wall, or even recognized the true path of righteousness much earlier. Ethics is often in the eye of the beholder, and high standards can be expensive. The point is that low standards can be expensive too.

b. **Environment** Environmentalism is not a fad. While much environmentally favorable legislation has been passed by Congress, the Clean Air Act and the Superfund Amendments and Reauthorization Act are two examples, companies are expected by the public and *by their employees* to treat the environment kindly. Can there still be a major corporation in the U.S. that does not have some form of recycling program?[3] Do not all consumer products now come in more environmentally responsible packaging and contain fewer toxic chemicals, from ozone-friendly hairspray to biodegradable disposable diapers? The cost to clean up all the declared hazardous waste sites in the U.S. is estimated at $750 billion. Hoechst recently announced that it will spend $500 to $600 million over the next five years to reduce emissions at its 21 U.S. production plants. Respect for the environment must be part of every ethical corporation's approach to business.

c. **Employment Conditions** Employees are expecting more and more of their employers. At a minimum they are expected to provide a clean, safe, and healthy place to work. Additionally, demands are rising for accommodations to changing family life styles, for example with respect to child care. With health and pension costs skyrocketing, trade unions now routinely demand comprehensive packages to fulfil these needs. Employers are also responsible for ensuring that hiring and promotion practices are fair and that employees are not discriminated against.

All of these trends are costly, but with planning can be incorporated into budgets. The danger, however, is that some single incident will reverse years of proactive behavior. American Cyanamid thought it was doing the right thing in 1981 when it banned "fertile women" from a production line that would have exposed them to lead, a fetus-threatening substance. Presumably American Cyanamid felt it had found a creative solution that avoided closing down the line completely without discriminating against women (at least all women). But five young women had themselves sterilized in order to keep their jobs and American Cyanamid was not only in the courts, it was in the public eye.

If smokers can sue tobacco companies for encouraging their habit, might lawsuits be in the offing where employees charge employers with failing to stop a known drug habit, or failing to serve low cholesterol alternatives in the cafeteria? Employers cannot be expected to foresee every trend and pay for every new program that is dreamed up. But it is important for *someone* to seek proactive, cost-effective ways to meet the changing societal goals of its many partners.

---

[3] G. C. Lodge and J. F. Rayport, "Knee—Deep and Rising: America's Recycling Costs," *Harvard Business Review,* September–October 1991.

Table 6.1

	The Evolution of Risk Management	
Decade	**The Problem**	**The "Answer"**
1950s	Catastrophe Protection	Insurance Buying
1960s	Insurance Costs	Risk Management as a Staff Function
1970s	Inadequacy and Volatility of Insurance Markets	Captives as an Alternative Funding Mechanism for Risk Financing
1980s	Volatility of Commodity Prices, Interest and Exchange Rates	Currency Hedging, Interest Rate Swaps and other financial risk management techniques
1990s	Greater Concentration and Interdependence of Values and Corporate Accountability	Companywide Risk Management Mentality

Our Proposal

Ten years ago, American-made products suffered because of management's lack of priority regarding quality. Management treated quality as a variable to be traded off against cost as a means of maximizing profit. The Japanese provided a demonstration that a zero-defect policy was not only attainable, but profitable.[4] Short-term losses in profitability were more than offset by long run gains in customer goodwill and employee satisfaction with a job well done.

Our proposal is that companies should approach all of their activities with a zero-defect attitude. Instead of regarding ethics as a dimension to be traded off against expense and effort, we suggest that a high ethical standard provides long-term paybacks in customer and employee goodwill. A zero-defect approach to the environment may be technically impossible, but it is the appropriate benchmark for corporate activity.

We recognize that tradeoffs must always be made, if not explicitly then implicitly. But we urge that a manager's first impulse should always be to consider doing the job right the first time.

The development of a *risk management mentality* is a low cost, high return activity that is a protective shield against the ever increasing threats surrounding corporate assets. (See Figure 6.2). We do not recommend avoiding entrepreneurial activities on the grounds that there may be a chance of loss; doing business always involves taking calculated risks. Nor do we recommend insuring everything in sight. We are talking about risk as a chance of loss where control is possible, realistic, and necessary. The little losses that happen every day due to inefficiency will not threaten corporate existence, but if their trend is increasing they may eventually lead to a major crisis that will have major effect on corporate assets. Unseen hazards will then become clearly visible.

---

[4]D. Garrin, "Quality on the Line," *Harvard Business Review,* September–October 1983.

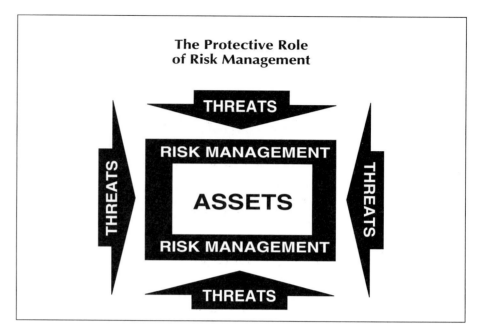

Figure 6.2

New manufacturing technology has brought extreme flexibility, customized products, shorter distribution runs along with new operation management systems such as Just In Time, Optimized Production Technology, Flexible Manufacturing Systems and Material Requirement Planning into larger production centers to achieve economies of scale. But the firm must remember to identify how these new techniques can affect the exposure to loss throughout the entire value chain. Long, hard-fought and expensive efforts that improve your competitiveness can prove to be a major unprotected asset if risk management is not integrated with your business strategies.

Many industries have already added environmental performance as part of their quality management programs. Such evaluations help to prevent pollution and to go beyond governmental regulations. Some corporations are combining health, safety, and environmental issues under one department. In the same way that product safety starts at the design stage of product development, so all business actions must be decided with a risk management mentality.

A zero-defect standard, which has become accepted in a manufacturing context, should also be the benchmark of corporate activities. Rather than associating risk management only with insurance, corporations would be better off treating insurance as a last resort. Such an attitude would lead to a wariness of unwarranted risk-taking that would soon extend to protection of the assets that cannot be insured: goodwill, competitive advantage and to a certain extent revenues. (See Figure 6.3.)

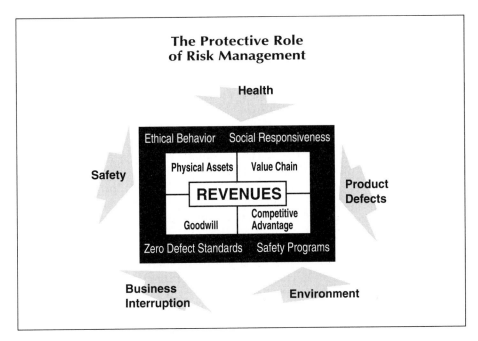

Figure 6.3

A review of where a project or decision might lead the company to an exposure should be done in all phases of a company's activities. This is not an onerous burden, simply a new one. Just as it took a few years to accustom ourselves to the notion that one shouldn't think about how to trade-off quality with cost, we now propose considering what might go wrong.

Activities like quality control, recycling, gender neutral language, and ethics, each sounded at first like the latest nuisance come along to tax us. But after getting over the initial mental hurdle, it immediately becomes apparent that we should have been doing them all along. Quality control makes sense because it means doing it right the first time. The spin-off value of increased customer satisfaction and employee feelings of self-worth offset any short run gains. So, too, with a risk management mentality. It provides your corporation with a dependable, consistent level of quality protection of its assets.

Risk management is also a powerful leadership tool to achieve excellence in everything: morale, productivity, quality, socially responsible public perception and trust, internal and external environment, and quality of work life. Quality risk management is the most positive message a corporation can give to its partners and to society.

It Works

DuPont has every reason to be a leader in risk management. Its origins as a manufacturer of explosives suggest a rationale for a history of caution. The corporate mission describes its contribution to society as a combination of the "usefulness of its products and the safety of their operation." New employees are warned, as a condition of their employment, not to perform a task that is unsafe. Any accident serious enough to keep any one of DuPont's employees off the job for a day or more is reported to the chairman within 24 hours. Such attention to detail has given DuPont an enviable corporate safety record. Figures for the National Safety Council show that DuPont's 1989 performance in lost work time cases, which represent more serious injuries, is 20 times safer than the rate for the chemical industry taken together, and 60 times safer than the rate for all industry. (A DuPont employee is many times safer at work than at home.) According to the director of safety and occupational health at Dupont, if the company had the average injury rate experienced throughout the chemical industry, it would require nearly $2 billion a year in additional sales to pay the cost.[5] It is reasonable to assume that such a corporate attention to detail will ensure that DuPont will suffer few losses due to business interruptions.

When DuPont saw the writing on the wall with respect to CFCs, it unilaterally promised to halt production by the year 2000, despite having no guaranteed replacement. Whether this was an ethical stand or not, common sense tells us the CFC issue will not go away, and DuPont's decision, while aggressive, made sense. Perhaps it learned from the problems Westinghouse has had shaking off allegations that they carelessly exposed its workers to PCB contamination before it was banned in the workplace by the EPA in 1979. Westinghouse also agreed, in 1983, to clean up a PCB-contaminated landfill in Bloomington, Indiana at an estimated cost that could exceed $1 billion. DuPont also invests heavily in environmental initiatives. It manages 1000 square miles of land for wildlife habitat, recycles plastic waste, conducts research into environmentally beneficial fuels, and creates citizen advisory panels at major sites.

Conoco, a DuPont subsidiary, has also announced that it will use double-hulled oil tankers, in the hope of averting oil spills. DuPont estimates such tankers will cost 15% more than conventional tankers, and carry about 10% less oil. Undoubtedly it figures that is a small price to pay to avoid a repetition of Exxon's experience in cleaning up Prince William Sound and the attendant publicity that may dog Exxon for years. Recall that the accident was not an act of God; both the captain and the company were later convicted of misdemeanors. Nor was the Valdez incident a one-off experience for Exxon. On Christmas Eve of the same year (1989) a refinery blew up in Baton Rouge, Louisiana and the following New Year's Day a pipeline between New Jersey and New York City leaked 567,000 gallons of heating oil into the estuary. What is the cost of all this to Exxon? The oil spilled? The repair costs of the Valdez? The cleanup costs? The costs are more than all of these. Exxon was fortunate that a fledgling customer boycott of the pumps never succeeded, but customer goodwill must have taken a beating.

One of the world's largest aluminum producers, Pechiney, of France, has invested $33 million over the last five years to avoid what its risk manager described as "383 large loss possibilities worth $8.5 billion." Tallies as of 1990 show that this investment saved $360 million in potential losses, a better than ten fold return. The average frequency rate of lost-time accidents for Pechiney Group's eight largest French companies has dropped from 22.8 in 1986 to 15.8 in 1990.

Alain Neveu, Pechiney's risk manager, reckons its $5 million expenditure on loss prevention saved $273 million in losses when a potentially disastrous fire was put out in seconds at one of the company's strategically important plants. At this time, Pechiney was undertaking a $3.5 billion acquisition of Chicago-based American National Can, which has now made Pechiney the world leader in the packaging industry. This transaction would surely have been sidetracked had a major fire completely destroyed this plant, thus diverting management time and energy.

Companies are beginning to comprehend the coming collapse of the health and worker's compensation insurance systems, and are taking active steps by improving employee health (keep fit activities, healthier diets, and non-smoking

---

[5]W. J. Motel, "Safety Management at DuPont," speech to Manufacturer's Alliance for Productivity and Innovation, Washington D. C. March 26, 1991.

campaigns) and reducing the likelihood of work-related health problems. Pepsico, discovering that 45% of its medical costs came from 2% of its cases, now appoints case managers to coordinate the health care programs for individual patients. A Coca Cola bottling company has implemented an experimental back injury prevention program which has significantly reduced employee injuries. Marriott now actively manages its own claims administration for worker injuries. By so doing the company gets first-hand knowledge of problems so that they can be corrected at once. This allows creativity in reassigning and retraining workers who are unable to perform their existing jobs. Not only do such programs lower costs, they improve the morale of employees and, with it, the image of the corporation.

Many industries have already added environmental performance as part of their quality management programs. Procter and Gamble's liquid detergent plant in Lima, Ohio, used to discharge detergent into the municipal water treatment plant. Although the amount discharged was within permissible limits, plant management wished to cut the levels. Building its own water treatment facility to pre-treat the water before it was discharged would have been very costly and, in some sense, a redundancy. Instead P&G studied its entire process and discovered that much of the detergent emission was caused by faulty filters, leaks, and loading spills. By retraining workers and modifying maintenance procedures, it was able to reduce detergent emission by nearly 60%, which in itself was a cost saving.

Risk management can be as simple as having all of your data backed up at a separate location or implementing good disaster preparedness plan. Digital Equipment Corporation backs up EDP tapes daily and stores them in a separate building or another fire zone from the original tapes. It also is making sure that each of its corporate locations has developed a disaster recovery plan. You may think that the time and energy spent at developing such a plan is not worth it. But, on March 6, 1990, a fire broke out at the Basingstoke, UK office of Digital Equipment Co. Ltd. The implementation of a crisis management program has enabled DEC to only suffer a minimal impact on business and none on customer services. All 400 regular staff and approximately 100 contractors and visitors were evacuated from the building within five minutes. Systems were operational over a period of from one hour to six days after the fire. The central computer room was protected by a halon fire extinguishing system and by firefighters who wrapped cabinets in plastic sheeting. While suffering smoke damage, nearly $18 million worth of computer, data network, and telephone switching gear were salvaged. After the majority of data was recovered from back-up and employees were located to other sites, only alternative computers on which to run the systems were needed to restart operations. This is risk management mentality in action!

A comprehensive risk-protection plan involves the following four steps:

1. The first step is to identify and *measure the value of all of your assets* and assess their potential vulnerability. You probably know the valuation of your physical assets (replacement values, not depreciated value), and perhaps a rough estimate of the value of your goodwill. You should also estimate the cost of a six-week business interruption, not only in terms of lost income and lost goodwill, but for the temporary, possibly permanent, advantage this would give your competitors.

STEPS TO COMPREHENSIVE PROTECTION

The following general principles capture our philosophy:

Rule 1: Act as if insurance is not an option. You will be more cautious, and prudent, if you believe there is no safety net. This is also good practice for the day when there might be no safety net.

Rule 2: Act as if your company is your number 1 product. Apply the same quality standards to the overall running of your company as you do to the manufacture of your product.

Rule 3: Act as if society is your number 1 customer. The customer is always right. So too is society.

Rule 4: Do things right the first time. This is the best mentality to govern decision making.

2. The second step is to identify important events that might occur in the near future: *what can possibly go wrong?* These could range from the recurring events normally handled by risk managers to legal changes, economic developments, and societal movements. Royal Dutch Shell's experience with Scenario Analysis[6] may be helpful in providing "big picture" possibilities for the future. Shell's 1970 analysis of Middle East nations forewarned it of the possibility of a cutback in production that was ultimately implemented in the OPEC agreements. Shell lost several hundred thousand barrels of Iraqi and Kuwaiti oil per day when the Gulf War began, but alternative, preapproved crudes were located and used due to a set of procedures that had been previously drafted. Many of these "what if ...?" scenarios may appear nightmarish, but you must realize that not only can they happen, they have probably already happened in some other corporation. Consider these "what if...?" questions:

   ‣ What will happen to your customers and their customers if your key manufacturing operation burns down to the ground?

   ‣ What will happen if product tampering forces you to take your products off the market for several months?

   ‣ What if you have invested heavily in a new product that will give you a significant competitive advantage and a key supplier suffers a major loss just before the product introduction?

3. The third step is to develop employee commitment to ongoing risk management process.

   Risk management requires great self-discipline and an emphasis on individual responsibility for the implementation of a successful zero-risk corporate process. Employees are close to the products and services, the suppliers and customers. They are the best ones to take the initiatives in their daily activities and make recommendations to protect the organization. It is important to emphasize the human factor of risk management because it is the bridge between quality risk management and quality engineering and environmental quality. Seventy percent of losses are caused by human error. When employees' ingenuity and risk consciousness are engaged, risk conditions change dramatically because risk control becomes second nature.

   Risk management actions could be the development of alternate suppliers, strict housekeeping and maintenance rules, training programs on safety, health and ethics, the duplication of facilities, the organization of crisis management teams, and disaster planning. As Salomon Brothers recently learned, attitudinal change begins at the top. The CEO is the Chief Risk Officer, but senior managers must also demonstrate their commitment to risk management and share this commitment with their employees by setting goals, evaluating and rewarding achievements so that it becomes a part of the corporate culture.

4. Having put your own house in order, the fourth and final step is to be sure that the *value chain* in which you lie is suitably protected. Even if you are invulnerable, the same might not be true of your suppliers, your distributors, even your customers.

   American Standard Inc. lost a personal injury case in which the cause was a replacement part not produced by the company but recommended as a replacement in its catalog. Customers can also be a threat. It is not sufficient to

---

[6]P. Wack, "Scenarios: Shooting the Rapids," *Harvard Business Review*, November–December 1985, pp. 139–150.

design a product to be reliable in the manner you intend it to be used, but rather to be reliable in a manner an ordinary person might use it. One driver exploded his Goodyear radial tire by driving over 100 mph and sued for damages. The argument that neither the car nor the tire were warranted for travel above 90 mph was deemed insufficient[7].

Start with your suppliers since you have the leverage to influence them and test their responsiveness. Gannett Co. Inc., a large newspaper publishing company, convinced its suppliers to have printing presses specially designed to accommodate fire protection devices. Bell Atlantic Co. worked with its suppliers to design a special cable wrapping that expands to eight times its original size when subjected to heat, thus, better protecting phone cables against fire and smoke, while increasing the probability of providing a non-interrupted service to customers.

We know that a zero percent mishap rate is unattainable, even at infinite cost, but there is a lot to be said for developing an attitude of mind that abhors unnecessary risk[8]. Just as most soccer players would rather play offense rather than defense, so most managers we know would rather focus on risks to be undertaken than eliminated. But the world is headed in the direction of greater focus on public positioning, specialization, centralization, and inter-dependency. The diversification that was a natural fire-break between calamities has disappeared and a company's fortune can be made vulnerable to a single blow. The pressure to produce profits is now leading companies into cutting corners on risk management. You can get away with it for years—maybe forever—but if it strikes it can be fatal.

It was near-fatal for Union Carbide in Bhopal, India, where the company had reduced the number of its safety personnel during the five years before the accident in November 1984 that killed more than 3,000 people. The company has survived, but the aftermath of the accident has been a constant focus to this day and has had a worldwide effect on the chemical industry.

In the "new" Union Carbide, executive bonuses are affected by how well the company has decreased its environmental risk. It is now leading cleanup efforts by creating new processes, which include removing dioxin from contaminated soil and eliminating polychlorinated biphenyls or PCBs. It also has an environmental audit program headed by its Vice President of Health, Safety and Environmental Affairs who reports directly to Union Carbide's chairman.

Risk management must be an integral part of a corporation's strategy to maintain and increase its value as both an economic and social entity. Ironically, it seems that a corporation needs to suffer a crisis that jeopardizes its financial stability in order to realize the critical role risk management plays in assuring corporate competitiveness and survival.

Do not cling to the notion that risk is a job to be delegated to a staff risk manager who buys insurance and runs risk management awareness programs in his/her spare time. There is much more to loss prevention investments than just insurance reduction paybacks. Risk management is still too insurance-focused and not geared enough towards risk assessment and control. For these reasons we feel it has not yet reached its full potential. Risk management has too wide a range of complex implications and is too critical to corporate success

---

[7] M. Manley, "Product Liability: You're more exposed than you think," *Harvard Business Review,* September–October 1987, pp. 28–41.

[8] R. B. Gallagher, "Risk Management: New Phase of Cost Control," *Harvard Business Review,* September–October 1956, pp. 76–86.

C.V. Culbertsen, J.D. Wods, "Charge total casualty claims against the operating unit's profit," *Harvard Business Review*, September–October 1981, pp. 6–12.

to be the domain of a service function of a few persons. We believe there is a need for an overall active organizational response to corporate risk that integrates the business functions and strategic decision making. Buying insurance without the systemic and comprehensive risk management process we have described is the most expensive way of minimizing a corporation's risk exposure. Risk is a management challenge that is at the intersection of all business functions. This is why risk management represents a new, additional way to assess and appraise strategic alternatives.

Conclusion

Unwarranted risk is an inefficiency that can be cured. It should not be ignored as simply an intangible companion of business activity or regarded as a detail to be worked out later. Risk is best reduced through vigilance and creativity at the time it is incurred.

A risk-free society is not our goal. But corporations have a risk capacity that is set, at least implicitly, by investors, bondholders, and the employee stakeholders. The normal risks of business—getting and keeping customers, battling competitors, gambling on investments for the future—are all substantial enough that risk-taking capacity should not be compromised. With the growing magnitude, complexity, and unknown future consequences of risks, the decision to go up the risk management learning curve is already overdue. By leading an active campaign to do things right the first time, to guard against unanticipated threats, and to carefully nurtured strategic gains, the company can ensure that it survives to enjoy the fruits of its labor.

Contracts and Incentives

Two people may fully intend cooperating in a venture, but the association may founder if the incentives of each are different. A legal contract can sometimes, but not always, correct this problem. Here we review some of the problems, discuss some guidelines for their solution, and establish some terminology. Some problems are provided by way of illustration.

Incentive Compatibility

Rule: *Each party should have the incentive to act in the interest of the group as a whole.*

Two partners in an entrepreneurial business venture each do a lot of travelling between Boston and Chicago. Each partner would, as an individual, be prepared to pay up to $100 for the privilege of flying first class rather than coach. The actual premium is $150 and so each "should" fly coach. But, as partners in the business venture, and thus sharing all costs equally, a decision by either of them to fly first class has an effective cost to themselves of only $75, since the non-flying partner will also be paying $75. If the partners fly together this incentive problem becomes readily apparent. If only one partner does all the flying this distortion in incentives may be disguised. One solution to this problem that corrects the incentives is for the partners to agree that the partnership will only reimburse the flier for coach fare. Any premium must be paid individually.

The lack of incentive compatibility is a widespread problem that can rarely be solved effectively. Employees have little financial incentive to save energy in the workplace or to be conservative in their use of the copying machine.

A fairly simple system exists for checking for a lack of incentive compatibility when the joint problem may be expressed as a decision tree.

Rule: *In a decision tree all parties should agree on the preferred alternative at each decision point (including contingent decisions) and each party should agree on the preferred outcome of each uncertainty.*

The need to agree on all decisions is clear, since otherwise conflict can arise. The need to agree on the outcome of uncertainties stems from the ability in practice for people to influence the outcome of uncertainties by suitable direction of their effort. If the decision tree does not satisfy this condition the contract should be rewritten with contingent sidepayments so as to create incentive compatibility.

Asymmetries

One difficulty to be surmounted in multiple-party agreements is that people may have different beliefs and preferences about the problem at hand.

As a simple example, suppose you and I are siblings who have been left $1,000 cash and an oil painting by a recently deceased uncle. The oil painting was painted by the uncle when he was a young man and has little or no market value. His will expresses the desire that we split his estate "equally." How should we do this? Let us suppose that you are very sentimental and would enjoy hanging the oil painting in your home whereas I would, at best, hide it in the attic. The noble thing to do would be for me to let you have the painting and then for us to split the cash equally. But I might propose that a fair way to divide the estate is to let you pick either the painting or the $1,000. If you pick the painting it must be because you value it at least as much as the cash so you are getting at least half of the estate. Of course you may argue that since I find the painting worthless I have, in effect, received the entire value of the estate. In solving problems like this, two guiding principles are:

▸ The negotiating procedure should induce honesty (or non-strategic behavior) in the parties involved.

▸ The negotiated solution should maximize the total value received by all parties. It is clear that I should not end up with the oil painting (which I might if we draw lots, or if I lie about its value to me).

Asymmetries can also occur if two people disagree on the likelihood of certain events (I think an event is quite likely to happen, but you don't) or if one person is more risk-averse than the other.

The following examples illustrate typical incentive problems. It is difficult to solve them precisely. They are presented to promote discussion.

1. You have seen some houses for sale that you like. They vary in price. In order to decide how much you can afford, you need a fair estimate of the value of your current home. You cannot wait until you sell your current house before selecting another house because the one you want may disappear in the interim.

   The local realtor will charge you a commission for selling your current house equal to 6% of its sale price. You must rely on the realtor for a fair estimate of your home's worth.

   a. Is it in the realtor's interest to tell you what the house is worth?

   b. Suppose the commission is charged as follows:

(i) The realtor provides an estimate E thousand dollars for the house's worth.

(ii) The realtor sells the house for S thousand dollars.

(iii) The realtor's commission is E $(S - \frac{1}{2}E)$.

For example, if the realtor estimates $120,000 and the sale price is $100,000 the commission will be

$$120 (100 - 60) = \$4,800 \quad .$$

What are the advantages and disadvantages of this commission arrangement?

2. The CEO of a company is trying to decide whether to spend $10 million on a new computer networking system to bring the company into the 1990s. The CEO is 64 years old, has never touched a computer in his life and doesn't really understand the benefits that computing power can bring. The company's two major divisions are headed by Alice and Bernard. It is generally agreed that Alice's division stands to benefit from the computer system more than Bernard's and so the question has arisen as to how the expense of the computer system will be charged to the divisions. Alice and Bernard receive bonuses that are tied closely to divisional performance. Alice has little idea what the system is worth to Bernard and Bernard has little idea what the system is worth to Alice. The CEO has little idea about the value to either.

Devise a procedure for deciding whether the computer system should be bought and how it should be charged to the divisions.

3. The CEO of a company is reflecting on appropriate bonuses to be paid to key employees for the calendar year just ending, as will the level of salary increases for the coming year. These amounts are not made public, but word inevitably gets around; employees who feel unjustly treated may leave or become unproductive through discontent. Even the task of determining the relative effectiveness of key employees is hampered by the different kinds of business they are in. Consider the example of an investment bank sales and trading department. Both salespeople and the traders have identifiable and quantifiable productivity measures (sales and trading profits/losses respectively). Nevertheless, it is unclear how the incentive structures should be designed. Should salespeople be paid on commission, and traders on a percent of annual profits, or should both be paid according to a more subjective evaluation process? Whatever system the CEO uses for distributing salaries and bonuses should achieve at least two goals:

▸ a person should be paid at least his or her "market value" so long as the person is worth that amount to the company

▸ a person should find his or her bonus and salary increase "fair" relative to the amounts received by other people within the company.

How should the CEO accomplish this?

DADE COUNTY RESOURCE RECOVERY PROJECT

On June 2, 1976, the Dade County Solid Waste Task Force ended its long search for a contractor to build and operate a resource recovery facility when it voted to recommend to the board of county commissioners that final contract negotiations be entered into with the New York firm of Black Clawson Fibreclaim, Inc., a wholly owned subsidiary of Parsons and Whittemore. The task force had been created in October 1970, with the charge of recommending how the county could improve its solid waste collection and disposal services. Now, with this vote, it looked like a firm contract might be signed by mid-1977. Major contract issues had, of course, been ironed out with Black Clawson already, but there remained a myriad of minor points to be settled. Not so minor was the separate contract that would have to be negotiated with Florida Power and Light Company for the sale of the steam that would be created by the resource recovery plant.

Nevertheless, Ray Goode, the Dade County manager, felt he could see the light at the end of the tunnel. Yet the last six years of effort might prove to have been the easy part, since there was no guarantee that the huge investment they would be making would solve their problems.

The Waste Disposal Problem

The United States generates 270 million tons of residential and commercial refuse annually and spends $4 billion in disposing of it. The problem of disposal is almost always solved by finding a hole in the ground, filling it with refuse and then covering it with soil—burying it. A number of factors are causing municipalities to seek alternatives to this process. First, there is an acute shortage of suitable dumping sites. For those that are suitable, not only must the refuse be transported considerable distances, and thus at considerable expense both in terms of fuel and in truck time, but since the holes may be located outside the community, their availability can be interrupted quite abruptly by the host authority. Second, environmental attitudes have become stricter so that even those landfill sites that are physically suitable may not meet environmental standards or may incur great costs to do so. Third, the only serious alternative currently used, incineration, has a slight disadvantage because it is a net consumer of fuel, usually oil.

Dade County is located in southeastern Florida. Most of its 1.3 million people live in the Miami metropolitan area. By the early 1970s, 4,200 tons of solid waste was being collected daily, six days per week, with estimates suggesting a likely doubling of the amount by 1990. Most of the waste was being disposed of in the 20 or so landfills around the county. Most of these landfills more closely resembled dumps and were receiving considerable attention by environmental organizations. The incinerators within the county were either in violation of air pollution regulations or were so close to residential areas that truck noise was a problem. With landfill space becoming scarce and expensive, and with most incinerators unable to meet emission standards, the county faced a waste disposal dilemma.

Harvard Business School case 9-182-167. Professor David E. Bell prepared this case. The information in it is based on public Dade County documents. Copyright © 1981 by the President and Fellows of Harvard College.

In November 1972, Dade County voters approved a $50 million "Decade of Progress" bond program for financing improvements in solid waste disposal. With this assurance of financing, the task force turned to private industry for proposals on how to solve, or at least alleviate, the disposal problem.

Request for Proposals

By September 1973, the task force had prepared and issued a request for proposals (RFP). The RFP asked for sealed bids to be submitted for the construction of two waste disposal facilities, one to handle 1,600 tons per day of solid waste at the Northwest 58th Street landfill site, the other to handle 1,200 tons per day at the site of the city of Miami incinerator. The plant sites would be rented to the contractor at a sum of $1 each for the duration of the contract and the contractor would not be responsible for property taxes.

Seventeen proposals were received. Bidders proposed systems which ranged from shredding (only) to composting. Most proposals lacked specifics about markets for products and environmental controls, and none of the proposals was clear on contract terms. Since the sealed bid procedure ruled out negotiating with the proposers, in December 1973 all bids were rejected.

The county then conducted interviews with many of the companies that had submitted bids, in order to learn more about available technologies and financing alternatives. The evaluation committee concluded that the county could procure a technically feasible but innovative resource recovery system for waste disposal if the county shared in some of the risks. It was also determined that when future regulatory requirements were taken into consideration, net disposal costs from private industry were competitive with disposal costs at its landfills and incinerators. Currently, landfills costs were running at $3.12 per ton exclusive of land amortization. New landfills meeting state environmental laws were costing about $9.00 per ton. The operating and amortization costs of the incinerator amounted to $12.89 per ton.

On the basis of feedback from the potential bidders, the RFP was revised and now asked for one large facility processing 18,000 tons per week instead of two sites. It eliminated the joint financing concept and required prospective bidders to arrange financing. The county also required the bidder to arrange financing for the electricity generating station to be purchased on an installment basis by FPL but fully owned and operated by them. Cost for construction and installation of equipment (estimated at $18 million) in the generating station would not be included in any debt service to the county. Finally, the RFP stipulated that only that portion of the tipping fee reflecting operating cost could be escalated annually, using the relative change in the United States Consumer Price Index from the execution date of the contract.

The redraft became the final version of the RFP. It was issued at the end of July 1974, with a requirement that proposals be submitted in November 1974. The county commissioners waived requirements for competitive bids and authorized the task force to conduct further negotiations following their evaluation of proposals.

Ten proposals were received by the county. It soon became apparent that the concept of private financing, but public ownership, would prevent private companies from realizing tax benefits. The concept also appeared to create legal problems (under state law) with respect to the county issuing pollution control revenue bonds. Both conditions meant that county disposal costs would be higher. It also was clear that the cost of the facility had risen beyond the $50 million general obligation bond issue for solid waste which had been authorized by Dade County voters in 1972. Hence the county could not finance the facility through issuing general obligation bonds. Evaluation also uncovered the fact that some of the proposers did not have the financial capability to arrange financing for the facility and, with one possible exception, none of the remaining proposers appeared capable or willing to finance the project on the basis of corporate credit without some form of financing participation by the county. Faced with this dilemma, the county retained the services of The First Boston Corporation to develop a new financing plan and to confirm Dade's finding on unwillingness by proposers to finance without some form of participation by the county. In the interim, the county advised each proposer that it was willing and capable of participating in the eventual financing of the facility.

Realizing that negotiations with FPL were going to be protracted and difficult, legal counsel recommended that the county negotiate with leading candidates and execute a contract with the successful bidder. It was felt that this approach would facilitate the eventual conclusion of negotiations between FPL and the county.

In June 1975, the county commissioners approved the committee's recommendation that simultaneous but separate negotiations be undertaken with Universal Oil Products (UOP) and Black Clawson on basic guarantees and definition of terms dealing with, but not limited to:

- precise capital cost;
- tipping fee;
- recovered materials;
- operating performance;
- escalation of operating costs;
- factors involved in financing the project.

The county also determined that it would only use pollution control bonds for the long-term purchase of the facility. That is, it would enter into a turnkey contract for the purchase of the facility from UOP or Black Clawson. It was the county's perception that the major risks associated with the project would occur during the construction and testing period. Therefore, the task force indicated to UOP and Black Clawson that the agreed-upon purchase price would not be paid until the county had accepted the facility. Thus, both companies would have to provide construction financing.

Selection of Black Clawson

In late April 1976, the county's legal counsel instructed UOP and Black Clawson to submit their final and best offers. Final bids were received on May 11, 1976. The task force and its legal counsel and financial and engineering consultants evaluated the two proposals and met separately with each company approximately a week later to clarify various issues.

In addition to the more extensive material-recovery capability of the Black Clawson system, the choice of Black Clawson over UOP was based on the following factors:

- Black Clawson offered to assume more risks than UOP even though it required the county to pay 60% of the construction price at the time the construction was completed, while UOP did not require payment until the county accepted the facility. The factors weighing the decision against UOP were:

▶ If the construction was not completed due to no fault of UOP, and the construction loan was due, the county would have to pay the full amount.

▶ If, after three years under the operations agreement, there were three consecutive years in which there were losses of at least $500,000 per year, UOP could terminate the contract. UOP could also terminate if it had an accumulated loss of $3 million. (Black Clawson's proposal did not limit its liability for operating losses.)

▶ UOP would require adjustments in the tipping fee if the BTU content of the waste changed from that established in the first year of operation. It also reserved the right to adjust the tipping fee as a result of any changes in laws which affected the composition of the county's waste.

▶ The capital cost component of the tipping fee was higher under the UOP proposal than under Black Clawson's; escalation of construction cost would be operable for a longer period under the UOP proposal than under Black Clawson's; and UOP had a slightly longer construction period than Black Clawson.

▶ UOP had a higher operating component of the net tipping fee than Black Clawson ($0.80 vs. $0.25), although the task force realized that it was difficult to make strict comparisons because each company had treated costs and revenues somewhat differently.

▶ Black Clawson's successful arrangement of financing for the Hempstead, New York project gave their Dade County financing proposal slightly more credibility than UOP's.

▶ The county's independent engineering evaluation rated the Black Clawson system superior overall to UOP's, based upon criteria including:

  • resource recovery effectiveness;

  • system controllability;

  • plant safety and environmental effects;

  • system flexibility.

▶ UOP's system rated lower on environmental factors than Black Clawson's with respect to: reduction in volume of waste; the willingness of Black Clawson to handle sewage sludge as solid waste; UOP's need to discharge liquid waste (Black Clawson had an enclosed system requiring no such discharge); and the slight advantage of burning a homogenized fuel in the Black Clawson system as it related to air quality.

The Current Situation

In mid-June 1976, the county commissioners authorized Ray Goode, the county manager, to commence final negotiations with Black Clawson, based on the provisional agreement outlined in Appendix A. Appendix B describes the way the proposed resource recovery facility would work.

As well as these negotiations, other matters would have to be cleared away before construction could begin. In addition to negotiating with Florida Power and Light, the county had to secure state financing and Black Clawson would have to secure various permits before starting construction.

The county estimated that it would require approximately six months to one year to obtain approval of an Environmental Impact Statement and to secure a National Pollution Discharge Elimination System (NPDES) permit from the EPA. It was understood that until such approvals were obtained, the county could not notify Black Clawson to commence construction. If the delay lasted one year, the incremental cost to the project reportedly would amount to $650,000 due to construction price escalation.

Issuance of state pollution control bonds was dependent upon approval of the Black Clawson and FPL contracts by the state. The state apparently could require modifications to the terms and conditions of each of these contracts as part of its approval powers. The county submitted the Black Clawson agreement to the state for informational purposes. The Division of Bond Finance had indicated that it would begin no formal action until such time as it had both contracts before it. The county estimated that it would take about six months from the time when both contracts were before the division before state bonds could be sold.

APPENDIX A: DADE COUNTY RESOURCE RECOVERY PROJECT

Summary of Contractual Agreements with Black Clawson

The contracts with Black Clawson are subject to each party being able to obtain financing to enable each party to perform its obligations. The contracts are also subject to the county being able to successfully negotiate an agreement with Florida Power and Light (FPL) for the purchase of steam.

The main features of the *facility purchase agreement* are as follows:

▶ The base construction price including interest, but excluding sales taxes, is $82,182,000 based upon the cost of labor, machinery, and equipment prevailing on June 1, 1976.

▶ The base construction price is to be adjusted upward or downward as follows:

  · Fifty-four percent of the construction price times the percentage by which the Bureau of Labor Statistics Wholesale Price Index, or its successor index, changes between June 1, 1976, and the month in which the last piece of major equipment is received at the construction site; and

  · Forty-six percent of the construction price times the percentage by which the Engineering News Record National Building Cost Index changes between June 1, 1976, and the completion date. (The completion date is to be 30 months from whenever the county authorizes Black Clawson to commence construction.)

▶ Upon the physical completion of the facility, but prior to testing and acceptance by the county, Black Clawson is to be paid 60% of the construction price as adjusted. At the time the facility operates at 80% of its capacity an additional 20% of the construction price will be paid. For operations between 80% and 100% of capacity, the county is obligated to pay 5% when operations reach 90% of capacity, and another 5% when they reach 95% and the remaining 10% upon operations at 100% capacity.

▶ If the facility cannot process 12,600 tons per week on or before the 30th month following the notice of construction commencement by the county, Black Clawson must pay the county $5,000 per day for each day that it is not able to process such volume, unless the failure is due to a condition of

Force Majeure. If the facility is unable to process 12,600 tons per week within 42 months from the commencement date, the county may terminate the agreement and seek damages. However, if the facility is capable of processing 12,600 tons per week prior to 30 months after the commencement date, the county will pay Black Clawson $5,000 per day for each day in which the facility is capable of processing said tonnage per week, up until the 30th month is reached. The county, under such circumstances, may request Black Clawson to commence operations per the operations agreement even though the construction completion date has not been reached.

▶ As part of the construction price, Black Clawson is required to develop a landfill area which will meet all rules and regulations of the county and state. Because of the high water table, the landfill must have a system for collecting and treating leachate. Also included in the construction price is a pathological waste incinerator capable of handling up to two tons per day. Pathological wastes are defined as animal and human remains, animal carcasses of 125 pounds or less, and contaminated clothing, instruments, and bandages associated with hospital operations.

▶ The county does not take title to the facility until such time as it makes payments of 60% of the construction price. Until such time as the county accepts the facility or pays 100% of the purchase price, Black Clawson is totally responsible for correcting or replacing any loss or damage to the facility equipment or landfill. The company, during this period, is in no way relieved of fulfilling its obligations to the county.

▶ Black Clawson guarantees that the facility shall be capable of processing 18,000 tons per week within 120 days of the completion date and in accordance with acceptance criteria. (The acceptance criteria also apply to the production of electricity.) Within 90 days following completion of construction, Black Clawson, at its own cost, must conduct a test run in the presence of a county representative and a mutually agreed upon independent engineering firm for a period of four weeks in order to determine whether the facility can operate at its design capacity of 18,000 tons per week. If the facility successfully operates at design capacity over the test run period, then the county must accept the facility. During the period of the test runs, as the facility demonstrates that it can operate at 80%, 90%, and 95% of design capacity, the county will make additional payments on the construction price as previously described. However, if the facility fails to meet either air pollution or ash residue tests (even though operating at acceptable percentages of design capacity), such failure shall be deemed a failure to meet acceptance criteria. This failure would relieve the county of making additional payments to Black Clawson until such time as both the air pollution and ash residue tests are satisfied. Failure of the facility to reach design capacity within 12 months of the completion date gives the county the option to terminate its obligation to make any additional construction payments to Black Clawson, provided it gives 60-days' notice of such intent and the facility is unable to meet design capacity within that 60-day period. If the facility has reached at least 80% of design capacity, but less than full design capacity during the 60 days, the county is only obligated to make payment proportional to the percentage of design capacity reached. If only 80% of design capacity is achieved, however, the county is not obligated to pay any portion of the 40% of the construction price outstanding. Black Clawson, however, must continue to do whatever is required to bring the facility up to full design capacity. The county also has the right to seek whatever damages it deems warranted from Black Clawson where design capacity is not achieved.

▶ *Force Majeure* is defined as any act beyond the control of either party. The completion period shall be extended for a period equivalent to that for which a condition of *Force Majeure* exists.

▶ Any default by Black Clawson lasting more than 30 days entitles the county to either terminate the agreement, or to complete construction on its own account using all necessary proprietary information of Black Clawson, or to seek payments for damages, or all of the preceding.

▶ The construction contract may be amended if so required because of the terms and conditions established in an agreement with Florida Power and Light.

▶ Any amendments to the agreement desired by the county shall not be effective unless approved in writing by the construction lenders of Black Clawson.

The main features of the operations (management) agreement are:

▶ The period of operation by Black Clawson is 20 years from the completion date. The period of performance may be extended by mutual agreement for as little as one year and not more than 10 years.

▶ Black Clawson is totally responsible for the operations of the facility and the landfill, including the landfilling of demolition debris, and all cost associated therewith, except sales taxes, franchise taxes imposed by the county on electricity used by the facility, and state and local taxes on electricity, water, gas, etc.

▶ The county may deliver up to 1,500 tons per week in excess of the minimum guaranteed delivery of 18,000 tons per week unless Black Clawson is unable to process or store such excess. The county may deliver up to 300 tons per week of demolition debris and up to two tons per day of pathological waste to the facility.

▶ The facility shall remain open to receive delivery of refuse 10 hours per day, six days per week, and eight hours on Sunday.

▶ Title to refuse and reclaimed materials belongs to Black Clawson.[9]

▶ Commencing the day after completion of construction, Black Clawson must accept delivery of any refuse up to the minimum guaranteed and dispose of said wastes. However, Black Clawson is required to first segregate ferrous, nonferrous metals, glass, and combustibles and recycle and sell all that can be marketed. The company is required to process all refuse capable of being processed by the facility up to full design capacity. That portion which cannot be processed must be landfilled. Black Clawson is required under any case to process or landfill whether or not the facility is accepted by the county at a reduced design capacity. In the event all or a portion of the facility is unable to process solid waste, Black Clawson must first store up to two days or 6,000 tons and then landfill the remaining deliveries. In the event the capacity of county landfill is reached, Black Clawson is responsible for acquiring additional acreage, but the county agrees to use its power of eminent domain if required. If Black Clawson is able to process solid waste prior to the completion date, it shall notify the

---

[9] The gross revenues to the operation of a resource recovery plant in Saugus, Massachusetts, is composed, approximately, of 53% dump fees, 41% steam revenues and 6% from reclaimed materials.

county which shall then make deliveries to the facility. During this period, the county will pay for the pickup of all unreclaimed waste and dispose the same at a landfill site other than that provided by it to Black Clawson.

▸ During emergencies caused by labor strikes, hurricanes, or other natural disasters, Black Clawson must process solid waste but may raise the service charge to the extent of actual premium labor costs, overhead, and cost of materials. If emergency operations result in greater than normal usage of the landfill site, the county at its cost shall obtain, provide, and develop additional land in as close proximity to the landfill site as possible.

▸ The county does not guarantee the quality or composition of solid waste delivered to the facility (see Exhibit 1).

▸ The base tipping fee paid by the county to Black Clawson is $0.25 per ton for each ton of solid waste, $4.50 per ton of demolition debris, and $77 per ton of pathological wastes. The county must pay a minimum tipping fee for 14,000 tons per week based on an average over a monthly period. In the event of a shortfall in waste deliveries, the county must also pay a percentage of the O&M cost per week which is equivalent to the ratio of the shortfall to the minimum guaranteed tonnage, plus all penalties paid by Black Clawson to FPL due to its inability to deliver minimum amounts of steam.

▸ The tipping fee in each year shall be adjusted subsequent to June 1, 1976, to reflect changes in the cost of doing business as follows:

  · $0.125 shall be adjusted by 100% of the net change in the national consumer price index; and

  · $0.125 shall be adjusted by 109% of the net change in the U.S. Wholesale Price Index.

▸ Black Clawson is entitled to receive all revenues from the recovery of materials.[10] The county guarantees that Black Clawson shall receive $6.8 million annually in steam payments. Any projected annual shortfall in that amount will be made up by the county to Black Clawson, unless the anticipated shortfall is a result of failures by the company. However, any steam payments received by Black Clawson in excess of projected annual payments are to be shared by the county and the company on a 50–50 basis.[11]

▸ Any expenditures to change the facility as a result of changes in existing law, regulations, or industry codes (except those affecting the quality and composition of the county's solid waste) are to be borne by the county. The tipping fee also shall be adjusted to reflect any increases in operating costs caused by changes or alterations to the facility.

▸ *Force Majeure* is defined as any act beyond the control of either parties which prevent them from carrying out their performance. If a *Force Majeure* condition prevents Black Clawson from operating the facility for more than 48 hours, the county has the right upon 12 hours notice and at its own expense to operate the facility and landfill. Where the county exercises this right, the tipping fee paid by the county is to be reduced to reflect the reduced services performed by Black Clawson. However, Black Clawson is still entitled to all revenues from the sale of recovered materials and steam.

---

[10] Estimated by Black Clawson at about $1.14 per ton of refuse.

[11] Steam revenues estimated by Black Clawson at about $4.34 per ton of refuse.

> ‣ The county has the right to terminate the operations agreement and to take over the facility and the landfill and to operate either if Black Clawson defaults because of:
>> · Insolvency or filing of bankruptcy by Black Clawson or Parsons & Whittemore;
>> · Black Clawson fails to process 12,600 tons per week (the minimum quantity of waste) after 90 days of completion for a period of 60 consecutive days, and fails to remedy or commence remedy of such default within 30 days of receiving a notice of default from the county; and
>> · Black Clawson fails to perform or observe any obligation under the operation or construction contracts and fails to correct such breach within 30 days of notice by the county, unless the time period for correction requires more than 30 days. In the case of any default by the county, Black Clawson is only entitled to damages and, where applicable, specific performance.
>
> ‣ To the extent that the operations agreement is affected by any subsequent Steam Purchase Agreement with FPL, it is to be amended or modified.
>
> ‣ Any dispute related to the operations agreement is to be settled by arbitration in accordance with the rules of the American Arbitration Association.

Exhibit 1 _____

GARBAGE OR RESIDENTIAL WASTE COMPOSITION

(Dade County's estimate of current waste composition. For the information of proposers only, not guaranteed.)

Garbage (55% of total refuse)	Percent by Weight
Food waste	16
Garden waste	8
Paper products	47
Plastics, rubber, leather	3
Textiles	3
Wood	3
Ferrous metals	7
Aluminum	1
Glass and ceramics	8
Rock, dirt, ash, etc.	4
Trash (45% of total refuse)	
Metals (mostly ferrous)	20
Other noncumbustible (glass, dirt, rock, etc.)	5
Garden trash (tree cuttings, grass and bushes, palm fronds, etc.)	75

Assume total refuse of 936,000 tons/year.

APPENDIX B: DADE COUNTY RESOURCE RECOVERY PROJECT

Brief Description of the Black Clawson's Proposed Recovery System

The resource recovery system will process up to 3,000 tons of waste per day, six days per week. The recovery process includes waterwall incineration to produce steam for conversion into electricity by a 70 Mw power plant. It is estimated that approximately 150 workers will be employed at the recovery facility.

The recovery system employs Black Clawson's "Hydrasposal Process," a wet-processing technique for size reduction and classification of solid waste. The processing technology is based on systems commonly used by the pulp and paper industry. In addition to segregation of combustible materials, the Black Clawson process recovers ferrous, aluminum, a mixture of copper, brass, zinc and magnesium, and color-sorted glass. Of the input solid waste, about 11% (by weight) remains as process residue for landfilling. Also included in the recovery system are separate lines for processing bulky waste such as white goods and yard waste, and for incinerating pathological waste.

After weighing, trucks unload refuse at one of the 19 tipping stations into an enclosed, relatively shallow, storage pit having a capacity of 6,000 tons. Heavy tractors are driven across this waste to compact it, and to move the refuse into conveyor hoppers. From the hoppers the refuse is carried by conveyors to four parallel lines of wet-processing equipment, each rated at 33 tons per hour. Each line consists of a hydrapulper, junk remover, dump pump, and two liquid cyclone separators. Each line feeds into ferrous metal, aluminum, nonferrous metal, and glass separation subsystems. The combustible fraction is dewatered and burned in waterwall boilers.

At the bottom of each pulper is a screen with one-inch holes through which pulped waste as a water slurry is pumped to a liquid cyclone for further processing. Oversized wastes, such as tin cans, metal, large pieces of rubber, stones, etc., cannot be ground or pulped and are ejected from the pulper through a slot located near the bottom of the pulping tub into a bucket elevator, or junk remover. Recycled water is introduced into the bucket in order to carry lighter objects back into the pulper for further grinding and pulping.

The lighter organic combustible fraction is separated from the heavier inorganic component in the liquid cyclone. The heavy fraction is ejected from the bottom of the cyclone where it is elutriated with water to wash out and retrieve most of the organics entrapped near the bottom of the cyclone. This washing forms a vortex of water containing the organics which flow upward and out of the center of the cyclone into a surge chest. The inorganics are introduced into a spiral classifier to remove any residual combustibles. The latter are transferred to the surge chest while the inorganic materials (50% ferrous metal in the form of tin cans, and 50% consisting of nonferrous metal, large chunks of glass, some wood, and pieces of rubber) are conveyed at high speed past an electromagnetic separator. Magnetic materials are deposited into a ferrous metal hopper while the nonferrous material drops into another hopper where it is passed over a grizzly screen. Large stones and other large objects are removed by the grizzly and become part of the nonrecoverable residue. Nonferrous metals, large pieces of glass, and other materials (such as buttons and broken china) are conveyed from the grizzly back to the hydrapulper for further regrinding.

Ultimately, reprocessed nonferrous metals and other materials are conveyed past a second magnet to recover any ferrous residue not originally separated following processing in the liquid cyclone. Aluminum foil and light sheet aluminum are separated from the remaining nonferrous and other materials on an air-aspirated shaking table. The balance is then further separated into electrical nonconductors and conductors on a high tension electrostatic separator. Materials which are poor conductors, such as glass and ceramics, receive an electrical charge, while conductors, such as nonferrous metals and crystalline stones, lose theirs. The noncharged materials fall into one hopper and the charged materials fall into another. The metallic value of the noncharged materials is recovered by running the mixture through a crusher which flattens metallic particles, but reduces the nonmetallics to a powder. These two types of materials are finally separated by screening.

Glass is recovered from the charged material hopper by means of an optical transparency scanner which separates out opaque materials, such as ceramics. The remaining mixed glass is sorted into clear, amber and green by means of an optical color separator.

The combustible material which is conveyed into the surge chest is thoroughly blended and pumped to a two-stage dewatering press. The dewatering process raises the solid content to 50% from the 3% content of the original slurry. The resultant combustible material is conveyed pneumatically to live-bottom metering bins at the boilers. Fuel production in excess of boiler requirements is transported on a shuttle conveyor to fuel storage for future use—primarily Sundays.

Steam is produced by two waterwall boilers equipped with two-stage particulate gas cleaning equipment. The boilers are designed to operate using only recovered organic fuel. However, oil burners are provided in order to assure the production of steam during scheduled and unscheduled periods of downtime. Recovered fuel is burned on an air-swept spreader stoker. Approximately one-third of the fuel is burned in suspension while the other two-thirds is burned on the traveling grate of the stoker. Ash is stored in a silo with two days' capacity.

The steam is supplied at 600 psig and 750°F to two 35 M hydrogen-cooled turbo generators. Condensate from the turbine provides low pressure steam from boiler room auxiliaries. Electricity is generated at 13.8 kv, which is transformed and fed to Florida Power and Light's 240 kv distribution line.

The generating plant will be equipped with mechanical force-draft cooling towers. Blowdown from the cooling towers is to be used to make up water in the waste processing plant.

At capacity, the recovery system will process 936,000 tons of solid waste per year, and will produce annually:

‣ 442 million kilowatt-hours of electricity
‣ 65,520 tons of ferrous
‣ 7,020 tons of aluminum
‣ 4,680 tons of other nonferrous metals
‣ 37,400 tons of color-sorted glass.

▼   ▼   ▼

RCI Inc. (A)

The following is a simplified business situation in which RCI must negotiate with Southeastern Electric Company for sale of steam during the calendar year 1993. The information in Part I of the case is known to both parties. The information in Part II is strictly internal to RCI. As this case is intended as an exercise, please ignore the effects of taxes and the time value of money.

Part I

You are vice president of research and development for RCI Inc., a company founded in the 1930's on the basis of one producing oil well. That well had long since dried up and RCI has no current oil producing facilities, but the money had financed RCI's growth into a large diversified company whose motivation was still to take calculated risks in projects that could produce energy. You recently negotiated a contract to build and operate a resource recovery facility for Westborough County. The plant will receive all of Westborough's residential and commercial refuse, recover usable materials for resale, and burn the residue, both to reduce it in size for landfill purposes and to produce steam which may then be sold.

You are confident that the construction will take exactly one year, starting January 1, 1992 and will cost $50 million. RCI's size had given it a major advantage in bidding for the original contract because smaller businesses had been unable to find commercial loans due to the technological uncertainty surrounding the plant design. RCI had chosen to fund the project out of retained earnings. Westborough is committed to paying 5 equal installments of $10 million when the plant is 20, 40, 60, 80, and 100% complete. RCI negotiated away a profit on the construction phase of the enterprise in return for exclusive title to the by-products of the plant, the recovered materials, and steam.

When operational (January 1, 1993) the plant will produce steam with an annual energy equivalent of 100,000 barrels of oil. You have identified two possible customers for the steam. Acme Company has agreed to purchase all of your steam output during the six winter months, November to April, inclusive, at a 20% discount from the price of oil prevailing on January 1st of each year. They would be happy to commence this agreement on either January 1, 1993 or January 1, 1994.

The Southeastern Electric Company has expressed a willingness to discuss the purchase of all of RCI's output of steam during the year 1993. On January 1, 1994 Southeastern will convert from oil to 100% nuclear energy and will then have no further use for the steam. If Southeastern agrees to purchase the steam, it will have to build a generating facility near the RCI plant to convert the steam into electricity. Construction of this facility would take one year and cost $1 million. The facility's location and design is such that it is of no use to anyone but Southeastern, and will have no salvage value if not needed by them.

Part II

The principal risk in the construction phase of the plant is that it may prove to be technologically unfeasible. If so, this will not be apparent until Westborough officials test the plant prior to handing over the final construction payment of

Harvard Business School case 9-182-277. Professor David E. Bell prepared this case. Copyright © 1982 by the President and Fellows of Harvard College.

$10 million. Of course, this amount would not be forthcoming if the plant did not work. Plants with similar, but not identical, technologies have been largely unsuccessful but RCI was proceeding on the presumption that it had the engineers to correct the difficulties. While these engineers profess 100% confidence in their ability to make the plant work, you feel that a probability of 0.7 summarizes your belief that the plant will work. (Assume that the plant either works to specifications or does not and has zero salvage value.)

The sale of steam represents your principal source of revenue. You believe that the current oil price of $35 per barrel could be anywhere between $30 and $50 by January 1, 1993, with all intermediate prices equally likely. Your plan is to negotiate a one-year contract with Southeastern for 1993 and then switch to supplying the Acme Company on a part-time basis thereafter on the terms outlined above. You currently see no other prospects for selling steam. The deal with Acme is sufficiently attractive to make the whole venture economically viable.

Your skill as a negotiator will be judged on the "value added" by your negotiations with Southeastern, using the various probabilities and dollar figures given above.

Calendar

1 Oct 91	"Now"
1 Jan 92	Construction begins on resource recovery plant and, if necessary, on generating facility.
1 Jan 93	If plant works, steam is supplied to Acme or Southeastern as appropriate.
1 Jan 94	Steam is supplied only to Acme, and then only in the winter months.

▼   ▼   ▼

CASE SOUTHEASTERN ELECTRIC COMPANY (A)

The following is a simplified business situation in which Southeastern Electric Company is to negotiate with RCI Inc. for purchase of steam during the calendar year 1993. The information in Part I of this case is known to both parties. The information in Part II is strictly internal to Southeastern. As this case is intended as an exercise, please ignore the effects of taxes and the time value of money.

Part I

RCI Inc. is a major diversified company with a 50-year history of investing in longshots, stemming from its initial success with an oil well (long since dried up). Though RCI has no current interests in oil, it does specialize in finding ways of producing energy. Consistent with this strategy, RCI has agreed to build and operate a resource recovery facility for Westborough County. On completion, the plant will receive all of Westborough's residential and commercial refuse, recover usable materials for resale, and burn the residue, both to reduce it in size for landfill purposes and to produce steam which may then be sold.

You have been put in charge of negotiating with RCI for purchase of that steam during the calendar year 1993. On January 1, 1994, Southeastern will convert from oil to 100% nuclear energy and will thus have no further use for the steam. RCI had been unable to obtain a commercial loan for the project but had apparently funded the project internally. This was quite consistent with RCI's reputation for investing in projects with potential. The terms of RCI's contract with Westborough require the county to pay 5 equal installments of $10 million when the plant is 20, 40, 60, 80, and 100% complete. You share RCI's belief that construction will cost exactly $50 million and take exactly one year (the calendar year 1992). RCI apparently negotiated away any construction profit in return for exclusive title to all by-products of the plant, including steam. When operational, the plant will produce steam with an annual usable energy equivalent of 100,000 barrels of oil.

You have learned that Acme Company has offered to buy all of RCI's steam for the six winter months (November to April, inclusive) of each year at a 20% discount rate from the price of oil prevailing on January 1st of each year. Any deal between Southeastern and RCI for 1993 would not affect this offer for subsequent years.

Acme intends to use the steam directly for its internal heating system, but Southeastern requires electricity and would need to build a generating facility near the RCI plant to convert the steam into electricity. Such a generating facility would take one year to build at a cost of $1,000,000. The facility's location and design is such that it is of no use to anyone but Southeastern, and will have no salvage value if not needed by them.

Part II

Southeastern has been hurt greatly in the past by vast swings in the price of oil. Its own forecasts suggest that by January 1, 1993 the price of oil could be anywhere between $30 and $50 per barrel, with all intermediate prices equally likely.

The deal with RCI is potentially attractive, not only as a way to soften the impact of oil price movements, but also as a gesture of goodwill towards the spirit of environmental preservation and energy conservation at a time when you are receiving bad publicity from opponents of nuclear power. However, Southeastern is concerned by the failure rate of resource recovery facilities similar to that being built by RCI. You know that these plants either work to specifications or fail completely (with zero salvage value) and that this uncertainty is not resolved until the plant is inspected by Westborough prior to the final installment payment of $10 million (which will be withheld if the plant does not work). You estimate the probability that the plant will work as 0.4.

You realize that Southeastern considers that being seen as accommodating as possible to resource recovery efforts is crucial to its image. However, you also realize that the company has a commitment to its customers and that you will be judged on the "value added" (calculated in terms of the probabilities and dollar figures given above) to the utility by the contract you sign.

Calendar

1 Oct 91	"Now"
1 Jan 92	Construction begins on resource recovery plant and, if necessary, on generating facility.
1 Jan 93	If plant works, steam is supplied to Acme or Southeastern as appropriate.
1 Jan 94	Steam is supplied only to Acme, and then only in the winter months.

▼   ▼   ▼

Harvard Business School case 9-182-280. Professor David E. Bell prepared this case. Copyright © 1982 by the President and Fellows of Harvard College.

EXERCISES ON PERSONAL SAFETY

1. On July 12, 1983, the EPA asked the citizens of Tacoma, Washington to help decide whether they would accept some risk of cancer from arsenic in the air in order to avoid the closing of a copper smelting plant that provided 800 jobs.[12]

   As an air pollutant, arsenic, a deadly poison, has been found to cause lung cancer and other illnesses. While the plant had met federal guidelines until then, new federal regulations, if imposed, would require it to lower its emissions to 172 million grams per year from 282 million grams.

   The EPA estimated that the risk of contracting lung cancer for most people exposed to the arsenic currently being emitted was about 9 in 100, over a lifetime. They estimated that about four Tacoma residents per year died from this cause, out of a total of between 71-94 dying from lung cancer from all causes.

   The new standard would lower the chances of contracting lung cancer from the arsenic emissions to 2 in 100, according to the EPA, and reduce the number of annual deaths to one per year. With current technologies, the risk could not be reduced to zero without effectively closing the plant, which was estimated to pump about $20 million per year into the local economy.

   Asarco, the company operating the plant, said it would have to spend $4.4 million to meet the new arsenic standard, if imposed.

   Do you think it is in the best interests of the citizens of Tacoma to impose the new standard? Should the correct standard of emissions be zero? How do you think the citizens of Tacoma would actually vote on these issues? What about the plant workers?

2. In 1980, a movie stuntman, James J. Nickerson, was asked to perform a stunt for the movie "Cannonball Run" in which he was to weave a car, at high speed, between four oncoming vehicles. The car slammed into a van, however, leaving Nickerson with a shattered hip, a fractured arm, and head wounds that required 100 stitches. His passenger, 22 year-old Heidi Von Beltz, was injured even more seriously, and as a result is quadriplegic.[13]

   In a deposition in a resulting lawsuit, Nickerson said that the car, an Aston Martin, had "faulty suspension, smooth tires, marginal steering, and no seat belts." Nickerson, asked why, knowing what he did about the car, he nevertheless had driven it, replied "If I said 'Hey I'm not getting in this car until there's seat belts in it', well, stunt man X would have been in the car and doing the shot instead of me. And I needed the money."

   What psychological factors might have contributed to Nickerson ignoring the dangers and doing the stunt anyway? Can an argument be made that Nickerson may well have made a rational decision by driving the car?

---

[12] This description abstracted from a *New York Times* article of 7/13/83, "A City Weighs Cancer Risk Against Lost Jobs".

[13] This question is based on an article in the *New York Times Magazine* of 12/5/83.

AMERICAN CYANAMID COMPANY

In June, 1981, Nina Klein, Corporate Medical Director of a large, international U.S. based chemical company, was rereading a memorandum she had just received from the Chief Executive Officer.

The company was proposing to implement a new set of safety standards, to take account of recent federal and state legislation. The new standards were to focus particularly on reproductive hazards in the workplace. Dr. Klein had been asked for her suggestions in formulating the standards.

While she had been cognizant of the major issues for some time, there were still a number of questions regarding the company's legal and economic liability, and social responsibility, which she had not yet resolved for herself.

As she sat enjoying the late afternoon sunshine, Dr. Klein collected her thoughts on the subject by recalling the kinds of provisions included in the safety standards of chemical companies similar to her own.

In particular, she recalled the fetus protection policy implemented by American Cyanamid three years earlier, which had led to a number of as yet unresolved lawsuits. American Cyanamid was still fighting actions by the Occupational Safety and Health Administration (OSHA), the American Civil Liberties Union (ACLU), and individuals who claimed that the fetus protection policy had forced women employees to choose between their jobs and their fertility.

As Dr. Klein mused on the arguments propounded by the various litigants, she wondered what lessons could be learned from the events at Cyanamid's Willow Island plant that would assist her in making proposals for her own company's safety standards.

American Cyanamid Company was incorporated in Maine in 1907 and grew fairly rapidly through related acquisitions in the chemical industry. It now had over $3 billion of revenues derived from operations in 125 countries.

The company was engaged in the manufacture and sale of a highly diversified line of agricultural, medical, specialty chemical, consumer, and formica products. Of approximately 44,000 employees, 48% were paid hourly. A large proportion of these hourly-paid employees represented by plant local unions of the International Chemical Workers Union, and the Oil, Chemical, and Atomic Workers Union.

The Willow Island Plant

Cyanamid's plant at Willow Island, West Virginia, was one of the more important production facilities in the United States, even though it employed a relatively small number of people. Here, Cyanamid manufactured pigments, dyestuffs, animal feed supplements, melamine, platinum catalysts, plastic antioxidants, and specialty chemicals. The plant represented an important source of employment to an industrially depressed area.

Harvard Business School case 9-181-131. Research Assistant, Nadia Woloshyn prepared this case from public information under the supervision of Professor David E. Bell. Copyright © 1981 by the President and Fellows of Harvard College.

American Cyanamid's New Safety Standards

Very few women were employed as production workers by American Cyanamid until 1974, when things began to change. By the end of 1977, twenty-three women were working on production lines at Willow Island. Legislative activity throughout the 70s forced companies to become increasingly alert to the hazards of female exposure to fetotoxins, any substances especially hazardous to fetuses.

Accordingly, in September, 1977, American Cyanamid began a corporate-wide campaign to revise safety standards, with particular attention to suspected fetotoxins. From a large list of suspected fetotoxins, five chemicals were identified as being especially hazardous to fetuses. These were lead, hydrazine hydrate, hydrazine sulfate, and two pharmaceuticals, Thiotepa and Methotrexate. For each substance, the company established exposure levels it considered safe for a healthy adult and for a developing fetus. These levels were usually determined by information available in published literature on toxins. Typically, the safe levels for adult exposure were five to ten times higher for an adult than for a fetus. In the case of lead, the setting of the standards took more than a year.

The Fetus Protection Policy

In January 1978, the American Cyanamid Company announced to employees of its Willow Island pigments manufacturing plant that it intended to implement what it called the "fetus protection policy." This policy, as ultimately implemented, excluded women aged 16 through 50 from production jobs in the lead pigments department unless they could prove that they had been surgically sterilized. The stated purpose of the policy was to protect the fetuses of women exposed to lead, particularly during early pregnancy when the employee might not know of her pregnancy. Similar policies were already practiced in the chemical industry, and had been implemented by Allied Chemical, DuPont, Dow Chemical, and General Motors, in areas where workers were exposed to lead.

Twenty-three women at Willow Island were warned at this time that they were working with potentially fetotoxic substances and that new company policies would require their transfer to other work areas if their exposure was found to be hazardous. By October, 1978, the policy was put into effect. The only affected area of the Willow Island plant was the lead chromate pigment manufacturing area where eight women worked.

Events Resulting from the Fetus Protection Policy

Between February and July 1978, five women employed in the lead pigments department submitted to surgical sterilization in a hospital not associated with American Cyanamid. The women later claimed that there was considerable confusion over the date when the policy would be implemented, and over its actual effect in practice. They also claimed that they were advised there would not be enough new jobs to go around after their transfer from the lead chromate pigment area; and as a consequence they risked losing their jobs or facing demotion once the guidelines went into effect.

American Cyanamid, on the other hand, contended that it actively discouraged the five women from undergoing sterilization, and that it offered them perfectly acceptable alternatives in the form of actual or promised jobs with similar status at the same pay level. Nevertheless, the corporate medical director D. Robert Clyne (now retired), agreed that, "If a women of childbearing age is sterile, she is allowed to work in the pigments area."

As of 1981, the case was still in litigation, and it was not clear where the blame lay. It was, however, certain that the situation was aggravated by the small size of the Willow Island facility. Equivalent jobs were not immediately available for the women, who faced transfer temporarily to lower-status jobs, although with retention of pay for 90 days. It was also certain that the policy caused so much anxiety among those affected that five women chose sterilization over anticipated unemployment or demotion. The youngest woman to undergo the surgery was twenty-five, according to Joan Burton of the American Civil Liberties Union.

Two other female women elected to change jobs rather than undergo sterilization. Both were offered janitorial jobs, with the same pay as their previous jobs for 90 days and with special access to other openings in the plant as they became available. Both were offered new jobs at their old pay level during the 90-day period. One took the new job. The other chose to retain the janitorial job, at a lower salary, because the new job involved shift work.

Lawsuits Against American Cyanamid

Shortly after the initial policy announcement in January 1978, the Oil, Chemical, and Atomic Workers Union (OCAW) and fourteen women members of the union filed complaints against the company's policy with OSHA, the West Virginia Human Rights Commission and with the Equal Employment Opportunity Commission in West Virginia or in Washington, D.C. The union's arbitration grievance and the West Virginia Human Rights Commission investigation, were subsequently withdrawn or dismissed.

In January 1979, however, OSHA inspectors visited the Willow Island plant for an investigation of the charges made by OCAW and the fourteen women. As a result of the investigation, OSHA brought citations against American Cyanamid. The first citation contended that American Cyanamid was in violation of the lead standard and lead chromate standard mandated by federal law. The exposure level allowed according to industry standards set by OSHA in April, 1979, was 50 micrograms per cubic meter, but 200 micrograms per cubic meter were being permitted as an interim compliance level for pigment plants. The willful and serious violations specified by the OSHA investigation included: failure to identify an area with lead chromate exposure as a regulated area; overexposure to coal dust and noise; allowing workers to use personal protection equipment improperly; permitting workers to consume food and beverages in a lead exposed area.

Willful violations, according to OSHA definition, existed where evidence showed that the employer committed an intentional and knowing act as contrasted with inadvertent violation, and the employer was conscious of the fact that what it was doing was a violation; or, even though an employer was not consciously in violation of the OSHA Act, it was aware that the hazardous condition existed and made no reasonable effort to eliminate the condition. Willful violations carried proposed penalties of up to $10,00 each.

Serious violations were defined as those where there was a substantial probability of death or serious physical harm resulting and the employer knew, or could have known with reasonable diligence, of the existence of the hazard. Such violations carried mandatory proposed penalties of up to $1,000 each.

OSHA also cited American Cyanamid under the general duty clause of the Occupational Safety and Health Act of 1970. This was the first time that clause had been used to justify an OSHA citation and represented an attempt by

OSHA to expand its authority over the setting of the safety standards in the workplace. The purpose of the act was "to assure so far as possible every working many and woman in the nation safe and healthful working conditions and to preserve our human resources." The general duty clause required each employer to furnish employment and a place of employment free of recognized hazards causing or likely to cause death or serious physical harm. The Act did not, however, define the term "hazard."

By October 1979, OSHA had proposed the maximum fine allowable by law, $10,000, and ordered the company to halt the regulatory violations. American Cyanamid contested the fine and the citations within the fifteen days allowable for contesting, and in August 1980 the case was heard by William Brennan, an administrative law judge, sitting in Hyattsville, MD.

The citations were dismissed by Brennan on two grounds: firstly, the OSHA had issued the citations after the six month statute of limitation had expired. Although the policies mandating exclusion had been announced early in 1978, they were not implemented until October 1978, and OSHA did not issue citations until the middle of 1979. The delays that occurred were partly a result of confusion about the actual effect of Cyanamid's new policies, and partly because OSHA's legal powers in this area had not been clarified by case law. As a result, the second ground for dismissal of the citations was that OSHA has no jurisdiction over exclusionary policies. OSHA appealed the administrative judge's decision to the OSHA Review Commission, a federal adjudicatory agency designed to hear employer/employee disputes arising from OSHA inspections.

On April 28, 1981, the Review Commission decided that American Cyanamid was not in violation of the general duty clause. The Commission explained that the fetus protection policy was neither a work process nor a work material, and it manifestly could not alter the physical integrity of employees while they were engaged in work or work-related activities. An employee's decision to undergo sterilization in order to gain or retain employment grew out of economic and social factors which operated primarily outside the workplace. The employer neither controlled nor created these factors as it created or controlled work processes and materials. Therefore the policy was not a hazard in the meaning of the general duty clause.

The Review Commission's decision was then appealable by OSHA to the circuit courts. As of 1981 it had not been announced what action OSHA would take.

American Civil Liberties Suit

A second suit against American Cyanamid was brought on January 29, 1980. Thirteen women, represented by the American Civil Liberties Union, filed a class action suit alleging violation of Title VII of the 1964 Civil Rights Act; and in particular, that Cyanamid's program wrongfully discriminated against the plaintiffs on the basis of sex, invaded their privacy, perpetrated a fraud, and intentionally inflicted emotional distress upon them. One of the principal allegations of the complaint was that Cyanamid imposed surgical sterilization as a term and condition of continued employment.

The Civil Rights Act upheld the right of employees to hold jobs without suffering discrimination and without threat to reproductive capacity and genetic stability. Among the women represented in this action were four out of the five sterilized women, and a number of applicants for employment at the Willow Island plant who were refused work, they claimed, on discriminatory grounds.

Dr. Klein knew that the suit was still in process: if ACLU should win its case, the women would be entitled to be put in positions they would have been in if no discrimination had occurred, and entitled to receive any money lost through discriminatory practices. American Cyanamid would therefore have to restore to them job opportunities and promotional opportunities. The question of reversing the surgical sterilization also arose. In certain circumstances it was possible to reverse sterilization, although the outcome of such operations in the past had been very uncertain. In addition, the women might be entitled to substantial damages under state tort claims filed at the same time.

The trial was expected to take place at the end of 1981.

Shareholders' Campaign

American Cyanamid faced attack from a third group. A shareholders' campaign mounted jointly by the International Chemical Workers Union (ICWU) and the Interfaith Center for Corporate Public Responsibility (CCPR) demanded that American Cyanamid establish a public responsibility committee composed of non-employee board members; the committee was to be an impartial body set up to study the fetus protection policy and corporate safety standards.

The ICCPR was a shareholder of American Cyanamid, and the ICWU held shares in Cyanamid through members who had received stock options as part of their compensation. The ICCPR held shares in a large number of US corporations. One of its functions was to use its influence as a shareholder to make corporations aware of their social responsibilities. While there were a number of companies that had implemented an exclusionary policy similar to Cyanamid's, the ICCPR selected Cyanamid as a target case. It was felt that in view of the publicity surrounding the sterilizations, Cyanamid would be particularly sensitive, and therefore responsive to, the issue.

Initially, the Board of Directors refused to establish a public responsibility committee stating that the current mechanism for reviewing safety standards was perfectly adequate. However, on the 31st of January, 1980, a few days after its earlier statement, the Board of Directors, threatened by shareholder resolutions, acceded to the request. The reason for Cyanamid's about-face was unclear, but the ICWU claimed that Cyanamid was particularly concerned about OSHA citations, shortly to come before OSHARC, and about the Equal Opportunity Commission's guidelines which were to be published in February 1980.

The public responsibility committee established by American Cyanamid originally consisted of three members, one of whom later withdrew from the committee. The two remaining members were: Paul MacAvoy, Milton Steinbach Professor of Organization and Management and Economics at Yale University; and George L. Schultz, a private investor. Their report was expected towards the autumn of 1981.

Complaints Filed with the Equal Employment Opportunity Commission

Complaints filed with the EEOC by the original fourteen women and OCAW were still pending in 1981. The EEOC had taken no action, but had the authority to impose penalties for sex discrimination. The EEOC had however, a history of involvement in the safety and discrimination issue in general.

Equal Employment Opportunity Commission Guidelines

In April, 1978, the EEOC issued a policy statement that fell short of making a decision on exclusionary work practices, but offered some guidelines. It stated that exclusionary employment actions taken hastily or without regard for rigorous adherence to acceptable scientific processes might be viewed as unlawful discrimination. Employers had to make sure that such practices not be instituted without making a serious effort to find alternative methods with a less exclusionary impact.

On February 1, 1980, the EEOC and the Office of Federal Contract Compliance issued proposed guidelines that were somewhat more specific and would have the effect of placing "protective exclusions" within the jurisdiction of the section of the Civil Rights Act of 1964 that prohibited job discrimination. The guidelines, briefly, suggested that an employer's conduct which treated men differently from women raised a presumption of a violation of Title VII. An apparently neutral employment policy, which nevertheless adversely affected either men or women, was an unlawful employment practice. If a workplace hazard was known to affect the fetus through either parent, an exclusionary policy directed only at women would be unlawful. If the hazard was scientifically shown to affect the fetus through women only, the class excluded must be limited to pregnant women and not all women of child-bearing capacity.

A *temporary* exclusion policy, introduced to protect women only, would be allowed provided that the policy was directed only at the individuals who might suffer harm; that it was not introduced until suitable alternatives had been adopted or examined; and provided that an employer could show that it had thoroughly searched the scientific literature and could find no evidence of a similar hazard for the nonexcluded sex. Companies had to begin, within six months of the commencement of the exclusionary policy, research projects to find out whether the chemicals in question also produced adverse reproductive effects in the nonexcluded sex. These research projects had to be conducted under "accepted scientific methods" and produce results within two years. The EEOC solicited industry opinions on the guidelines and received critical responses. Unions, women's, and public interest groups supported the guidelines in principle, but found them too vague and subject to misinterpretation. As a result of the lack of support, EEOC withdrew the proposed guidelines on January 13, 1981, stating that,

"Upon reviewing the comments, the agencies have concluded that the most appropriate method of eliminating employment discrimination in the workplace where there is potential exposure to reproductive hazards is through investigation and enforcement of the law on a case by case basis, rather than by the issuance of interpretive guidelines."

Shut-down of Lead Chromate Pigment Unit at Willow Island

On January 15, 1980, American Cyanamid closed down its lead chromate unit at Willow Island, citing adverse profitability of the operation. Poor profitability was due, the company said, to increased government regulation and the decreasing use of lead chromate pigments in paint. The unit was one of ten production lines at Willow Island. American Cyanamid was thought to have lost some orders after the shut-down because the unit acted as a source for other divisions of the company. Any financial loss, however, was temporary and minimal, especially in view of the probability that the unit would have been phased out in due course as other less hazardous substitutes became readily available in the marketplace. Sixty plant personnel were laid off as a result of the shut-down.

Summary of Issues

The issues raised were emotional ones, and aroused considerable anger among the people most closely involved with the various suits against American Cyanamid. A causal comment of one ICWU official was typical: "If a company knew that the result of exposure to fetotoxins would be spontaneous abortion or still birth, they would be happy to allow women to work in areas where they risked exposure. The company's concern is to avoid expensive lawsuits that might be brought by damaged, but surviving, fetuses."

Existing Legislation Affecting Fetotoxins

The law in this area was ill-defined as of 1981. State law in West Virginia was also, according to an attorney in the Attorney General's office of West Virginia, somewhat developed. Environmental laws in this state were still relatively new, and many of the issues in the Cyanamid case had not previously arisen.

Federal law was essentially contained in the OSHA Act of 1970 and the Toxic Substances Control Act of 1977. The Acts differentiated between postconception effects and preconception effects on the fetus; and between *teratogens* and *mutagens*. Teratogens were agents affecting development of the fetus where only the mother's exposure could endanger the fetus. Mutagens were preconception toxins that altered adults' gametes in such a way as to produce mutations in later offspring.

Although the toxic effects of many chemicals were simply not known, in the case of lead, there was considerable evidence that harm could accrue of the male reproductive system as well as to the female. A 1974 study had shown that men with levels of blood lead above 60 micrograms (the federal safety standard) suffered reproductive problems; and OSHA explicitly mentioned dangers to male workers in the new lead standards of April, 1979. "Male workers may be rendered infertile or impotent and both men and women are subject to genetic damage which may affect both the course and outcome of pregnancy." Lead was therefore widely regarded as a *mutagen*.

In theory, an employer discovering a mutagen in the workplace had to address the following issues: Does it affect males in a comparable way to females? Can exposure be controlled in some way short of prohibiting access to the workplace of vulnerable groups? Alternative protective measures might include the use of work assignment adjustments, engineering controls, and personal protective equipment.

The issue of an employer's liability to a fetus or ultimately born child was also unclear. Legal liability of an employer however, might arise from a number of sources:

▶ The employer might be violating a *standard expressly regulated by OSHA*.

▶ The employer might be violating the *OSHA general duty clause*.

▶ The employer might be liable to claim by an injured *employee* under state *workmen's compensation statutes* or other occupational illness statutes.

▶ Under certain circumstances, the employee might be barred by workmen's compensation from bringing *tort action* against the employer.

▶ An ultimately born child injured as a result of its parent's exposure to an occupational mutagen, might bring a *personal injury lawsuit*, where the employer had substantial liability in tort.

It should be emphasized that an employer would normally face considerably higher costs and damages under a personal injury suit than under a workmen's compensation suit.

Arguments for American Cyanamid's Fetus Protection Policy

American Cyanamid contended first of all that it "absolutely discouraged any surgery to preclude child bearing potential." Jack E. White, plant manager at Willow Island, stated, "Our doctor met with local union committee members who represent the females to explain the company position in this matter." Acceptable alternatives were offered in the form of actual or promised jobs with similar status at the same pay level.

It also contended, in the company of Dow, DuPont, Allied Chemical, and other chemical manufacturers with exclusionary policies, that federal safety standards were often technically or economically unattainable. A case in point was the new lead standard, where the level of pollution of 50 micrograms per cubic meter had not yet been reached even with engineering controls and personal protective apparel. Perry Gehring of Dow Chemical stated that, "If the cost of implementing good industrial hygiene is going to risk exponentially to reach a certain low level for uniquely fetal toxins, then it is justified to take women out of the workplace."

The focus of concern of chemical companies was not so much the health hazards to their employees, who were protected under the worker's compensation act, but to the fetus. Bruce Karrh, medical director of DuPont stated, "When we remove a woman it is not to protect her reproductive capacity but to protect her fetus."

Further, chemical companies were reluctant to allow women to sign waivers of responsibility for their unborn children. They claimed the unborn children had legal rights that the mothers could not waive and that, if they did not protect the fetus, they would leave themselves open to claims for damages on behalf of children born with birth defects.

Finally, chemical companies were reluctant to allow fertile women in areas exposed to fetotoxins, regardless of whether they intended to become pregnant or not. Major malformations occurred from the 14th to the 40th day of pregnancy when the major organ systems were being formed. It was usually not possible to detect pregnancy in workers and remove them to a safe workplace before that critical period. While there were methods of ensuring that pregnancies did not take place, or that they were terminated very early in the life of the embryo, these would probably be resisted as unacceptable intrusions into the privacy of employees.

Arguments against American Cyanamid's Fetus Protection Policy

Critics of the exclusionary policies attacked the chemical companies' position on a number of grounds.

Eula Bingham, formerly of OSHA, felt that such policies allowed companies to avoid real efforts to clean up the workplace in favor of the cheaper and easier alternative of removing those employees most susceptible to the danger.

Further, it had not been proven that a toxic substance that affected the fetus through the mother did not also have a deleterious effect on the male reproductive system. Anthony Robbins, director of NIOSH, stated that, "There is no reason to believe that the genetic material of a male worker is in any way more resistant to toxic occupational injury than that of the female." There was, in fact, growing evidence to show that a father's exposure to toxic substances might affect the embryo. Dr. Channing Meyer, environmental health specialist at the University of Cincinnati: "Interference with the normal development of human sperm may result in reduced numbers of sperm, improperly shaped sperm, abnormal sperm movement, and genetic abnormalities in the sperm cell."

Male workers' exposure to toxins could affect the fetus directly through interference in sperm development, and indirectly through carrying toxins from the workplace to the home. In August 1980, the United States Court of Appeals for the District of Columbia Circuit upheld the portion of the OSHA standard that provided the same safeguards for both men and women working with lead, which was commonly regarded as being hazardous to the male reproductive system. Petitions regarding the standard were brought by a variety of parties, including the United Steelworkers of America, the United Automobile Workers, General Motors Corporation, National Construction Association, and others who said the standard was too strict; other unions, however, wanted the standard stricter. The decision was being appealed to the Supreme Court.

Women's rights groups were concerned that the policies would contribute to the myth of 'permanent pregnancy'; that is, that all fertile women at any one time are assumed to be pregnant. The right and ability of women to make a choice about pregnancy should not be curtailed. Eighty percent of blue collar workers then used some form of contraception. Exclusionary policies seemed to deny the fact that women were now free to make their own choice about childbearing.

Finally, the ICWU and other groups were concerned about the dangers inherent in discriminating on genetic grounds. Should the exclusionary policies be allowed to stand, it might open a path to companies screening out other minority groups on the basis of 'genetic susceptibility.' The *New York Times* published a series of articles in February 1980, on this subject. Excerpts from the articles follow:

> Petrochemical companies have quietly tested thousands of American workers to determine if any of the genes they were born with are what industry doctors call 'defective,' making the employees especially vulnerable to certain chemicals in the workplace. The process is called genetic screening...
>
> Employers say the purpose of the tests is to provide a protective barrier keeping 'hypersusceptible' workers away from industrial poisons...
>
> Some scientists, union leaders, and industrial hygienists reject assertions that the tests protect the workers...
>
> They say the genetic approach is indeed a barrier, but one that threatens workers with sexual, racial, or ethnic discrimination. They oppose an employment philosophy that would label a particular group of people as unfit for certain jobs because of their genetic make-up. This approach shifts the focus of the problem to the genes of the workers, rather than to the presence of industrial poisons in the workplace.

▼   ▼   ▼

BREAKFAST FOODS CORPORATION (B)

John Morgan, CEO of Breakfast Foods Corporation (BF, Makers of "Wheatflakes" and other brands), was chairing a meeting of his senior VPs. They were discussing possible reasons for the rather sudden decline of BF's stock price, a decline made more marked by the corresponding rise in the stock of their chief rival, MC (Morning Cereal, Inc.).

Ron Sykes, the marketing VP, had just finished making the observation that BF's success with its purchasing of raw materials, principally wheat, had not been so good of late while MC was apparently having some luck, when David Baker, Morgan's general assistant, interrupted. "We should never have hired a risk manager."

John sighed. He had been expecting something like this. The new risk manager was Christine Aquilino, a recent Harvard Business School graduate. John had sensed that David, a Stanford graduate hired a year earlier, might resent the publicity and carte blanche given to Christine, who had already announced plans to actively hedge BF's interest rate and foreign currency exposures.

David continued, "Since shareholders of BF are diversified they do not care about unsystematic risks, so it is a wasteful exercise on our part to try and manage them."

Don Phillips, VP Production, interrupted, "Chris spent $500 the other day on fire extinguishers for the new machine shop. I can see now that that was a mistake."

"Obviously I'm not talking about risk management strategies that have a positive expected return," said David, "but actions like hedging with futures are definitely a waste of time for us. Modigliani and Miller showed that shareholders were indifferent to the debt/equity ratio of a company on the grounds that shareholders could always leverage their shares themselves. The implication is, that since the debt/equity ratio makes no difference, a company shouldn't waste resources to alter it. Isn't that right, Arthur?"

Arthur Barnes, VP Finance, with his eyes fixed on the ceiling, simply said, "You've no idea how thankful I am all this kind of stuff came out after I left graduate school."

"Well, anyway," continued David, "the argument is the same with managing risk, if shareholders want to hedge foreign currency or wheat prices they can do so themselves. *We* shouldn't spend money, salaries for example, to do this on their behalf."

John Morgan spoke up. "Right now I'm beginning to think of other ways we might save on salaries, but if I understand you, David, at least Christine is doing the company no harm."

David jumped back in, "Actually it's worse than that. Common stock is essentially a call option on the firm's assets, whose 'exercise price' is the amount the firm has promised to pay to the bondholders. Since the value of an option increases with variability in the underlying asset, it's inevitable that taking action to reduce risk in BF will lead to a lower stock price. Appointing a risk manager is a blessing to our bondholders, not our stockholders."

Before Baker could use the example he had brought to clarify the matter (see Exhibit 1), Ron Sykes interrupted. "I know Harvard MBAs are expensive, maybe even overpriced, but this is the first time I've heard of a company wiping $60 million off its stock price because it hired one." Sykes was trying not to laugh.

Harvard Business School case 9-183-135. Professor David E. Bell prepared this case. Copyright © 1982 by the President and Fellows of Harvard College.

Arthur Barnes chimed in, "David, why don't you and your pals buy a controlling share of BF, fire the risk manager, and share in the windfall $60 million profit?"

Morgan could not resist adding, with a straight face, "You are right, David. I'm going to call up Mitchell (CEO at MC) and suggest that each December 31 we toss a coin for $25 million. That should really get our stock price up."

Sykes: "To get back to business, what I was about to say is, I wonder if there is any chance of luring Harry Simpson back from MC. I've been looking at his old forecast record..."

Exhibit 1

Imagine a company whose only asset will be worth either $0 or $200 in six months time. The company has $100 in debt. The company could choose to hedge the value of its asset by use of the futures market. This would assure the company of $100 in revenues. We may compare the possible actions as follows:

	Asset Value	Gain from Futures	Payoff to Debtholders	Payoff to Stockholders
No Hedge	$ 0	$ 0	$ 0	$ 0
	200	0	100	100
Hedge	$ 0	$ 100	$100	$ 0
	200	−100	100	0

Average Gains to Shareholders: No Hedge = $50
                                 Hedge = $ 0

▼   ▼   ▼

INDEX

S

value chain, risk management and, 220–21
variability, uncertainty and, 39–41
variable-price contracts, 44
variance
    assumption of investor agreement on, 11, 12
    defined, 4
    formula, of portfolio, 7
    as measure of risk, 38
    minimum, of portfolio, 8–9
    for risk analysis of two investments, 15

weather-related business losses, insurance for, 139–40
weighted assessments, 136

weights, in preference analysis, 120, 136
White, Jack E., 247
whole-life insurance, 69–70, 73
    dividends from, 69
    level premiums, 69
    surrender values, 69–70
    vs. term insurance, 70
William Taylor and Associates caselet, 122–23
women, fetus protection/discrimination policy, 240–48
worker's compensation insurance, 99
Wright, Elizur, 69

zero-defect standard, risk management and, 215–17